The Aftermath of the Global Crisis in the European Union

The Aftermath of the Global Crisis in the European Union

Edited by

Beáta Farkas

CAMBRIDGE
SCHOLARS
PUBLISHING

The Aftermath of the Global Crisis in the European Union,
Edited by Beáta Farkas

This book first published 2013

Cambridge Scholars Publishing

12 Back Chapman Street, Newcastle upon Tyne, NE6 2XX, UK

British Library Cataloguing in Publication Data
A catalogue record for this book is available from the British Library

ISBN (10): 1-4438-4620-1, ISBN (13): 978-1-4438-4620-2

Table of Contents

List of Figures

LIST OF TABLES

INTRODUCTION

We cannot be completely certain about the ultimate end of the 2008 world-wide economic and fiscal crises; however, we can be assured that it has made permanent changes to the economic and financial systems. In this volume, monographs are selected to reflect on the long term impacts of these crises within the European Union (EU). Three main topics are covered: economic growth, EU fiscal and monetary policy issues, and special challenges for the new member and Mediterranean states (in the so-called cohesion countries).

Europe is being battered by multiple, interrelated crises. Economic and financial issues triggered the public financial and Euro crises, leading to political and social ones not only within some member states but also at the EU level. These crises add to a difficult long-term trajectory as Europe struggles to maintain its economic, social and environmental models in light of resilient challenges such as demographic change, resource scarcity, rising inequalities and the need to transform Europe's societies driven by climate change and increasing competition from emerging economies. *Fabian Zuleeg* analyses these processes and presents the conditions necessary to avoid stagnation in Europe during the next decade.

Matti Viren applies econometrical analysis to find explanations for the slowdown in European economic growth. He presents empirical analyses using European cross-country data. Special attention is paid to institutional and structural factors that are often assumed to affect aggregate growth: the functioning of labour markets, availability of labour and capital and the size of government. His results reinforce the notion that accelerating growth in Europe is not completely unrealistic. However, it is only possible through unpopular reforms.

The Japanese experience of struggling with decades of recession represents a real threat for Europe. *Masahiko Yoshii* examines what happened during the last twenty years in Japan. He studies what policies were implemented and why they were ineffective. He draws conclusions on lessons learnt and applies them to the current European crisis.

The common European Union budget is a special field of fiscal policy. *Gabriele Cipriani* provides insights on a particular aspect of national and union level budgeting. The economic and financial crisis creates the need for a more targeted and results-driven public expenditure policy a priority, demonstrating and acknowledging that EU actions add value to national policies and address individuals' concerns more effectively than "national" or "local" ones may provide an example of "best practices" for national spending. The opportunity is to identify and promote best practices in planning, management and reporting to achieve public objectives.

The euro-area has deep-rooted problems and, despite the various attempts to resolve the crisis, no solutions have been offered to the most pressing of these problems. *Zsolt Darvas* summarises ten major roots of the euro-crisis and assesses the policy responses to these issues. This is followed by a closer examination of the most pressing problem that also constitutes the most serious threat to the integrity of the euro-area: the dreary economic outlook of southern euro-area member states. He concludes that instead of exiting or breaking-up the euro, the common interest lies in finding ways to offer improved prospects for these countries. A substantial amount of measures need to be accomplished in these countries, but other euro-area partners, the so-called 'northern' members, as well as European institutions, will also have a decisive role in supporting the development process in Southern Europe. In the medium term, additional intuitional changes will be necessary to complement the currently planned overhaul of the euro-area's institutional framework.

Miklós Losoncz supplements the previous study and scrutinises the latest developments in the sovereign debt crisis and the experience of and the issues in crisis management in the European Monetary Union (EMU). He focuses on an analysis of the relationship between the institutional system and the operation of the EMU and the study of the sovereign debt crisis. He discusses the measures introduced thus far that have weakened the three pillars of the EMU and provides options for the EU to manage the unfolding sovereign debt crisis going forward.

One of the most important objectives of European integration is to reduce the economic gap between the more developed and less developed member states. European convergence is based on foreign capital inflows. *Beáta Farkas* demonstrates that this model provided substantial opportunities for Mediterranean and post-socialist member states; the success of convergence in the European integration process is unique. As a consequence of the crisis, the foreign capital inflows in Europe will decline and the convergence process will be slowed. Under these circumstances, it will be extremely important to promote the positive spill-over effects of foreign direct investment through economic policy. Both national and European policies should focus on the problems of the dual economies in the less developed member states and the development of an internationally competitive domestic economy to bridge the current productivity gap between foreign and domestic companies. The global crisis also necessitates some changes to the concept of integration.

The crisis that broke out and struck in waves brought to the surface, not only the consequences of the shift in the hub of world economic development, and the structural problems of the European economy, but also the differences in the capabilities, governance and approaches that existed between "Eastern Bloc" countries that joined the EU later (the "EU-10"), in addition to the differences that had already existed between this group and the older members of the European Union. From this perspective, *Árpád Kovács* reviews the common features of, approaches to, and differences in public finance among these nations.

Gábor Dávid Kiss and *Andreász Kosztopulosz* address the impacts of the crisis on monetary policy in three Central-East European countries, Poland, the Czech Republic, and Hungary. They analyse the euro-zone's daily bond and currency benchmark's impacts on their Czech, Hungarian and Polish counterparts between 2002 and 2010. They also examine the impact of monetary policy changes by the US Federal Reserve and the European Central Bank (ECB). Despite the fact that the Central-East European countries follow an ECB-compatible monetary policy; their fundamental differences resulted in increased risk premiums on extreme days. This risk premium represents increased losses given unfavourable events, while the ECB's and the Fed's monetary expansion has a limited impact on the Central-East European countries. As EU members, these countries are required to maintain the free movement of capital and allow the application of various financial innovations and will have to introduce the euro in the future. The authors conclude that they have to follow an inflation-targeting monetary policy but also need to improve their institutional capacities to substantially increase their focus on financial stability and regional cooperation.

The crisis in Greece remains the focus of the attention of researchers and analysts worldwide. Although several alternative explanations of the causes and implications of the crisis in Greece have been produced, the literature lacks a focused discussion on the role of fiscal policy in addressing the crisis. Against this background, *Anna Visvizi*'s objective is to dwell on the question of how the crisis in Greece was addressed and – in this context – how to conceive of the specific role that fiscal policy played in the process of addressing Greece's fiscal imbalance.

In recent years, Hungarian economic policy has been the focus of international interest. Having played a leading role in the 1990s, Hungary now lags behind due to public and private sector indebtedness, which is well documented in the literature. *Péter Mihályi*'s study analyses one other important, but less understood cause of the economic slowdown: the productivity of domestic enterprises remained low. The country lacks large-scale enterprises, which maximise worker output through economies of scale and scope. Thus, there is a need for a concentration of ownership in fixed capital, as well as in natural resources (e.g., agricultural land and forests). Such a strategy would require, first, a rapid consolidation of micro- and small enterprises into transparently functioning medium-sized and large firms.

These monographs present a comprehensive picture of the different aspects and levels of the crisis. The studies not only confront us with serious challenges but also offer potential solutions.

—The Editor

CHAPTER ONE

PERSPECTIVES OF GROWTH

Europe in Crisis: A Lost Decade or Stronger Future?

FABIAN ZULEEG

1. Introduction

Europe has been battered by the global financial and economic crisis, which has turned into a sovereign debt crisis that is not only threatening the Economic and Monetary Union and the common currency of the 17 countries of the euro zone, but the whole European integration process. In this immediate climate of crisis, requiring ever-greater political and economic sacrifices to keep all countries within the euro zone, too little attention is being paid to the long-term challenges Europe faces.

Europe is facing a daunting set of challenges, which will require significant reforms to maintain Europe's economic and social model. Dealing with climate change, population ageing, increasing inequality, rising unemployment, resource scarcity and global competition will require a deeply rooted change in how Europeans live. Furthermore, these challenges are being aggravated by the crisis, and the sovereign debt crisis will limit what public money can do in future years. Europe will need to get used to a very different world, which is characterised by trade-offs and sacrifices.

2. Is the European model special?

To assess the threat posed by these long-term challenges, including the long-term impacts of the current crisis, we first have to determine what makes Europe special. What makes the European model uniquely European?

The first and striking issue that can be observed is, of course, that there is significant diversity. Even on a very broad macroeconomic level, many have classified Europe's economies and social systems into different categories, for example, into a Nordic, a Continental, an Anglo-Saxon and a Mediterranean model, all with separate characteristics (Sapir 2006). The accession of the formerly centrally planned Central and Eastern European countries has, if anything, made the diversity even wider[1], also adding countries with significantly lower Gross Domestic Product (GDP) per capita than in the previous European Union (EU).

However, even this broad categorisation can easily be called into question. For example, where do countries such as France, which arguably share some aspects of both the Mediterranean and the Continental model, belong? Do all Nordic countries share a similar economic policy approach? The euro crisis has also shown that rather than increasing convergence, which arguably was the case in the pre-crisis period for countries such as Poland, Ireland and Spain, we are facing a period of fragmentation, with some countries falling further and further behind.

Looking at this evidence of continuing diversity and divergence, it could be concluded that there is no such thing as a European model. There are, however, clear indications that such a European model exists. This is more apparent when looking at the situation from the outside and in comparison to the rest of the world.

A case in point is the size and role of government. Typically, the European model entails a larger government sector with comparatively high public spending. Government expenditure stood at 49.1% in the EU-27 in 2011 (Wahrig and Gancedo Vallina 2012), compared to the OECD average total outlays of 43.2% (OECD 2012). This level does not necessarily mean high public deficits: some countries with the highest levels of public spending have sound public finances, while other countries with low public spending have significant deficit problems.

There are typically two reasons for the high level of public spending: a relatively generous social net (social security) and the provision of universal public services (for example, health and education). This pattern of public spending reflects the values of Europeans: while there is a belief in the basic principle of a capitalist market economy, there is also a strong notion that the "US-style" free market capitalism has to be tempered by the state. In essence, the preference of Europeans is for what is termed the "social market economy" or the "welfare state." In recent decades, Europeans' concern for social issues has been complemented by a strong emphasis on environmental concerns, including combating climate change.

The European model is thus closely aligned with the concept of sustainable development, with economic growth complemented by social and environmental protection. This concept is reflected in the debate at the European level about whether Europeans need and should forego a certain

---

[1] Beáta Farkas (2011) argues that there is a separate model for Central and Eastern Europe.

level of economic growth to maintain high levels of environmental protection (by reducing resource consumption) and social cohesion (by reducing incentives for profit-making through redistribution). This, in part, reflects the high standard of living that has already been reached across the EU. However, we should also note that for those countries where incomes are lower, more emphasis is generally put on economic growth and competition between individuals as an important driver for the economy.

The general concern for sustainable development is integrated into policy at the European level, which in turn reinforces a pan-European model. By emphasising the protection of the environment and of workers, the EU has created a pan-European standard, which in turn defines Europe's unique economic, social and environmental model. Because accession to the EU requires acceptance of the existing legal framework (the *acquis communautaire*), the EU also effectively transfers these values to new members.

3. Europe's long-term challenges

Over recent decades, the Member States of the EU have increasingly felt their economic, social and environmental model to be under threat by a range of global and European long-term challenges.

3.1. Globalisation

One of the key challenges arises from Europe's apparent ambivalence to the globalisation process. Europe is clearly one of the key beneficiaries of globalisation: European economies are among the world's greatest traders and have managed to raise their standards of living significantly through integration into the global economy.[2]

However, in recent years, for many Europeans the threats from globalisation have come more to the forefront, be it culturally, through the movement of people, or through intensified competition. Increasingly, there is a perception that Europe is not keeping up with its key competitors: neither with the more developed economies, such as the US, that manage to outpace European productivity developments through innovation and entrepreneurship, nor with the developing countries that have far lower wages. In both cases, the fear persists that higher European

---

[2] See for example the argument made by José Manuel Durão Barroso (2008), President of the European Commission, referring to Daniel Hamilton and Joseph Quinlan's book "Globalization and Europe: Prospering in the New Whirled Order".

taxes, as well as higher social and environmental standards, reduce the ability of Europeans to compete.

While this argument has to be taken with a large pinch of salt – after all, many European countries have competed very effectively for a long time, and the overall European trade position is close to balance – this poses a significant challenge to Europe's approach to globalisation.

First, global competition emphasises the need for quality of public spending. If public spending is simply an additional cost, the EU is unlikely to retain its competitive edge. If the spending helps to increase Europe's productivity and economic capacity, for example by increasing human capital and necessary infrastructure, it can add to the overall performance of an economy.

Second, there is a significant challenge for low-skilled jobs that can be outsourced to emerging economies. This threat is not for low-skilled jobs per se – there are many jobs that are difficult to outsource, for example in the area of personal care. However, in sectors where it is easy to transport the final product, such as basic manufacturing, labour-intensive industries tend to migrate to lower wage cost countries. This can create persistent long-term unemployment, especially for low-skilled workers.

Third, globalisation and especially global competition can put intense pressure on companies to consider their cost basis carefully, potentially relocating or investing in countries with lower taxes, reduced environmental and social standards, or a faster growing market. Companies that do not adjust to the reality of global competition will eventually have to close down.

Together, this adds up to a significant challenge to Europe's economic and social model. Economies characterised by high public spending without the resulting increase in productive capacity, long-term unemployment problems, a complex and bureaucratic business environment and low investment will struggle to maintain their highly valued lifestyles. While some European economies can concurrently maintain their economic and social model and retain their competitiveness, others struggle.[3]

3.2. Resource competition

Globalisation is also aggravating the global resource challenge. Economic progress still relies on increased consumption of natural

---

[3] In the global competitiveness index, Northern and Western European countries dominate the top 10 with Sweden (3rd), Finland (4th), Germany (6th), the Netherlands (7th), Denmark (8th) and the United Kingdom (10th). In contrast France is only 18th, and Greece is down to 90th (World Economic Forum 2012).

resources. The increased demand from the growing middle classes in countries such as India and China is creating a strong upward pressure on prices for all resources. While the economic crisis is, to some extent, reducing demand and thus the upward pressure on prices, this relief is only temporary.

This upward pressure on resources will most obviously affect energy, in particular oil, but will also affect energy sources such as coal that were less affected in the past. The types of price spikes observed just prior to the crisis, which were intensified by conflict, are likely to recur. This then affects all of the economy because input prices are higher, leading to inflation and lower growth, but also higher food prices. This development is mirrored by other resources, such as minerals, commodities or rare earths. In particular parts of the world, there will also be an increasing pressure on water resources.

For the EU countries, this resource competition will limit the growth potential and increase inflationary pressure. Given that growth rates are significantly lower than in emerging economies, the EU provides fewer economic opportunities, which will make it increasingly difficult to access the resources that are needed. While it is undoubtedly true that emerging and developing economies will be even more affected, this provides little comfort for the EU.

In addition to physical resources, there will be intensive competition for human resources, especially in relation to scarce, superior and soft skills (Collett and Zuleeg 2008). To attract these types of skills in the future, European countries can no longer rely on passively attracting immigrants and filtering out those that are considered desirable. Rather, European countries will have to actively compete for these migrants.

3.3. Increasing inequality and rising unemployment

Migration and the increasing diversity of Europe's societies have undoubtedly contributed to Europe's economic success in the post-World War II period. However, increasing diversity has also created longer-term issues that are difficult to resolve. In particular, the integration of some of the migrant communities has proven difficult, with many children from migrant backgrounds underperforming in education and, subsequently, being insufficiently integrated into the labour market. This deficiency perpetuates social integration problems for these communities.

However, the problem of inequality does not only affect migrant communities. While recent decades have led to an increase in living standards for many, there has also been a persistence of disadvantage for some groups. The impact of globalisation noted above can make it difficult to reintegrate the long-term unemployed into the labour market, frequently resulting in low aspirations being transmitted to future generations. In recent years, inequalities in Europe have been rising, a problem likely to be aggravated by the economic crisis (European Trade Union Institute 2012).

There is an on-going debate in Europe regarding how far inequality affects economic performance and imposes costs on all of society.[4] However, having groups in society that are permanently excluded clearly adds a burden to social protection systems. And given Europe's demographic profile, Europe cannot afford the long-term costs associated with under-utilised human resources.

3.4. Demographic change

Demographic change, in particular the combination of low fertility and increasing life expectancy, will have a profound impact on European societies. While the demographic projections differ significantly between countries, the common feature for European countries will be population ageing: "Population ageing is undoubtedly going to be a key demographic challenge in many European countries over the next fifty years" (Lanzieri 2011). This development will have a transformative impact on European society, which is hard to appreciate in its entirety.

Of course, migration can have a mitigating impact. However, the scale of migration that would be needed to reverse population ageing is very high: "In order to prevent a decline in the working-age population, the annual number of migrants would need to nearly double compared to recent experience" (UN 2001). In any case, it would only be a temporary fix because migrant populations also tend to age at similar rates once integrated.

There are clearly challenges from population ageing that affect the welfare state. There is increasing pressure on health, care and pension systems, while, at the same time, the ratio of those paying into the public system to those receiving support is reduced. The obvious way to address this issue is by altering public support systems, for example by increasing the retirement age. However, this in and of itself is not enough, even if it was widely accepted as a step in the right direction. It is crucial to ensure that changes to entitlement increase the propensity of individuals to stay in the labour market; for example, apart from a potentially small reduction in

---

[4] With significant debate triggered by the publication of Wilkinson and Pickett (2009).

public support costs, there is no gain if people, instead of retiring, become unemployed.

Keeping all groups engaged in the labour market (i.e., the elderly but also other groups with a tendency to drop out, such as those with caring responsibilities, a migration background or with health problems) is the key to addressing the impact of population ageing.[5]

Higher labour market participation also addresses the challenge of growth: an ageing population would automatically reduce the growth rate unless counteracted by such a development. But achieving higher labour market participation is a significant challenge, especially in light of the difficult labour market situation across Europe with unsustainably high unemployment in many countries. Once again, the current crisis is aggravating the long-term challenges Europe faces.

3.5. Climate change

One final challenge Europe faces is truly global in nature: how to mitigate climate change and how to limit global temperature increases. The challenge of dealing with climate change is, however, qualitatively different from the other challenges noted above, which makes finding a policy solution even more difficult.

Why is climate change different? The key reason is that whatever Europe does with regard to its own emissions will have little impact on the overall picture. The growth in the emission of greenhouse gases takes place clearly outside of Europe, with the biggest increases in countries such as China. While higher emissions in these countries are driven by an understandable desire to create economic growth in emerging economies, it does aggravate the climate change challenge: even a reduction of emissions in Europe is quickly outweighed by developments elsewhere. In addition, the other major historical perpetrator of emissions, the US, is showing little leadership or motivation on this issue.

These issues lead some to conclude that Europe should give up on attempting to combat climate change and just adapt to its effects while ignoring our global responsibilities. However, this is a very negative agenda with the obvious drawback that it could result in the destruction of the global climate system. A more positive approach is to develop Europe as a positive example of how environmental sustainability can be combined or even drive economic growth. Such a green growth scenario

[5] The European Policy Centre (EPC) has developed the Labour Market Adjusted Dependency Ration which clearly shows the combined impact of labour market participation rates and ageing populations (Guerzoni and Zuleeg 2011).

might well become the standard that other countries aspire to, but it is difficult to implement. It is a slow process because of significant political and economic transition costs, and it has yet to receive the genuine backing of member states. And once again, the crisis is also hindering this process, with many arguing that now is not the right time to be too ambitious and that we should rather focus on jobs, even if this means that the long-term transformation is delayed.

4. The crisis: from bad to worse

The economic and financial crisis, which has battered Europe over the last three years or so, has aggravated these long-term challenges and has added some new and pressing issues that need to be tackled, not least the unsustainable public debt situation in many European countries. The crisis should thus not be understood as a cyclical downturn from which Europe will emerge unscathed. Rather, it is a deep-seated structural crisis that will profoundly threaten Europe's economic and social model. While the overall impact will crucially depend on how policy reacts to the crisis, it is already clear that the on-going transformation will impose significant transition costs on all of Europe.

The first issue the EU will have to address is the aggregated growth crisis. The long-term challenges noted above have already tended to reduce Europe's growth rate. While policy can do much to reduce this impact, overall it remains a challenge to have strongly growing economies when faced with low-cost global competition and an ageing workforce. The unsustainable public debt situation in many countries further aggravates the situation: fiscal consolidation implies lower government spending, which will tend to reduce growth rates.

Dealing with Europe's aggregated growth crisis is tricky at the best of times. Even before the economic crisis hit, European attempts to reinvigorate the EU economy were less than convincing. At first, European worries were raised by competition from the US, driven by impressive increases in productivity, and, subsequently, by competition from the emerging economies, led by China. The Europeans responded with a European growth strategy, the Lisbon strategy, aiming to generate growth and jobs in Europe. However, despite some revisions over time, the strategy lacked decisive implementation tools. Consequently, while some countries in Europe made great advances, others continued to lag behind. Even before the crisis hit, it was clear that the Lisbon agenda had not significantly shifted the EU's growth performance.

The revised version of the Lisbon strategy, Europe 2020, contains some provisions that will, in principle, drive implementation more strongly, including, for example, provisions to link any European money to the strategic objectives in Europe 2020. There are also moves to develop the single market further, for example by creating a digital single market for Europe's citizens. There are also some attempts to address the impact of the crisis, for example by making credit or alternative financial instruments more widely available. While these are important initiatives, which, if implemented,[6] can have an impact on Europe's long-term growth rate, they are in themselves insufficient.

5. Divergence, not convergence

The solutions for the aggregated growth crisis also have the potential to aggravate Europe's other growth crisis: the increasing gap between the good performers and those lagging behind. The measures noted above, such as a better functioning single market, tend to benefit most those countries that have an economy geared towards trade. In a world of scarce and expensive capital, investments will go to the countries that are performing better.

In the pre-crisis environment, it looked easier: private capital would flow to the peripheral countries, often generated by high savings rates in countries such as Germany, and public spending could be financed cheaply. Now, however, neither of these routes is open to the countries in crisis. Global investors will avoid crisis countries, not least because of the political and economic uncertainty such a crisis brings. In the current climate, the risks outweigh the possibilities of making returns. The reality is that crisis countries will need to receive support from those performing better. True, there is already significant funding being provided to prop up banking systems and to help governments that struggle to finance their public debt at reasonable rates. However, the crisis countries will also need support to encourage private investment and enable public investment, for example in education (Zuleeg and Emmanouilidis 2011).

The need of the crisis countries for investment and growth also needs to be reflected in the reform programmes the crisis countries have to implement. One of the great paradoxes of the crisis is that fiscal consolidation tends to reduce growth, but without growth, fiscal consolidation becomes near impossible. Europe's approach to dealing with

[6] The EPC's (2012) Digital Single Market project estimates that completing only this aspect of the Single market would add at least 4% to EU GDP by 2020.

the euro crisis in the absence of positive external growth impulses is thus doomed to failure: not only is the fiscal consolidation not working, the political constituency for further reform is continually weakened. In the medium term, many electorates will question the purpose of reform: is it to help the weaker economies to improve, or is it just a means to preserve the euro? In either case, the perceived pain of reform is likely to outweigh the benefits.

The recent summit in Brussels made some moves in the right direction[7], for example by redirecting unused structural funds to the crisis countries and by enabling the European Investment Bank (EIB) to expand its lending operations. However, overcoming the growth divergence between the better performing countries and those in crisis will require significantly more action, for example by developing new financing mechanisms, providing guarantees for private sector investments and by redesigning the European budget (Zuleeg 2012).

There is, however, little apparent appetite in Brussels for continuing in this course of action. Providing the current help for the crisis countries is already observed as stretching what citizens can bear. There is also concern about the potential moral hazard involved. If the crisis countries receive this support, will they not just fall back into bad habits? Many also note that the countries most affected by the euro crisis are not the only ones that need support. Countries outside the euro zone are also suffering, and the Central and Eastern European accession countries are still relatively poor when compared to the EU average GDP.

6. Prospects: stagnation and imbalances?

Europe's long-term challenges, together with the impact of the crisis, are putting European countries in a very difficult situation. It can be argued that Europe is facing a "perfect storm" with all the negative impacts reinforcing each other, potentially destroying EU citizens' faith in their trusted system and, thus, potentially destabilising Europe's economic and social model and the European integration process. If no sustainable solutions can be found for the challenges arising from globalisation, population ageing, resource scarcity, rising inequalities and climate change, and if the aggregated growth crisis and the divergence of the crisis countries from the better performing ones continue, it is difficult to see how Europe could emerge from its current economic doldrums.

---

[7] See European Council (2012) which introduced a "Compact for Growth and Jobs."

Europe might then be facing a situation similar to Japan, with a long-term decline. This does not necessarily imply a dramatic collapse, but the European economy would lose dynamism and be left behind. In the longer term, this would also mean falling standards of living and a state that can no longer play the role of providing public services and social protection for all.

However, the situation in Europe could turn out even worse, given Europe's complexity. Europe is not one country, but 27 (soon 28), with very different prospects and needs. A sluggish European economy also means that the catch-up process for the Central and Eastern Europeans would significantly slow down. There would be increasing imbalances within the euro zone. Some countries would try to shield their social market economy from the turmoil elsewhere, for example by limiting free movement of people, while others would struggle to provide even the most basic services. All in all, this does not look like a situation that would be to the benefit of Europe's citizens: disintegration and perpetual crisis. Indeed, the core fabric of the European model would be threatened.

So what can be done? Policy can still have a decisive role to play if it can activate Europe's assets. However, this cannot be accomplished with traditional policy approaches. Adapting to the long-term challenges and the crisis will require systemic change. To rescue Europe's economic, social and environmental model – the very essence of the European project – it will not only need to be altered but also reinvented. Only if public services are an asset to economic growth, for example by effectively activating all those outside the labour market, can the system become truly sustainable. Europe's economic and social model must be a competitive factor in our relations with the rest of the world, helping us to develop new growth and employment patterns and attracting the best talent from across the world. If this crisis is to be taken as an opportunity for fundamental reform, it might well lead to the eventual re-emergence of European strength.

This vision relies on an ability to carry it out. However, many countries in Europe have already lost this freedom of movement, or they never had the resources in the first place. So transforming Europe's economic, social and environmental model depends on joint EU action. Individual countries can do a great deal, but the high degree of interdependence and the need to show solidarity with those who do not have the means to carry out this process makes a pan-European approach a necessity. The crisis also aggravates the following need: solving the euro crisis must be an essential part of the way forward and can only be accomplished by moving forward together, towards a 'more Europe' solution.

Such fundamental change in Europe cannot happen without engaging Europe's citizens. We are no longer talking about some institutional change at the European level, which citizens hardly care about and are even less likely to understand. We are talking about the whole direction of the European integration process, and we are talking about the fundamental nature of the economic, social and environmental model and how it can be revitalised and preserved.

Europe's leaders must explain these fundamental choices to their citizens and sketch out a positive way forward. Without such an open debate around Europe's future, we will face growing imbalances and economic stagnation. The technical resolution of the euro crisis and even the challenge of current youth unemployment are only elements of this wider question. The future of the EU's economic, social and environmental model should take central stage in the current debate.

References

Barroso J. M. D. 2008. "Globalisation and Europe: Prospering in the New Whirled Order." Brussels. http://transatlantic.sais-jhu.edu/transatlantic-topics/Articles/economy//2.28.08barroso_globalization_europe_remarks.pdf

Collett, E. and Zuleeg, F. 2008. "Soft, Scarce, and Super Skills: Sourcing the Next Generation of Migrant Workers in Europe." Migration Policy Institute. http://www.migrationpolicy.org/transatlantic/scarceskills.pdf

EPC. 2012. Digital Single Market project website. http:// www.epc.eu/dsm

European Council. 2012. "Conclusions of 28/29 June 2012." http://www.consilium.europa.eu/uedocs/cms_data/docs/pressdata/en/ec/131388.pdf

European Trade Union Institute. 2012. "Benchmarking Working Europe." http://www.etui.org/News/Social-inequality-worsening-in-European-Union

Farkas, B. 2011. "The Central and Eastern European Model of Capitalism." *Post-Communist Economies* 23, 1: 15-34. http://papers.ssrn.com/sol3/papers.cfm?abstract_id=1965290

Guerzoni, B. and Zuleeg, F. 2011. "Working Away at the Cost of Ageing - the labour market adjusted dependency ratio". EPC Issue Paper 64. http://www.epc.eu/documents/uploads/pub_1265_working_away_at_the_cost_of_ageing.pdf

Lanzieri, G. 2011. "The greying of the baby boomers – A century-long view of ageing in European". Statistics in focus. Eurostat.

http://epp.eurostat.ec.europa.eu/statistics_explained/index.php/Population_projections

OECD. 2012. "Economic Outlook 2012." No. 91. http://statlinks.oecdcode.org/122012011P1T105.XLS

Sapir, A. 2006. "Globalization and the Reform of European Social Models." *Journal of Common Market Studies* 44, 2: 369–390. http://www.ulb.ac.be/cours/delaet/econ076/docs/sapir.pdf

UN. 2011. Replacement Migration: Is it a solution to declining and ageing populations? http://www.un.org/esa/population/publications/ReplMigED/migration.htm

Wahrig, L. and Gancedo Vallina, I. 2012. "EU-27 government revenue and expenditure stood at 44.6% and 49.1% of GDP respectively in 2011." Statistics in focus 27/2012. Eurostat. http://epp.eurostat.ec.europa.eu/cache/ITY_OFFPUB/KS-SF-12-027/EN/KS-SF-12-027-EN.PDF

Wilkinson, R. and Pickett, K. 2009. *The Spirit Level*. London: Penguin.

World Economic Forum. 2012. "Global Competitiveness Report 2011-2012." http://www.weforum.org/reports/global-competitiveness-report-2011-2012

Zuleeg, F. 2012. "Is Europe addressing the wrong growth crisis?" EPC Commentary, May 2012. http://www.epc.eu/pub_details.php?pub_id=2039&year=2012

Zuleeg, F. and Emmanouilidis, J. 2011. "A New Deal to help save the euro." EPC Commentary. May 2011. http://www.epc.eu/pub_details.php?pub_id=1277

How to Accelerate Growth in Europe?

Matti Viren

1. Introduction

Most people would likely agree that Europe suffers from a growth slowdown. The GDP growth in Europe has lagged behind the GDP growth in the US and has been far worse than the GDP growth in the Newly Industrialized Countries, particularly China (cf. Figure 2-1 for the US-Europe comparison). Quite clearly, there is a declining trend in economic growth rates for Europe during the post-WWII period; although there are substantial growth differences among European countries, the overall trend is similar for all of the EU countries (Figure 2-2). During 1998–2011, GDP has grown by 1.7% annually in EU-27 and 1.5% annually in the euro-area. Moreover, these numbers are misleadingly high, given that in most EU/EMU countries, fiscal expansion exaggerates the true equilibrium growth rate.[1] The growth prospects appear no better for Europe; the estimates of annual GDP growth for the near future are in the one per cent range, and the long-term prospects are sometimes even worse due to poor demographic developments (see Figure 2-8 for several extreme examples).

However, what is the reason for slow or rapid economic growth? Growth theory does not provide us with a clear answer to this question. To phrase this conclusion in a different manner, the story is far from simple, as one may agree after consulting, for example, Acemoglu (2009). The classical Solow model states that it is (exogenous) technological progress that can keep output growing in the long run (in the short run, capital deepening can also produce output growth; however, diminishing returns will eventually make increased capital impotent). The new growth theory provides a somewhat more optimistic perspective for growth policies. However, alternative versions of this new growth theory generate different

[1] See, e.g., Snower et al. (2011) for an illustration of how to compute the impact of unsustainable fiscal policy on output growth and obtain an estimate of the corresponding equilibrium growth path.

recommendations. In particular, according to the AK model, the way to sustain high growth rates is to save a large fraction of GDP, a portion of which will find its way into financing a higher rate of technological progress and thereby stimulate faster growth. By contrast, the Schumpeterian view states that innovation and therefore productivity growth and convergence can be fostered by the following measures: better protection of (intellectual) property rights, which improves the extent to which successful innovators can appropriate the rents from their innovations; better financial development, which provides easier financing of new and innovative ideas; a higher stock of educated labour, which improves the ability of individuals either to imitate more advanced technologies or to innovate; and macroeconomic stability, which ensures low (risk-adjusted) equilibrium interest rates and encourages individuals to engage in long-term growth-enhancing investments (cf., e.g., Aghinon and Durlauf 2007). These recommendations are sensible, and to a certain extent, they are incorporated into the various programs that have been created to stimulate growth in Europe (cf., e.g., EU Commission 2010).[2] However, the recommendations are rather abstract, and it is not easy to quantify the importance of different factors for the growth process.

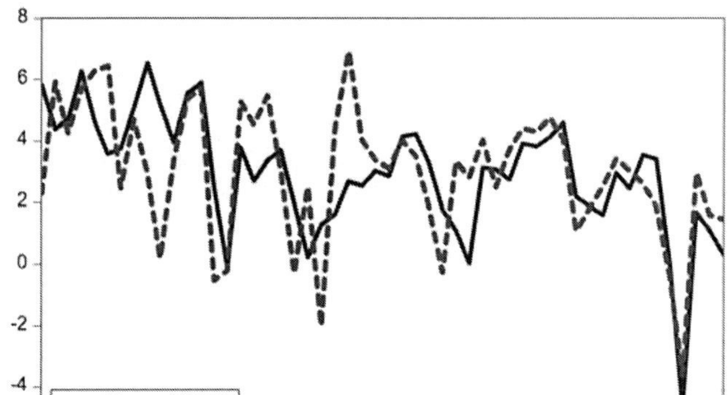

Fig. 2-1 GDP growth rates in the EU and in the US
Source: AMECO database

[2] The Commission program attempts to incorporate all possible issues, and therefore it produces results that are not very concrete but are instead a collection of aims and intentions.

The poor growth numbers have, however, prompted various attempts to quantify the importance of possible growth factors (see, e.g., Collingnon 2011 and Barro and Sala-i-Martin 1998). The assessment of growth factor importance is also the purpose of this paper. What makes this paper somewhat different from most previous analyses is its emphasis on "deep" background variables. Thus, rather than examining the national accounts numbers to evaluate factors such as exports and investment, we attempt to discover the relationships between key institutional and structural variables and the growth of output. To a certain extent, our variables correspond to those of the growth factors of the aforementioned "new growth theory", but one cannot really characterise the empirical analysis as a test of this theory. As mentioned, we focus only on the EU countries in this study, and therefore the special features of developing countries do not play a role in this investigation.

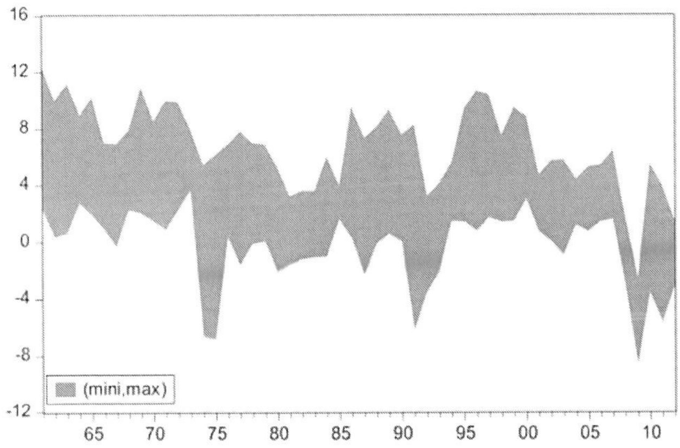

Fig. 2-2 Range of cross-country growth rates of GDP
Source: Author's calculation based on AMECO database

Thus, we attempt to quantify the importance of several commonly presented explanations for the slowdown of growth in Europe, beginning with the (poor) functioning of the labour market, the (adverse) development of price competitiveness and the (excessive) growth of government. In many respects, the labour market plays the key role in the economy because it determines both the use of the labour input and the level of overall competitiveness of a nation. Obviously, the functioning of the labour market is not independent of the public sector. A large government is almost inevitably associated with a large tax wedge, and the functioning of the labour market appears to be critically dependent on the size of the tax wedge. It may be fair to say that the harmful consequences of a high tax wedge are exceptionally well and unambiguously documented in the literature (see, e.g., OECD 2006).[3]

The empirical model uses certain alternative indicators for these institutional and structural factors. The idea is that these factors affect growth via productive inputs and (total factor) productivity. Thus, we do not attempt to identify any behavioural relationships, and we therefore have no (testable) parametric restrictions. Obviously, the estimates can be interpreted as the outcomes of a reduced form model; however, the "door is left open" for alternative interpretations and conclusions.

With respect to the structure of the remainder of the paper, the estimating equation is introduced in section 2, and the corresponding estimation results are reviewed in section 3. Finally, several concluding remarks are provided in section 4.

2. The model

To predict the GDP growth g $(= \Delta \log(y))$, we utilise the following simple linear equation:

$$g_{it} = a_{i0} + a_1 ws_t + a_2 fx_t + a_2 tax_t + a_4 dep_t + a_5 hours_t +$$
$$a_6 tt_t + a_7 rr_t + u_{it}$$

where the variables on the right-hand side of the equation are as follows:

- The wage share, ws (the inverse of the profit share)
- The real exchange rate, fx (an increase in fx implies an appreciation in the exchange rate)
- The gross tax rate, tax (or gov. expenditures, $govexp$)
- The (needs-weighted) dependency ratio, dep
- Average working hours (HP trend), $hours$[4]
- The terms of trade (tt)
- The real interest rate, rr (in terms of bond yields)
- The error term (u).

---

[3] The OECD study arrives at very high employment (and unemployment) estimates resulting from the size of the tax wedge. Thus, for prime-age males, the elasticity of this factor was 0.3 and for prime-age females, the elasticity of this factor was 0.5.

[4] The HP trend is used to diminish the importance of the simultaneous cyclical (demand for labour) relationship between output and working hours.

With respect to the coefficient values, we expect $a_1 < 0, a_2 < 0, a_3 < 0, a_4 < 0, a_5 > 0, a_6 > 0$ and $a_7 < 0$.

For the wage share, we have two proxies. One of these proxies is a simple income-share of (gross) wages, which is denoted by ws, and the other proxy is an adjusted wage share, ws_a, which accounts for the difference between the total number of (paid) employees and total employment. Similarly, the size of government is measured both by the gross tax rate and by total expenditures with respect to GDP, $govexp$. Finally, competitiveness is measured not only by the real exchange rate fx but also by the (real) unit labour costs, ulc.

As a final check, we introduced a measure of high-tech industries into the model. This *hightech* variable represents the share of high industries of the value added of the total manufacturing industry. We would obviously expect that a more advanced structure of the economy allows for higher growth rates of exports and total output.

We use annual data from 15 EU countries for this study. The data span the 1971–2011 period, and include a total of 375 data points. With the *hightech* variable, only 253 data points were available. The main data source is the AMECO data bank, although dep values were obtained from the DICE data bank, values of the US GDP = USG (used as a control) were obtained from the NBER, the unadjusted ws values were obtained from OECD data, and the adjusted wage share (ws_a) data were obtained from AMECO. The *hightech* variable was derived from the OECD Stan database and it included the following ISIC categories: 3825 (office machinery & computers), 383 (electric machinery), 3845 (aerospace), and 385 (scientific industries); see Viren and Malkamäki (2002) for details.

The data for *dep* and *hours* (which are not frequently used in empirical analyses) are illustrated in Figures 2-4 and 2-5. Both of these variables evince a great deal of variability over time. The average working hours variable demonstrates more trend-like development, whereas the dependency ratio undergoes several long swings that correspond to various occurrences, such as demographic changes and changes in pension systems.

The estimates of the model are presented in Table 2-A1. The model is estimated using ordinary least squares (OLS), or generalised method of moments (GMM) in the case of dynamic panel settings (Arellano – Bond estimator). Additional variables in the model include the US GDP growth rate (USG) and the lagged dependent variable (g_{-1}). In most cases, we have included cross-section fixed effects (in one instance, fixed time effects are also included), although these effects are not displayed.

However, to indicate the flavour of the result, we report one set of estimates for the cross-section fixed effects in Figure 2-7 (which correspond to equation (2-4) in Table 2-A1). If the model included either period fixed effects or US GDP growth, the terms of trade variable, tt, became insignificant; thus, this variable is not included in the equations that are reported in Table 2-A1 (see, however, the results in Boxes 2-1 and 2-2).

Obviously, the cross-section fixed effects are not completely innocent because they capture most of the cross-sectional variance of output growth. Given the approach of the current paper, only the cross-sectional variation is of primary interest because we wish to know the determinants of the equilibrium growth rate, rather than the factors affecting cyclical (short-term) variations in output. It would therefore be useful to present at least one set of estimates that includes no fixed effects but only has a common constant term. Thus, we ask whether our explanatory variables can explain all of the changes (differences) in the examined GDP growth rates. This set of results is displayed below in Box 1. The magnitude of the coefficients is illustrated by computing the growth rate responses to an increase of one standard deviation in each right-hand-side variable (Figure 2-6).

Because we have so many alternative proxies available for functional income distribution, price competitiveness, and the size of the government, we created an additional experiment in which all of these variables are introduced into the estimating equation at the same time. The idea is simply to determine how robust the model is in terms of the measurements of different factors. The results are displayed in Box 2-2 in the Appendix.

In this study, we almost entirely report results that represent common coefficients for all countries (and years). However, we also estimate the models for individual countries. In the cases of individual countries, we are primarily interested in examining which types of convergence patterns can be detected from the data. An idea of the dispersion of data for individual countries can be obtained from Figures 2-2 and 2-3, which show the range of growth rates for the examined countries and the relationship between the standard deviations of growth rates and the mean growth rate. On the basis of these figures, it is a bit difficult to perceive that the dispersion would change over time (for instance, during the course of the EMU period), whereas it is easy to observe that the dispersion of growth rates is strongly related to the mean growth rates. This observation,

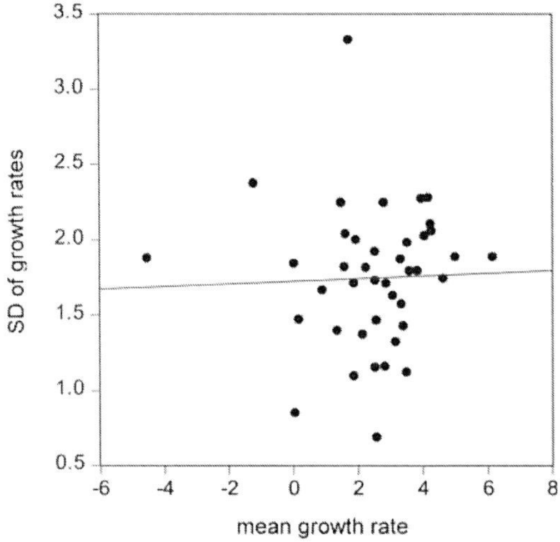

Fig. 2-3 Mean and standard deviation of growth rates
Source: Author's calculation based on AMECO database
Note: The mean and the standard deviations are derived for the cross-section data of EU 15 countries.

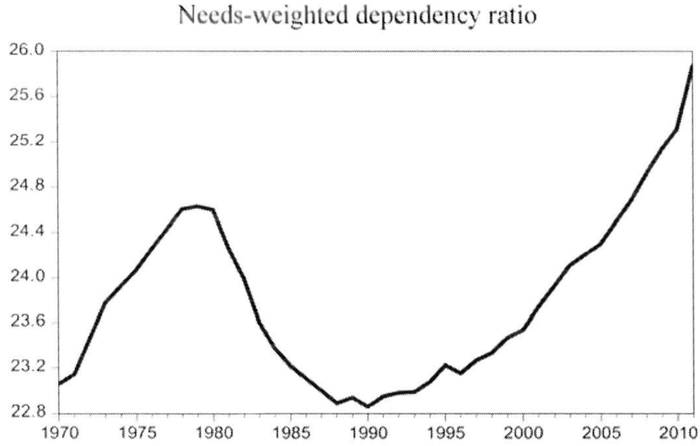

Fig. 2-4 The median dependency ratio in the EU
Source: Author's calculation based on DICE database

in turn, suggests that individual countries differ greatly in terms of output shocks, which is a phenomenon that creates obvious problems for common economic policies (this issue is more thoroughly analysed in Mayes and Viren (2011)).

Box 2-1

The estimates of the simplest equation

Growth rate of GDP =

−0.069	(3.66)	The wage share (t-ratio)
−0.053	(3.48)	The real exchange rate
−0.067	(2.85)	The government size (expenditures/GDP)
+0.006	(0.61)	The HP trend of average working hours (log)
−0.201	(2.91)	The needs-weighted dependency ratio
−0.015	(0.20)	The real interest rate
+0.033	(1.13)	The terms of trade
+0.374	(5.35)	constant

$R^2 = 0.242$; $SSE = 0.021$, $DW = 1.168$;

OLS with no fixed & random effects

Source: AMECO database

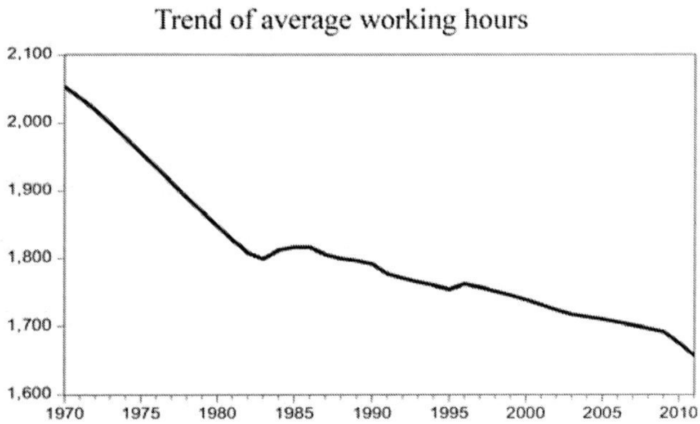

Fig. 2-5 The average working hours in the EU
Source: OECD/MEI database

3. Interpretations of the results

Overall, our simple model fits the data very well. In general, the coefficients have the correct signs and are of reasonable magnitude. Moreover, the results that are obtained are quite precise, which allows us to generate at least tentative policy conclusions.

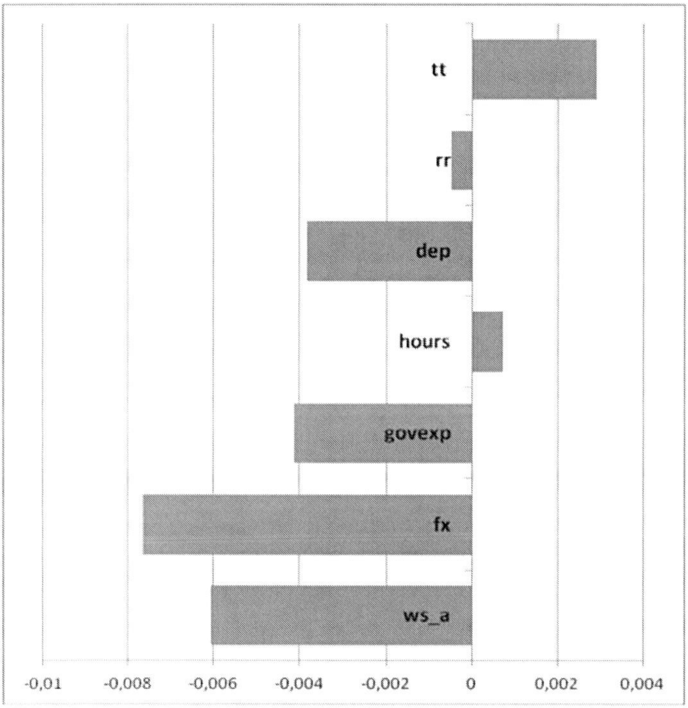

Fig. 2-6 Growth effects of one standard deviation increase in exogenous variables
Source: Author's calculation
Note: The values are related to estimates in Box 2-1.

The results also appear to be surprisingly robust in terms of various measures of the underlying variables (Box 2-A1). Thus, if we construct an extreme version of the model and include all alternative proxies of our variables, the only coefficient with an unexpected sign is the coefficient of the gross tax rate. This result clearly reflects the fact that the gross tax rate and the expenditures/GDP ratio are sufficiently similar that the coefficients of both variables cannot be correctly estimated from a single equation.

The reported cross-section fixed effects (Figure 2-7) demonstrate that Greece, Italy, Portugal and Spain are the poor performers among the 15 countries examined (even after controlling for the background variables). By contrast, the Nordic countries manage quite well. This finding may provide support for various interpretations of the observed differences, including distinctions in the quality of institutions, moral values and/or the credibility of economic policies.[5] Regarding convergence, there appears to be unconditional (but not conditional) convergence in terms of GDP.[6] With respect to other variables, the evidence is rather inconclusive. In terms of unit labour costs, certain striking exceptions can be detected (see Table 2-A2 in Appendix).

On the basis of the estimates derived in this study, the following guide for growth policies appears to be warranted: Keep the profit rate and the price competitiveness at a reasonable level (or improve them). Do not over-expand the welfare state. Larger governments are associated with slower growth rates.[7] Secure a sufficient labour supply. Longer workweeks generate better economic growth. Do not allow interest rates to exceed equilibrium levels, but instead keep the risk premiums as low as possible. Try to achieve a more advanced structure of production and exports.

Clearly, these recommendations largely match the recommendations that are provided by the new growth theory, despite the fact that we do not directly control variables that directly affect innovative activities. The only exception is the output share of high-tech industries (*hightech*). Including this variable does not, however, invalidate the other results and the variable makes a positive contribution to the explanation of differences in growth. The systematically positive and rather precise coefficient estimates suggest that countries that have managed to modernize their

---

[5] These interpretations obviously enter a topic that is rather thoroughly analysed by Barro and Sala-i-Martin (1998).

[6] The coefficient of $\log\left(\frac{y_{i,t-1}}{y_{ge,t-1}}\right)$, where ge refers to Germany, was calculated to be $-.043$ (3.26) in the unconditional convergence regression; however, if this variable is inserted, e.g., to equation (4) in Table 2-A1 as an additional regressor, the resulting coefficient is $-.019$ (0.75).

[7] This conclusion may be motivated by the idea that the there is a type of Laffer curve in the productivity of public sector services, as discussed by Koskela and Viren (2000). This notion also arises in the analysis of the extensive empirical evidence that was produced by Tanzi and Shuhknecht (2000).

industries seem to perform better than countries that stick to their old structures of production.

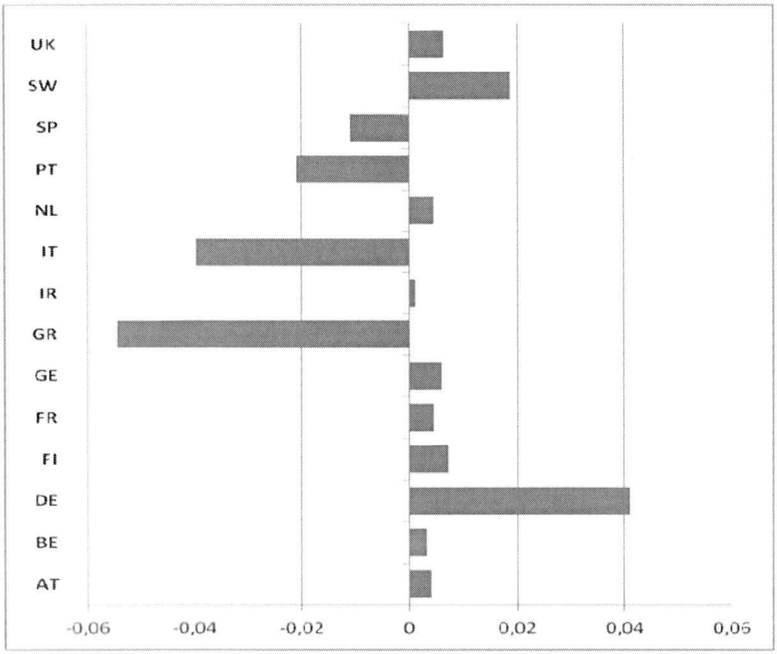

Fig. 2-7 Cross-section fixed effects
Source: Author's calculation
Note: These estimates are derived from equation 4 in Table 2-A1 and they represent a level-difference from predictions of the respective model.

From a policy perspective, our explanatory variables provide a plethora of possibilities for growth programs. These possibilities may be illustrated using the following simple calculation, which will at least provide an idea of the relevant magnitudes of various effects. Take the simplest equation reported in Box 2-1. Using the mean values of the time series for each variable, this equation implies that one may increase the mean growth rate from 2.4% to 3.4% by changing the right-hand-side variables in the following way:

- Wage share: 66% → 61%
- Government expenditure share: 48% → 43%

- (Annual) working hours: 1600 h → 1700 h
- Dependency ratio: 24% → 23%
- Real interest rate 3% → 2%.

This result implies that a revolution is not required to generate one per cent of additional growth each year: the "welfare state" does not need to be eliminated, wages do not need to be lowered to subsistence income levels, and working hours do not need to be increased to medieval levels. In fact, in most instances, significant improvements in economic growth could be produced by simply reverting to the conditions of approximately one decade ago. The changes that would be entailed in this reversion are still sufficiently great that they would not easily be sold to the general public within the median voter model. Given the gloomy prospects of most EU countries (Figure 2-8), however, the need for certain unpleasant reforms has become increasingly compelling.

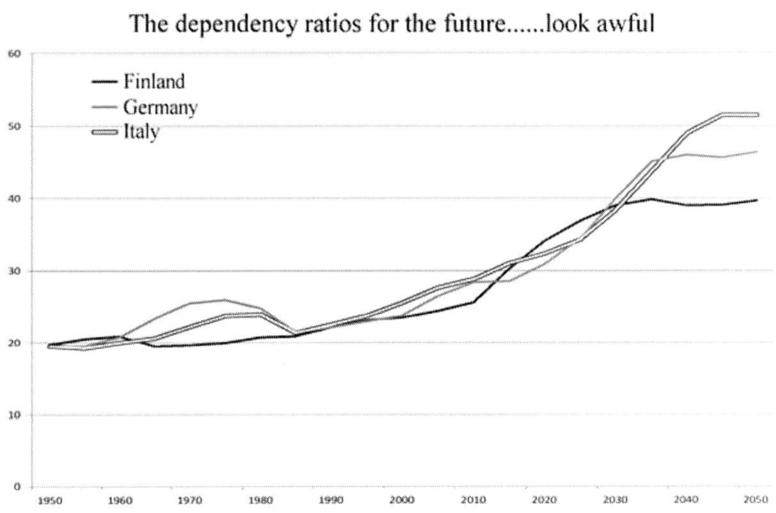

Fig. 2-8 Long-run forecasts of the dependency ratios
Source: Eurostat 2007 projections (European Commission 2007)

4. Conclusions

This paper shows that accelerating growth in Europe is not completely unrealistic. However, several unpopular reforms would be required to increase the labour supply, alleviate tax burdens and increase competitiveness. Obviously, these phenomena are not unrelated. Thus, by reducing the growth of the public sector and decreasing tax rates, one may increase both the labour supply and the competitiveness of the private sector. The future development of the public sector is indeed the key aspect of determining the future development of the economy. If the public sector can be maintained in a reasonable fashion, one may manage to achieve low tax rates and low tax wedges in labour markets, and one can also avoid fiscal crises and keep the risk premiums (of interest rates) low. Indeed, there are causal relationships in the opposite direction, as well; for instance, an increased labour supply (well-functioning labour markets) generates more tax revenues, allowing for lower tax rates and diminishes the risks of fiscal crises.

Although the message of this paper is clear and the results of the empirical analysis are quite unambiguous, there are several caveats that merit mention. Above all, it is worth noting that in this study, we have not considered either capital deepening (increasing investment and saving activity) or various other factors that may underlie total factor productivity, such as innovative activity and the adaptation of innovations, in any detail (cf. Kilponen and Viren (2010) for an assessment of the importance of these factors). Similarly, financial factors related to economic growth must be more deeply analysed (in accordance with the approach of, for example, Beck et al. (2005)). We also have not considered the implications of global developments, although these developments obviously affect the economic position of European countries relative to other countries. Our rather crude institutional and structural explanatory variables do not capture any of these considerations particularly well, and thus further analysis is certainly required.

Acknowledgement

Sami Oinonen's research assistance and financial support from the OP-Pohjola Research Foundation are gratefully acknowledged.

References

Acemoglu, D. 2009. *Introduction to Modern Economic Growth*. New York: Princeton University Press.

Aghinon, P and Durlauf, S. 2007. "From Growth Theory to Policy Design." Memo prepared for the World Bank Commission on Growth.

Barro, R. and Sala-i-Martin, X. 1998. *Economic growth*, 2nd edition. Cambridge MA: The MIT Press.

Beck, T. and Demirguc-Kunt, A. and Laeven, A. and Levine, R.. 2005. "Finance, Firma Size and Growth." World Bank Policy Research Working Paper 3485.

Collingnon, S. 2011. A New Growth Strategy for Europe. Paper presented at the 39th Economics Conference in the Austrian Central Bank. Printed in the proceedings publication "The Future of European Economic Integration: Some Economic Perspectives", 155–163.

European Commission. 2007. "Europe's demographic future: Facts and figures on challenges and opportunities." Brussels: European Commission.

—. 2010. "EUROPE2020: A European strategy for smart, sustainable and inclusive growth." Brussels: European Commission.

Kilponen, J. and Viren, M. 2010. "Why do growth rates differ? Evidence from cross-country data on private sector production." *Empirica* 37, 3: 311–328.

Koskela, E. and Viren, M. 2000. "Is There a Laffer Curve between Output and Public Sector Employment?" *Empirical Economics* 25, 4: 605–621.

Mayes, D. and Viren, M. 2011. *Asymmetry and aggregation in the Euro-area*. London: Palgarave-MacMillan.

OECD. 2006. "Reassessing the Role of Policies and Institutions for Labour Market Performance: A Quantitative Analysis." Chapter 7 in OECD Employment Outlook "Boosting Jobs and Incomes". Paris: OECD, 207–231.

Snower, D. and Burmeister, J. and M. Seidel. 2011. Dealing with the Eurozone debt crisis: A proposal for reforms. Kiel Policy Brief 33/2011. Kiel Institute for the World Economy.

Tanzi, V. and Shuhknecht, L. 2000. *Public spending in the 20th century: A global perspective*. Cambridge: Cambridge University Press.

Viren, M. and Malkamäki, M. 2002. "The Nordic Countries". In *Technological Innovation & Economic Performance* edited by Steil, B. and Victor, D. and Nelson, R., 200–226. Princeton: Princeton University Press.

Appendix

Box 2-A1

Panel data estimates with all alternative measures in the same equation

Growth rate of GDP =

–0.054 (2.27) The wage share (t-ratio)
–0.035 (2.04) The adjusted wage share
+0.006 (0.76) The terms of trade
–0.038 (2.63) The real exchange rate
–0.063 (2.52) The unit labour costs
+0.182 (3.80) The gross tax rate
–0.138 (3.88) The government size (expenditures/GDP)
+0.029 (1.85) The HP trend of average working hours (log)
–0.297 (4.27) The needs-weighted dependency ratio
–0.062 (0.88) The real interest rate
+0.571 (7.53) The US GDP growth rate
+2.846 (1.04) constant

$R^2 = 0.529$; $SSE = 0.016$, $DW = 1.346$;

OLS with no fixed & random effects

Note: See Box 2-1 for other details.

Table 2-A1 Estimation results

	1	2	3	4	5	5	6	7	8	9	10
ws_a	-0.27							-0.126			
	(4.63)							(3.17)			
ws		-0.309	-0.211	-0.297	-0.137	-0.179	-0.237		-0.191	-0.745	-0.213
		(4.23)	(3.63)	(4.77)	(1.47)	(3.04)	(4.41)		(3.75)	(2.43)	(3.23)
fx	-0.038	-0.033	-0.043	-0.038		-0.03	-0.03	-0.035	-0.038	-0.015	-0.019
log	(2.35)	(2.37)	(2.94)	(2.30)		(2.65)	(2.27)	(2.42)	(2.75)	(0.39)	(1.23)
ulc					-0.137						
					(4.68)						
tax	-0,015	-0.143		-0.112	-0.065	-0.1	-0.152			-0.225	-0.116
	(0.38)	(2.63)		(2.00)	(1.12)	(1.93)	(2.95)			(1.15)	(2.22)
govexp			-0.142					-0.085	-0.082		
			(4.69)					(2.88)	(2.29)		
hours	0.082	0.071	0.0433	0.027	0.071	0.059	0.038	0.042	0.027	0.089	0.057
log	(5.03)	(2.83)	(1.84)	(1.82)	(2.64)	(0.19)	(1.54)	(2.44)	(1.14)	(1.03)	(1.91)
rr	-0.081	-0.166	-0.037	-0.18	-0.162	-0.179	-0.094	-0.008	-0.042	-0.032	-0.131
	(1.46)	(2.87)	(0.54)	(3.20)	(2.89)	(2.30)	(1.77)	(0.13)	(0.65)	(0.74)	(1.76)
dep				-0.245	-0.369	0.019				-0.036	-0.286
				(2.15)	(3.10)	(0.20)				(1.15)	(2.24)
USg	0.589	0.692	0.643	0.646	0.57		0.665	0.591	0.634	0.441	0.345
	(7.97)	(8.52)	(8.11)	(7.82)	(7.48)		(6.65)	(8.35)	(8.03)	(4.70)	(4.46)
hightech											0.303
											(1.90)
g_1						0.347	0.303	0.232	0.251	0.411	
						(4.51)	(5.49)	(3.02)	(3.89	(3.13)	
panel	CS	CS	CS	CS	CS	CS&TS	CS	CS	CS	..	CS
R^2	0.529	0.495	0.526	0.505	0.561	0.787	0.579	0.595	0.576	..	0.41
SEE	0.0171	0.0166	0.0161	0.0165	0.0157	0.0115	0.0152	0.0159	0.0152	0.0177	0.0133
DW	1.43	1.43	1.45	1.44	1.37	1.85	1.98	1.81	1.89		1.3
J-test (n)	..	..		..		..	..	..		7.41 (14)	

Source: AMECO database

Numbers inside parentheses are corrected t-ratios. CS denotes cross-section fixed effects and TS period fixed effects (test statistics for the cross-section fixed effects always exceed conventional critical values). Estimates in column (9) are GMM estimates. The number of datapoints is 375. However, with equation 10 it is only 253.

Table 2-A2 Convergence of unit labour costs

	coefficient	t-ratio
All countries	-0.078	2.61
Individual coefficients		
Austria	+0.012	0.26
Belgium	+0.040	0.36
Denmark	0	0.01
Finland	-0.096	1.54
France	+0.048	0.85
Greece	-0.038	1.45
Ireland	-0.096	1.19
Italy	+0.050	0.45
Luxembourg	-0.466	2.34
Netherlands	-0.002	0.03
Portugal	-0.211	2.19
Spain	+0.029	0.23
Sweden	-0.03	0.43
UK	-0.018	0.29

Source: AMECO database
Note: On the first row, we have a common coefficient for all countries and on subsequent rows country-specific coefficients. Germany is the reference country in both experiments.

JAPAN'S TWO LOST DECADES: LESSONS FOR TODAY'S EURO CRISIS?

MASAHIKO YOSHII

1. Introduction

Japan experienced an economic boom in the middle of the 1980s. Commercial land prices in the Tokyo area increased by 57% in 1987, while those in the Osaka area rose by 36%, 36%, and 40% in 1988, 1989, and 1990, respectively. The Nikkei index increased from 12,565 yen in 1985 to 38,915 yen in December 1989. These increases led to capital gains from 1987–89 of 1,343 trillion yen, more than three times the Japanese GDP in 1989.

The boom ended in 1990 and 1991, and the Japanese economy has stagnated for the last twenty years. GDP increased slightly after the collapse but stagnated once again with the onset of the Asian financial crisis in 1997. Today, due to the Lehman Brothers shock in 2008, the GDP is almost as low as it was in 1991 (Fig. 3-1).

Economists have thoroughly studied the lost decades of the 1990s and 2000s.[1] The main issues are the following:

A) Why Japan has experienced such a long recession.
B) What remedies Japan should utilise to overcome the crisis:
    1) from the demand side: fiscal and/or monetary policies, and

[1] A number of books and articles have been published investigating why Japan experienced such a long recession. Okita (2010) discusses the Japanese post-war economy. Miyazaki (1992) is a memorable book on causes and impacts of the bubble. Chapter 19 of Hashimoto (2011) gives a very concise overview of the recession. Ogawa (2009), Kataoka (2010) and Otaki (2011) looked back the history of lost two decades. Itoh et al. (2005) and Iwata and Miyagawa (2003) collected discussions from both supply and demand sides. Todou (2011), Ono (2012) and many others discuss how to overcome the long recession from either the supply or demand side.

2) from the supply side: how to raise productivity through structural reform.

C) The effects of the lost decades:
1) on the Japanese economy,
2) on the ageing society, etc.

In this paper, we will summarise these discussions and attempt to draw lessons for today's European economy.

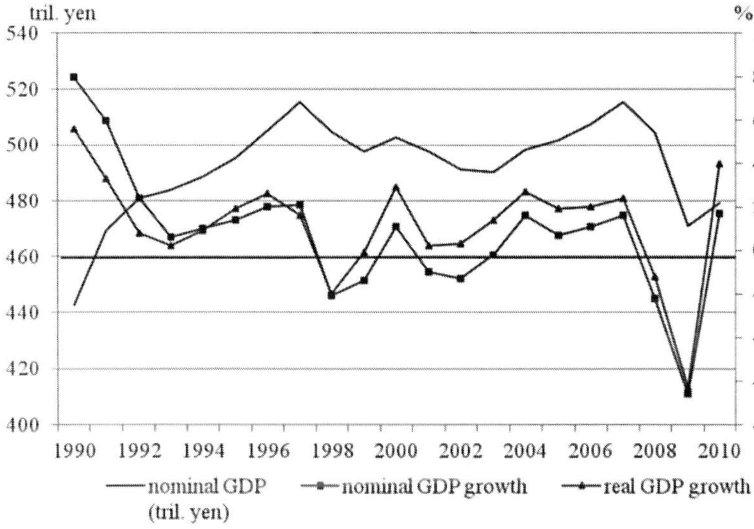

Fig. 3-1 GDP and its growth rate
Source: Cabinet Office (2011, 343)

2. After the feast

In 1991, the Japanese boom ended and the lost decades began. In the beginning, there were two serious problems: (1) an unused production capacity problem and (2) a balance sheet problem. During the bubble, Japanese companies expanded their production capacities on the assumption that the economic boom would never end. For example, the number of cars produced increased from 8.0 million in 1985 to 13.2 million in 1991, only to decrease to 10.8 million in 1995 (Statistics Bureau 2011a). With the bust, these capacities became excessive.

When the bubble burst in 1991, the capacity utilising rate of the manufacturing industry as a whole dropped from a rate of 100–110 to 90–100 (Fig. 3-2). The capacity utilisation rate of the automobile industry decreased drastically to a rate of 70–80; the steel industry soon fell to a similar level.

As Japanese companies reduced investment, productivity stagnated and, in the second half of the 1990s, unemployment began to increase.

The more serious problem was the balance sheet problem. With Japanese companies believing that land prices would remain high, they increased borrowing with land as collateral. When land prices began to fall, the land standard system – borrowing with land used as collateral → new production capacities → sales increase → profit increase → price increase → land price (collateral) hikes → borrowing – also collapsed, and non-performing loans abounded. The non-performing loan problem was most serious in the real estate, construction, and wholesale & retail sectors, as these three sectors very prominently expanded their capacities on the basis of the land standard system (Fig. 3-3).

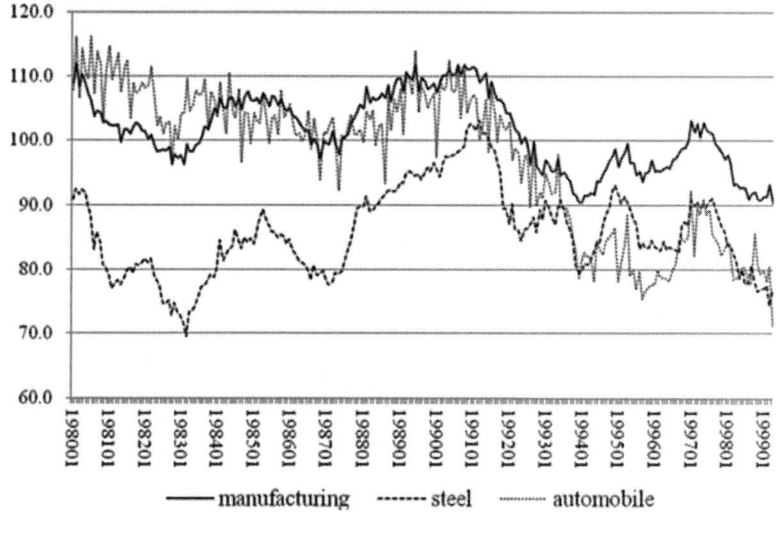

Fig. 3-2 Capacity utilisation rates
Source: Author's compilation based on the data of Ministry of Economy, Trade and Industry (2011)

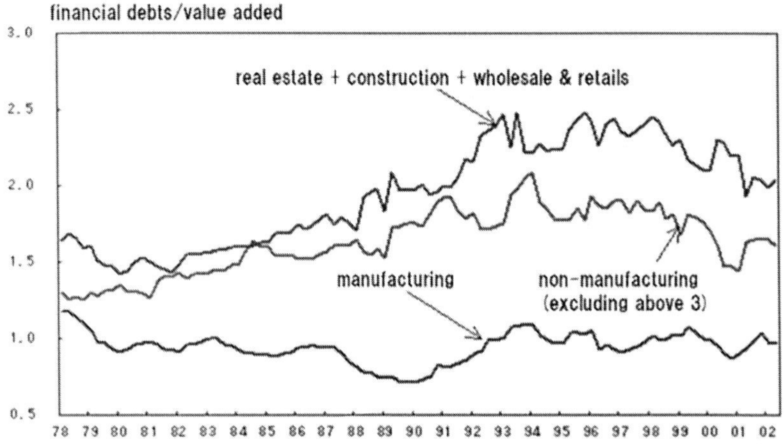

Fig. 3-3 Non-performing loan problems
Source: Cabinet Office (2002, 34)

Though Japanese banks faced increasing numbers of non-performing loans within the above three sectors, they, somewhat surprisingly, continued lending to these companies. The banks, companies, and government all believed that the economy would soon recover, but this was not to be. Some companies within these three sectors went bankrupt, and the non-performing loan problem was transferred onto the banking sector.

Figure 3-4 reveals that the non-performing loan problem first impacted the banking sector in 1995, four years after the bubble burst, and that it took nearly seven years to resolve. There are several reasons why this took so long. First, the companies, banks, and government all underestimated the seriousness of the recession. Second, in the beginning, the definition of non-performing loan was excessively narrowly defined by the government. Third, a debate on who was responsible for the costs of the non-performing loans took place. In particular, the general public could not consent to the idea that the non-financial sectors or the financial companies with non-performing loans would be bailed out by tax-payer money. Finally, the Ministry of Finance tried to sustain the convoy system (*Goso Sendan Houshiki*) by adjusting the banking regulations so that not even the worst-off banks would fall into bankruptcy. For example, each bank offered the same interest rate on deposits.

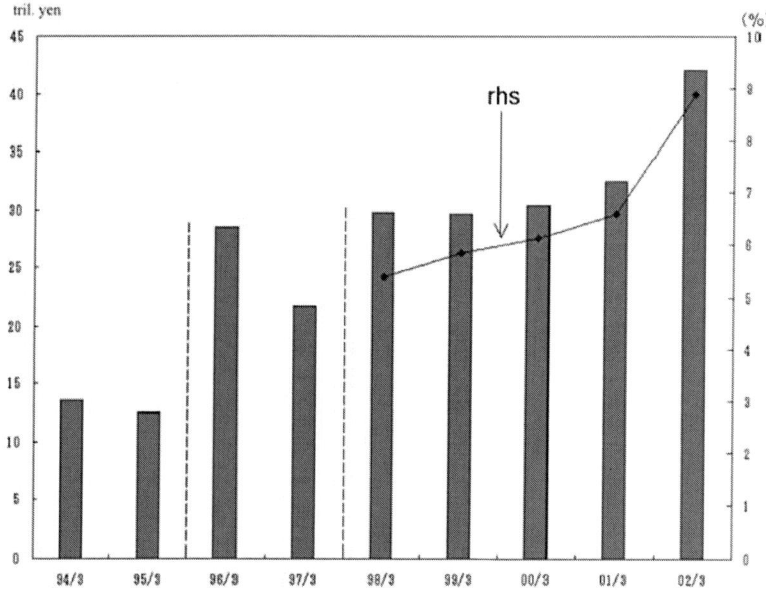

Fig. 3-4 Banking sector's non-performing loans
Source: Cabinet Office (2002, 47)

The situation dramatically changed in November 1997 when two large financial institutions went bankrupt. First, Hokkaido-Takushoku Bank, one of the largest Japanese banks, failed due to a resort development project in Hokkaido and closed its doors on 15 November. Then, Yamaichi Security, the second largest security company after Nomura, declared bankruptcy on 24 November due to enormous off-the-book liabilities.

Insolvencies occurred before these two large financial institutions went bankrupt. One example is a bankruptcy of Hyogo Bank several months after the Great Awaji Hanshin Earthquake, which hit Kobe, where the headquarters of the bank were located, in January 1995. The bankruptcies of Hokkaido-Takushoku Bank and Yamaichi Security signalled that the Ministry of Finance could no longer sustain the convoy system, resulting in the other large financial institutions substantially increasing the pace of their financial consolidations. This led to the establishment of mega-financial systems in Japan: four financial groups[2] and the independent Nomura Security.

Discussions on whether the government should inject capital into the large banks continued. On the one hand, it was difficult to convince the general public that financial institutions should be bailed out by tax-payer money. On the other hand, the large banks refused to accept the capital injections because they were afraid of being nationalised.

In October 2002, the Koizumi Cabinet settled on the "Program for Financial Revival", which dictated that the Financial Services Agency normalise the non-performing loans (NPLs) problem by reducing major banks' NPL ratio to approximately one-half (Financial Service Agency 2002).

In June 2003, the government injected two trillion yen into Resona Bank, whose financial condition was the worst among the mega-banks. Other mega-banks augmented their capital by issuing proffered stocks and allocating shares to third parties in order to avoid nationalisation.[3] As shown in Figure 3-5, the large banks' non-performing loans began to decrease from a peak of 25 trillion yen in the beginning of 2002. While 56 banks went bankrupt in 2001, only one bank has done so since 2002.

It took more than ten years after the collapse of the bubble to settle the non-performing loan problem. It is not difficult to imagine such an enduring experience significantly changing the behaviour of Japanese companies and households.

A) Banking sector:

The first consequence of the non-performing loan problem is that Japanese banks gradually became reluctant to extend credit to businesses, even those with healthy financial outlooks, to preserve the capital adequacy ratios defined by the Bank of International Settlement (BIS). The role of Japanese banks as funding centres diminished. The second consequence is that their role as main banks also decreased. The symbolic event was the merger of Sumitomo Bank, the main bank of the Sumitomo group, and Sakura Bank, the main bank of the Mitsui group, in 2001. The decrease of roles of main banks was not limited to large banks. As small banks' financial positions became more vulnerable and they became less willing to extend credit, their roles as main banks to small and medium enterprises (SMEs) also diminished.

---

[2] Mitsubishi Tokyo UFJ Financial Group, the Sumitomo Mitsui Financial Group, Mizuho Financial Group, and the Resona Group.

[3] Nishikawa (2011) described how the author, then governor of Sumitomo Mitsui Financial Group, overcame the non-performing loan problems.

B) Non-banking sectors:

Most companies within the non-banking sectors also made serious efforts to survive the non-performing loan problems. The easiest way was to reduce costs by curtailing investments and employment. However, this led to the fallacy of composition problem. The fact that investment demands and household incomes have not increased is one of the reasons why Japanese GDP has stagnated for the last twenty years. However, the more serious problem was that curtailing investments led to competitiveness losses within Japan's manufacturing industries. Whether the Japanese TFP (total factor productivities) has plateaued is one of the biggest discussions on the lost decades (Hayashi and Prescott 2002). Discussions on supply-side options ensued.

C) Households:

As mentioned in the previous paragraph, Japanese companies tried to curtail labour costs, and household incomes have stagnated for the last two decades. Additionally, deflation and household thriftiness led to decreases in consumption.

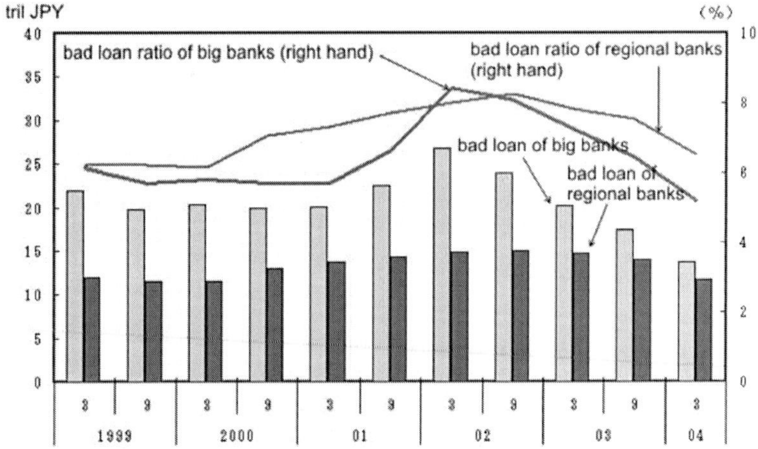

Fig. 3-5 Resolution of non-performing loans
Source: Cabinet Office (2004, 85)

3. Stimuli to recover

3.1 Timid attitude of the government in the 1990s

The Japanese government did not sit idly by as the economy faltered. At first, the government tried to support the economy from the demand side through active fiscal policies to increase public investments and reduce taxes. The Bank of Japan (BoJ) also relaxed monetary policy. The government also tried to support the economy from the supply side through structural policies. These measures were not successful.

First, let us look at the fiscal policy of the 1990s (Fig. 3-6). We notice the following points. Expenditures increased during the period at approximately the same pace. The government had no choice but to continue using active fiscal policies since the economy continued to stagnate for the next ten years. Second, tax revenue had significantly fallen. The government expected that reducing tax rates would save the economy and increase tax revenue. However, the expectation was not realistic. Third, because of increasing expenditures and decreasing tax revenue, the state debt has increased. However, looking at the figure in detail, we find that the deficit government bond, which is issued for the purpose of covering the budget deficit, was not issued until 1994. This might indicate that the government did not strongly intend to stimulate the economy at that time.

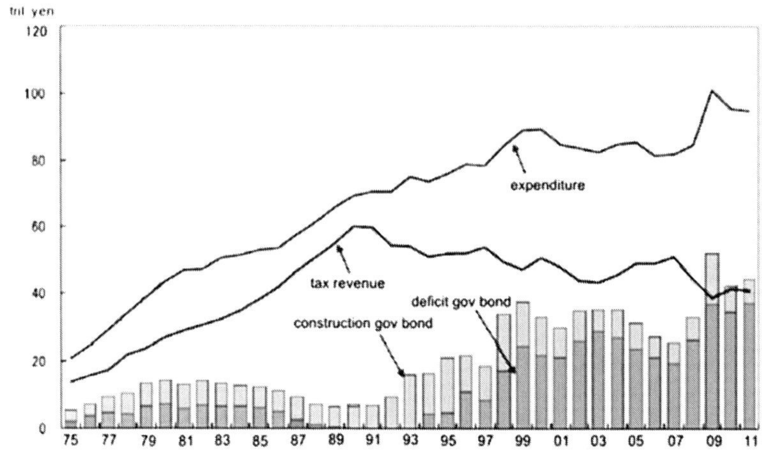

Fig. 3-6 Japanese central government budget
Source: Ministry of Finance (2011a)

Regarding the monetary policy of the 1990s, we notice the timid attitude of the Bank of Japan. After the official discount rate reached six per cent during 1990, it continued to decline. It was not until 1995, four years after the bubble burst, that it reached the bottom level (Fig. 3-7). From these facts, we may say that the BoJ might think that keeping the interest rate level high enough to hold down the land price hikes was still the priority task even after the bubble burst, that the BoJ also thought that the Japanese economy would recover soon, and that capital losses could be recovered in the near future.

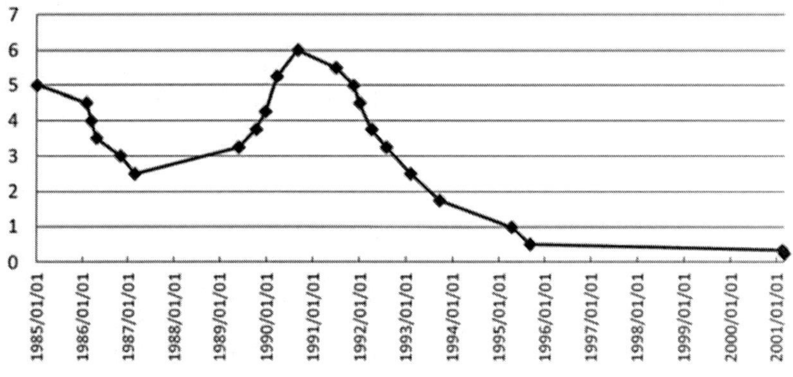

Fig. 3-7 Official discount rate
Source: Bank of Japan (2011)

3.2 The government policies of the 2000s

The 2000s were years of deflation. Returning to Figure 3-1, it shows that the nominal GDP growth rates have been less than the real GDP growth rates. That means that GDP deflators and price indices were negative during the 2000s. Because the macroeconomic environment changed in the 2000s, the Japanese government also changed their policies.

Referring to the government budget (Fig. 3-6), we find that the government (i.e., the Koizumi Cabinet between April 2001 and September 2006) tried to curtail expenditures and the issuing of state bonds. This fiscal approach saw modest success with a weak but extended boom in the middle of the 2000s.

The Lehman Brothers shock frustrated this fiscal strategy. Expenditures increased to 101 trillion yen in FY2009 from the previous year's 85 trillion yen, and state bond issuance increased by 20 trillion yen to 52 trillion yen in FY2009. The Japanese fiscal situation had reached a very dangerous point in that the value of the newly issued state bonds surpassed that of tax revenue.

Table 3-1 shows the overnight call rate target, which is today's policy interest rate. The BoJ has adopted a zero interest rate policy since 1999 (except for a short period between August 2000 and February 2001).

Table 3-1 Overnight call rate target

date	overnight rate target	remarks
2/1999	0.15%	zero interest rate policy
11/8/2000	0.25%	temporary lift
28/2/2001	0.15%	reintroduction
14/7/2006	0.25%	re-lift
21/2/2007	0.50%	
31/10/2008	0.30%	
19/12/2008	0.10%	
5/10/2010	0.0 – 0.1%	

Source: Authors own construction by The Bank of Japan

When the IT bubble burst in 2001, the BoJ had no room to lower the interest rate. Instead, the BoJ turned to an unconventional quantitative easing policy to broaden the monetary base by buying financial assets and injecting a pre-determined quantity of money into the economy. This increased the excess reserves of the banks. However, comparing how the monetary bases in the US, Japan, UK, Euro-area and China were broadened (Fig. 3-8), we note that the BoJ was very timid in broadening the monetary base during the 2000s. As a result of the BoJ failing to broaden the monetary base to an extent similar to the US or the ECB, some economists demanded that the BoJ introduce the inflation target policy[4] and more decisively broaden the monetary base.[5]

Let us summarise the reasons why the monetary policies were ineffective for the last two decades. First, the priority of the monetary policy remained controlling high land prices even after the burst of the bubble. Second, a de facto zero interest rate policy began at the end of the

[4] At the Monetary Policy Meeting on 14 February, 2012, The BoJ for the first time officially mentioned the inflation target, saying that The Bank judges "the price stability goal in the medium to long term" to be within a positive range of 2% or lower in terms of the year-on-year rate of change in the CPI and, more specifically, sets a goal at 1% for the time being.

[5] Moriyama (2011) is an example.

1990s but was only modest in effect. Third, a de jure zero interest policy was introduced in 1999 but was lifted while the recovery remained weak and the IT bubble had not yet burst. Fourth, quantitative easing was introduced, but the monetary base remained insufficiently large. In sum, the BoJ failed to introduce the bold policies necessary to overcome the stagnant economy of the last twenty years.

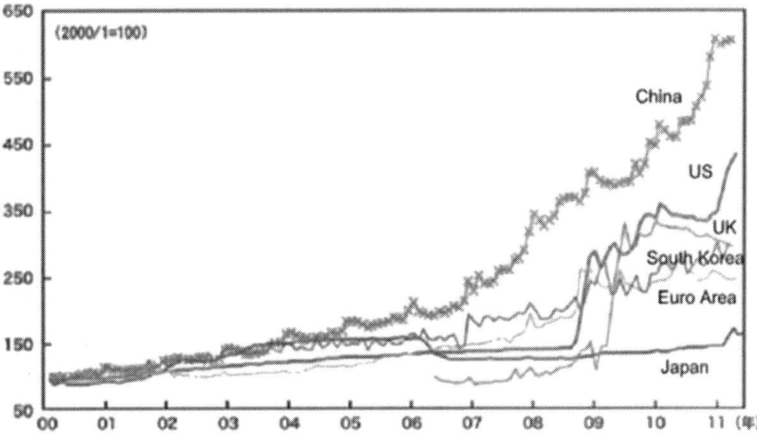

Fig. 3-8 Monetary base balance
Source: Daiwa Institute of Research (2011)

4. Structural reforms

In the previous sections, we have discussed how to increase demand via fiscal and monetary policy. However, policies from the supply side were also considered. These policies always emphasise the importance of breaking away from the Japanese economic system, which was admired with *Japan as Number One* in the 1980s (Vogel 1979).

A) Public structural reforms:

Public structural reforms were mainly driven by the Koizumi Cabinet. Prime Minister Koizumi emphasised it with the phrase "No Reform, No Growth." The three pillars of the reform were:

1. from public to private
    - privatisation of the postal and highway systems,
    - marketisation test,

    - deregulation of the labour market,
    - integration and abolition of public entities,[6]
    - promotion of special zones.
2. from centre to region
    - abolition and curtailment of state subsidies,
    - transfer of tax sources,
    - revision of local allocation tax grants.
3. other reforms
    - promotion of Free Trade Agreements and Economic Partnership Agreements,
    - medical system reform,
    - off-budget system reform.

The most debated reform was privatisation of the postal system. When the Postal Service Privatization Act was rejected by the Upper House in August 2005, Prime Minister Koizumi dissolved the Lower House and called a general election. After Koizumi won the election, the law was approved. The Japan Post System was divided into the Japan Post Service, Japan Post Bank, Japan Post Insurance, and Japan Post Network.[7]

Additionally, labour market reform increased the flexibility of the work force. The share of permanent workers decreased from approximately 75% in 2000 to approximately 65% in 2009.[8]

B) Private structural reforms:

Regarding private structural reform, breaking away from the Japanese economic system was the key idea. Some examples follow.

1. dismantling *keiretsu* (grouping)

Under the Japanese economic system, the sub-contracting system was widely used. Assembly (parent) companies purchased parts of the products from sub-contractors (child companies) under the same *keiretsu*. The *keiretsu* system began to be dismantled in 1999 when Carlos Ghosn became president of Nissan.

2. dismantling main banks

Mutual/cross holding of stocks among the group companies, with banks being at the top of the cross holding system, was very common. For example, Mitsubishi/Sumitomo/Mitsui Banks were the main banks of the

---

[6] National universities were transformed to national university corporations in April 2004.

[7] See the organization chart: http://www.japanpost.jp/en/group/map/.

[8] *Annual Report on Japanese Economy and Public Finance, FY2009.*

Mitsubishi/Sumitomo/Mitsui Groups. When these banks began to address their non-performing loan problems, they could not afford to maintain the main bank system.

3. corporate governance reform

Based on the life-long employment system in Japan, most presidents of large companies designated their successors, and outsider influence was very limited. In 2003, the Commercial Law was revised and some Japanese corporations introduced the committee system.[9]

5. The consequences of the lost decades

In the previous sections, we showed how the Japanese government and companies struggled to overcome the non-performing loan problem and the stagnant economy. The main consequences of the lost decades were the following.

A) Competitiveness loss

Has Japan regained its competitiveness? Japan's IMD World Competitiveness ranking is shown in Figure 3-9. Japan fell from its highest competitiveness ranking to today's ranking of just 26th. The fact that today's GDP is approximately the same as that of 1991 symbolises Japan's stalled competitiveness.

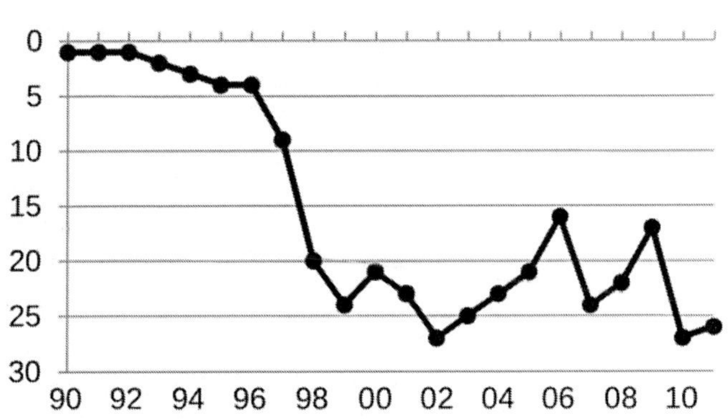

Fig. 3-9 Japanese competitiveness
Source: Kogures.com (2011)

[9] http://www.sony.net/SonyInfo/News/Press_Archive/200301/03-004E/

B) State debt

One of the greatest consequences is the state debt (Fig. 3-10). Because of increasing fiscal expenditures and the revenue gap since the end of the bubble, state debt has been increasing. Its accumulation accelerated particularly after the Lehman Brothers shock of 2008. The state debt at the end of Fiscal Year 2011 (March 2012) was 667 trillion yen, 141% of GDP. It should be noted that this debt is thc responsibility of the central government alone. Adding the local government debts, the figure increases to 894 trillion yen, 189% of GDP (Ministry of Finance 2011a). The general government debt, which includes the social security fund deficit, etc., is 1,024 trillion yen, almost 200% of GDP (Ministry of Finance 2011a).

These figures are the worst among advanced economies, even considering the Greek figures. However, the possibility of fiscal insolvency in the short term is limited since almost all of the state debt is held by the Japanese people.

The risk of fiscal insolvency in the long term, however, is high. As the Japanese society ages at an increasing rate, expenditures for social security will increase. At the same time, the Japanese saving ratio will decrease, leading to a current account deficit. These trends may force the Japanese credit rating to be lowered, increasing interest rates and making it more difficult to redeem government bonds.

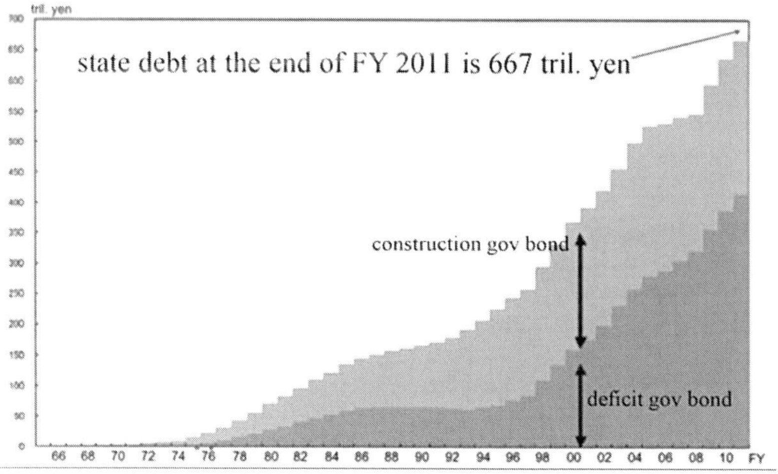

Fig. 3-10 Central government debts
Source: Ministry of Finance (2011b)

C) Public structural reforms

As mentioned earlier, the postal and highway systems, as well as other public corporation systems, were reformed in the 2000s. Before this, there were reforms of the national railway, telegraph and telephone, and tobacco and salt public corporations during the 1980s (today's Japan Railway (JR) networks, NTT groups (Nippon Telegraph and Telephone Corporation), and Japan Tobacco).

Except for some of the JR groups (JRs Hokkaido, Shikoku, Kyushu and Freight), which have never turned a profit due to their challenging geographical situations, shares of the formerly public corporations were sold to the public. They were, genuinely speaking, privatised.

Shares of the Japan Post and the Japan Highway groups, however, remain in the hands of the government. They were corporatized, but their privatisation, i.e. concrete tender programs, have not yet been finalised. Furthermore, due to the ousting of the Liberal Democratic Party, which had ruled Japanese politics for more than fifty years, in 2009, the privatisation program of the Japan Post group is now being reconsidered.

D) Private structural reforms

Regarding private company reforms, we have seen that corporate governance and other reforms were initiated in the 2000s, but they have not yet borne fruit. For example, Sony is thought to have lost its innovative edge (Tateishi 2011 and Tsujino 2011), has posted losses every year since FY2008, and has announced the dissolution of its joint venture with Samsung to produce LCD panels. Furthermore, window-dressing settlements of Olympus and unjust financing to the former chairperson by Daio Paper have revealed that corporate social responsibility has not penetrated sufficiently into Japanese corporations.

6. Conclusions

We summarise what we have discussed as follows.

In the 1990s:

- The Japanese government and private sector had optimistic views of the recession after the bubble burst in 1991. They thought the recession would come to an end soon and that the virtuous cycle of the Japanese economic system, including the land standard system, would work well again. This belief caused a delay in acknowledging the seriousness of the recession.
- The stimulus fiscal package was too little, too late.

- The monetary authority was afraid of the land price hikes and their monetary policies were timid.
- The collapse of the bubble caused the non-performing loan problems in the non-manufacturing three sectors and then in the banking sector. It was not until 2002 that the non-performing loan problem in the banking sector was resolved.
- GDP increased a little even after the collapse of the bubble, but stopped growing in 1997 when the Asian financial crisis took place.

In the 2000s:

- The non-performing loan problems were resolved in 2002 after the Koizumi Cabinet settled on the "Program for Financial Revival."
- In the process of resolving the non-performing loan problems, Japanese banks became reluctant to lend to companies, especially small and medium-sized enterprises.
- Even during the weak but long boom of the 2000s, Japan's state debt continued to increase. After the IT bubble burst in 2001 and the Lehman Brothers shock in 2008, extremely aggressive fiscal policies made the state debt situation much worse. Today, the state debt is valued at 200% of GDP.
- The state debt is a serious concern for the ageing society of Japan.
- The Japanese government tried to implement structural policies to raise productivity and increase the effectiveness of the economy. However, the government policies were not bold enough to be successful.
- Japanese companies tried to reform themselves. However, the reforms were insufficient and the Japanese economy has not recovered its competitiveness of the 1980s.

The EU economy has been seriously damaged by the Lehman Brothers shock and the euro crisis. Most EU member countries have accumulated large sovereign and private debts since 2008 (although the Japanese debt remains higher).

The EU economy is now searching for an exit from their unhealthy situation. The European Stability Mechanism (ESM), which will come into force in September 2012, is expected to reform the functioning of the euro zone. It is also expected to accelerate the fiscal consolidation process and to facilitate harmonisation of the fiscal systems among the member countries. The EU also adopted the "Europe 2020" strategy to increase its competitiveness.

However, the Japanese experience shows that these efforts will not bear fruit if the governments, the ECB, and the companies do not take prompt and decisive measures. If they do not, they may also experience at least two lost decades.

References

Bank of Japan. 2011. "Official Discount Rates." Institute for Monetary and Economic Studies. http://www.imes.boj.or.jp/english/hstat/data/rates/index.html

Cabinet Office. 2002. "White Paper on Japanese Economy and Public Finance."

—. 2004. "Annual Report on Japanese Economy and Public Finance, FY2004."

—. 2011. "White Paper on Japanese Economy and Public Finance."

Daiwa Institute of Research. 2011. "Changes in monetary base balance of major countries (in Japanese)."
http://kokka-vision.jp/_src /sc1203/92868CB4.pdf

Financial Service Agency. 2002. "Program for Financial Revival - Revival of the Japanese Economy through Resolving Non-Performing Loans Problems of Major Banks"
http://www.fsa.go.jp/news /newse/e20021030.pdf

Hashimoto, J. et al., eds. 2011. *On the Japanese Economy* (in Japanese), 3rd edition. Tokyo: Yuhikaku.

Hayashi, F. and Prescott E.C. 2002. "The 1990s in Japan: A Lost Decade." *Review of Economic Dynamics*, 5, 1: 206–235.

Itoh, T. et al., eds. 2005. *Japanese Economy under the Post Heisei Recession: Analyses by Policy-oriented Approach* (in Japanese). Tokyo: Nihon-Keizai-Shinbunsh.

Iwata, K. and Miyagawa, T., eds. 2003. *What is the True Cause of the Lost Decade* (in Japanese). Tokyo: Toyo-Keizai-Shinposha.

Kataoka, T. 2010. *Japan's 'Lost Two Decades': towards Economic Policies to Overcome the Deflation* (in Japanese). Tokyo: Fujiwara-shoten.

Kogures.com. 2011. "Trends in Japan's ranking in the IMD World Competitiveness Reports" (in Japanese). http://www.kogures.com /hitoshi/webtext/ref-data/imd-wcy-overall.html

Ministry of Economy, Trade and Industry. 2011. "Statistics, Indices of Industrial Production, Historical Data" (in Japanese).

http://www.meti.go.jp/statistics/tyo/iip/result/h2afdldj/csv/ha2ngsm2j.csv

Ministry of Finance. 2011a. "Budget, General Account Tax Revenues and Government Bond Issues (in Japanese)." http://www.zaisei.mof.go.jp

—. 2011b. "Japan's Fiscal Condition" (in Japanese). http://www.mof.go.jp/budget/fiscal_condition/related_data/sy014_23.pdf

Miyazaki, G. 1992. *Multiple Recession: towards a Prescription to overcome the Post-Bubble* (in Japanese). Tokyo: Chuo-Kouronsha.

Moriyama, K. 2011: *Isn't the Economic Growth Impossible any more* (in Japanese). Tokyo: Chuo-Kouronsha.

Nishikawa, Y. 2011. *The Last Banker* (in Japanese). Tokyo: Kodansha.

Ogawa, K. 2009: *The Truth of the "Lost Decade"* (in Japanese). Tokyo: Toyo–Keizai-Shinposha.

Okita Y. 2010. *On the Post-War Japanese Economy* (in Japanese). Tokyo: Toyo-Keizai-Shinposha.

Ono Y. 2012. *Economics of the Matured Society: How to Overcome the Long Recession* (in Japanese). Tokyo: Iwanami-shoten.

Otaki M., 2011. *Essence of the Heisei Recession: From the Employment and Financial Aspects* (in Japanese). Tokyo: Iwanami-shoten.

Statistics Bureau. 2011. "Historical Statistics of Japan." Ministry of Internal Affairs and Communications, Statistics Bureau. http://www.stat.go.jp/english/data/chouki/index.htm

Tateishi, Y. 2011. *Goodbye! Our SONY* (in Japanese). Tokyo: Bungei-Shunjusha.

Todou, Y. 2011. *Real Potentials of the Japanese Economy* (in Japanese). Tokyo: Chuo-Kouronsha,.

Tsujino, K. 2011. *All the Necessaries in Google were What I Learnt in SONY* (in Japanese). Tokyo: Shinchosha.

Vogel E. F., 1979. *Japan as Number One: Lessons for America*. Cambridge, Mass.: Harvard University Press.

CHAPTER TWO

CHALLENGES OF FISCAL AND MONETARY POLICY

The EU Budget: A "Trojan Horse" for Better National Spending?

Gabriele Cipriani[1]

1. Introduction

The legend of the Trojan Horse, told in Virgil's Aeneid, exemplifies a masterstroke of cunning. At the end of the 12th century BC, after ten years of war, the Greeks could not breach Troy's walls. Yet, the Trojans could not drive the Greeks away.

Then, the Greeks devised a plot. Pretending to admit defeat and to sail home, they left behind them a huge wooden horse as an offering to the goddess Athena. Thirty Greek warriors hid themselves inside the horse. In fact, the Greek fleet actually hid just nearby.

Smelling a trap, the priest Laocoon wanted to burn the horse and warned the Trojans:

> "O wretched countrymen! What fury reigns? What more than madness has possess'd your brains? Think you the Grecians from your coasts are gone? (…) Somewhat is sure design'd, by fraud or force: Trust not their presents, nor admit the horse" (Vergilius).

The Trojans ignored the warning and rolled the horse into the city as a reminder of their victory. During the night the Greek warriors came out of the horse and opened Troy's gates to the other Greek warriors. There was a big battle and the Greeks won.

The idea of a "Trojan Horse", meant as a way to put in place the conditions for achieving specific objectives, is somewhat implicit in the EU's actions, whose aim is to reach a better result than the member states

---

[1] The opinions expressed by the author in this publication in no way commit the European Court of Auditors to which he belongs. The author gratefully acknowledges the insightful comments as well as the editorial assistance received.

could achieve by themselves. This aim is the basis of the EU added value concept.

2. The EU fundamentals

The European Union originates from the member states' decision to pool selected aspects of their respective sovereign powers to attain objectives they have in common (Articles 1, 5(1)(2) of the Treaty on European Union (TEU)). The Union's competences, most of which are shared with the member states, are therefore based upon the achievement of these objectives.[2] The Union's competences imply the identification of "what" the EU should be doing and "how" it should be done. Here the principles of subsidiarity and proportionality come into play. Before launching an initiative, it is essential to systematically check (a) whether public action is really necessary, (b) whether action at the European level is the most appropriate, and (c) whether the measures chosen are proportionate to achieving those objectives (European Commission 2001, 11).

The subsidiarity principle, applicable in the areas of shared competence with the member states, requires one to demonstrate that the member states cannot sufficiently achieve the objectives of the proposed EU action, which can instead, by reason of its scale or effects, be better achieved by the Union (Art. 5(3) TEU). Subsidiarity implies weighing up all types of advantages and disadvantages and, finally, the exercise of political discretion. Subsidiarity is a dynamic concept that allows EU action to be expanded where the circumstances so require and, conversely,

---

[2] Art. 2 of the Treaty on the Functioning of the European Union establishes three categories of EU competences depending on the intervention field (exclusive, shared with the member states, and competence to carry out actions to support, coordinate or supplement the members states' actions). The European Union has exclusive competence in few areas (see Art. 3 TFEU). It is worth mentioning that Art. 4(1) TEU (and Declaration No. 18 in relation to the delimitation of competences attached to the Treaty of Lisbon) underlines that "competences not conferred upon the Union in the Treaties remain with the Member States". Protocol No. 25 on the exercise of shared competence clarifies that "when the Union has taken action in a certain area, the scope of this exercise of competence only covers those elements governed by the Union act in question and therefore does not cover the whole area". An increase or a reduction of EU competences can be decided in accordance with the Treaty's ordinary revision procedure provided for in Art. 48 TEU. The procedure can be initiated by the member states, the European Parliament or the Commission. A Treaty revision would require ratification by the member states in accordance with their respective constitutional requirements.

to be restricted or discontinued where it is no longer justified. One of the characteristics of EU action is therefore to be "inevitable" in terms of reaching a better result and making a real difference.[3] The underlying logic is that for every EU action, one should be able to convincingly answer the question: Why Europe?

Moreover, the content and form of any Union action should be limited to "what is necessary to achieve the objectives of the Treaties" (principle of proportionality) (Art. 5(4) TEU). All EU measures should leave as much scope for national decision as possible. This concept explains, for example, why the Union has no administration at the individual country level so that it must rely on each member state to implement its decisions. The EU's implementing power is consequently residual and not monopolistic. The EU administration is, in fact, a chain of national administrations (Sigma 1998, 13).

EU actions are pursued above all through EU legislation. The latter is at the root of a significant (and growing) part of national legislation and is therefore instrumental in bringing different national laws in line with each other and effecting changes in the member countries' basic economic, social and political structures. For governments, EU law might even represent a welcome externally imposed discipline for overcoming internal resistance to far-reaching domestic reforms (i.e., the "*vincolo esterno*" metaphor conceptualised by the Italians).

3. The EU budget

As observed by the President of the European Commission, the EU budget is one of the tools available to achieve the Union's objectives and, in particular, to foster change (Barroso 2008).

As a consequence of the European Union's unique framework, the EU budget represents a type of "rare bird" in all aspects, from its approval and

[3] For example, the European Parliament has underlined that the main purpose of EU budgetary spending is to create European added value (EAV) by pooling resources, acting as a catalyst and offering economies of scale, positive transboundary and spill-over effects thus contributing to the achievement of agreed common policy targets more effectively or faster and reducing national expenditure. EU spending must always aim at creating greater value than the aggregated individual spending of member states (see European Parliament 2011, para. 15).

financing, through the management of its revenue and expenditure, to holding to account for its implementation.[4]

The EU budget does not, in general, finance goods and services aimed directly at EU citizens.[5] A significant part of its expenditure (approximately one-third) is devoted to agricultural markets and direct payments to farmers. The rest is divided up into more than 70 spending programmes, covering a wide range of sectors and contributing to similar actions financed from national budgets (for example, providing funds for infrastructure and favouring productive investments, training, research and studies).[6] In quantitative terms, the EU funds represent a relatively marginal financial contribution to the far higher-funded national programmes.[7] In some cases (notably, Cohesion, Rural Development and Fisheries), the EU actions are co-financed by national budgets. As a result, the EU and the national budgets are closely interconnected.

The EU budget has evolved over the years from a primarily political instrument of compensation to an instrument for economic development and pan-European objectives. Currently, the budget is a hybrid between a political and an economic instrument. One example is its pivotal role in the development of the internal market by making it acceptable for the member states (Núñez Ferrer 2012, 8). The cohesion policy is another example where the policy's rationale goes well beyond its financial dimension because it focuses on a long term change in investment patterns and on overcoming structural barriers to development; in order words, a

---

[4] For a complete review of the EU budget process, see European Commission (2008a). For a critical analysis, see the numerous contributions presented in the context of the EU budget review (European Commission 2008c). My own considerations are developed in Cipriani (2007).

[5] BusinessDictionary.com defines a public good as an "item whose consumption is not decided by the individual consumer but by the society as a whole, and which is financed by taxation. A public good (or service) may be consumed without reducing the amount available for others, and cannot be withheld from those who do not pay for it. Public goods (and services) include economic statistics and other information, law-and-order enforcement, national defence, national parks, etc. No market exists for such goods, and they must be provided to everyone by the government."

[6] For an overview of the different programmes funded by the EU budget, see European Commission (2012c).

[7] For example, although taking approximately 1/3 of the EU budget resources, the cohesion policy is still a relatively small policy when compared to similar spending in member states. Another example is provided by the research domain, the bulk of whose public funding is provided by the national budgets (approximately 95%).

"Trojan Horse" to improve and modernise public administrations, to enhance transparency and to foster good governance (Hübner 2007, 3).

The concept of EU added value mentioned earlier implies the ability to do things that nobody else can (or will) do, with better results. For the EU budget, this added value means that one euro spent at the EU level can offer more than one euro spent at the national level (European Commission 2004, 5,8). The EU budget *raison d'être* is, therefore, to produce a better added value compared to national spending, not to replace it.

Yet, what can the EU budget do that the member states cannot do for themselves? Does the European Union's role in a given policy area necessarily require EU spending? Is an EU budget of over €130 billion needed?

There is no straightforward answer to these questions because there are no "objective" criteria for deciding whether a policy fulfils the conditions for EU financing.[8] For example, if funding for cohesion, agriculture and research can be traced back to the Treaty, the latter does not clarify what actions should be undertaken and how much money should be invested in those policies. This lack of clarity is why the European Court of Auditors has suggested that "[t]he concept of European added value should be articulated in a suitable political declaration or in EU legislation in order to provide guidance to the EU's political authorities to be used when choosing expenditure priorities" (European Court of Auditors 2010a, point 18).

In fact, because of the integration between the European states, "nearly all policies have a European dimension and a national dimension" (European Commission 2002, 20).[9] In practice, the decision to complement EU actions with spending measures is made on "political" grounds. In

---

[8] It is worth mentioning that, already in 1978, the Commission had tried to define the intervention of the EU budget on the basis of criteria such as "economies of scale", the "need for a global approach with the other policies funded" or the "reduction of the burden of national budgets" (see European Commission 1978, 6–8). However, these criteria turned out to be too vague to be applied. With the Lisbon Treaty, it would still be possible for the EU budget to intervene in all sectors. Indeed, while the Treaty establishes three types of categories and areas of EU competence (see note (i)), it does not provide operational criteria to define the EU area of intervention.

[9] For example, immigration, justice, taxation, the labour market, energy and telecommunications are all sectors in which responsibilities are still largely national but which doubtlessly have effects across frontiers.

given situations, on the basis of different arguments, the member states can decide that the "European" level is preferable to the national level.[10]

Without denying the difficulties and differences surrounding the concept of EU added value,[11] it appears reasonable to identify three main characteristics for EU expenditure: *catalytic* (making something happen that otherwise would not happen or would happen more slowly); *targeted* (concentrated on the best added value and the most effective results on the basis of evaluation and impact assessment); and *realistic* (objectives should be achievable).

The use of the EU budget to make something happen that otherwise would not happen is based on three elements.

There is first "money", earmarked for specific objectives and meant to increase the overall funds available nationally for a given policy. This can be relatively significant in some cases.[12]

Second, these funds are made available for spending according to specified rules that are instrumental to achieving the EU added value through a number of specific requirements concerning for example public procurement, competition, environment, financial management, audit and control. More recent tendencies aim to introduce other forms of conditionality, such as funding disbursements that are linked to the

---

[10] Gros (2008, 2) argues that the current composition of spending is the result of historical accidents and that the main legacy of the 'founding' compromises on Agriculture and Structural Funds is that the budget is basically seen as a vehicle for the redistribution of money between member states, rather than as a tool for fostering common goals.

[11] For example, Tarschys (2005) observes that the notion of European added value can often appear to be capable of justifying almost anything as a worthy target for European funding. To make the concept operational in policy-making practice, one should design procedures and methods for assessing how the specific programmes and projects rank. This assessment would speak in favour of a two-pronged strategy. First, there is a need to take a hard look at the economic elements involved. Returns could differ a great deal between various policy areas. The second part of the appraisal would aim at estimating the strength of the various proposals with regard to their contribution to European cohesion, in the widest sense of that word. As a result, the concept of European added value should be reserved for (i) investments where the limited scope of the member states and the existence of economic externalities reduce their propensity to take appropriate action and for (ii) programmes and projects likely to make substantial contributions to promoting the sense of community and effective interaction within the European Union.

[12] For example, for the 2007–13 period, some €348 billion are set aside for Cohesion (all Funds), €96 billion for Rural Development, and €50 billion for Research programmes.

achievement of results or the countries' compliance with the Stability and Growth Pact (European Commission 2011b, articles 11 and 21).

Third, the budget is implemented by the Commission on its own responsibility and with regard for the principles of sound financial management.[13] However, to reflect the EU model of governance *without government*, the EU spending programmes can be implemented through several management modes, which are very different in nature and which imply a variable intensity for the EU intervention.[14] This intensity concerns, in particular, the degree of decision by the Commission in granting the funds and its direct control at the level of the funds' beneficiaries.

For most of the expenditures (approximately 80%), there is "co-administration" with the member states based on a partnership (or "shared management"). This partnership means that in reality the financial implementation (Commission) is dissociated from the main decision-taking aspect (member states). In particular, the member states must satisfy themselves that the actions financed from the EU budget are actually carried out and implemented correctly, while the Commission has a supervisory role and is not expected to micro-manage the implementation of the spending programmes. This segregation of functions shows that the EU might well have a "shared competence" in terms of policy, without necessarily having a corresponding full competence in terms of implementation.

4. Beware of myths

When discussing EU expenditure, very often three "myths" come to light. The first myth is that significant spending is essential to achieve some public objectives. The second is that spending is a sufficient

[13] See Art. 17(1) TEU and 317 TFEU. In particular, Art. 17(1) TEU provides that the Commission shall execute the budget and "manage programmes". This addition from the Lisbon Treaty appears to indicate an enhancement of the Commission's role. One should also note that the "cooperation" with the member states in the budget implementation is related to specific tasks only and, therefore, it should not undermine the Commission's full responsibility (Art. 317 TFEU).

[14] Council Regulation (EC, Euratom) No 1605/2002 of 25 June 2002 on the Financial Regulation applicable to the general budget of the European Communities as amended last by Council Regulation (EC) No. 1525/2007 of 17 December 2007 provides for four different management modes: centralised management by the Commission (used mainly for administrative expenditure and internal policies), shared management with member states (namely agriculture and rural development, cohesion), decentralised management (external actions/pre-accession aid) with third countries and joint management (cooperation with international organisations).

condition for durable results. The third is that when EU payments are found to be irregular, recovery procedures can fully repair the damage to the EU budget.

4.1 No spending, no results

To what extent a given policy requires EU spending (or non-budgetary measures only) depends on an assessment of EU spending's added value compared to national spending. As has been observed, the strongest generators of economic expansion are most likely found in the regulatory sphere. The important engines for this development are the internal market, the monetary union and the growing mobility of skills and knowledge. In stimulating lasting growth, the EU's rules matter more than the EU's expenditures (Núñez Ferrer 2012, 43).

For example, crossing borders between some national rail systems remains complicated because many trans-European rail services are interrupted by required stops at border locations. Making progress on alleviating these constraints has the potential to facilitate improvements in trans-European transport that are of comparable scale to the performance gains that result from significant investments in infrastructure. As shown below, this progress would entail more co-operation between the member states' authorities than a financial investment in infrastructure (Box 4-1).

Box 4-1

25 minutes saved and 25 minutes delay on Priority Project 1

25 minutes	
The journey time saved by constructing a new high speed line between Nürnberg and Ingolstadt in Germany at an overall cost of 2,336 million euro (with EU co-financing of 134 million euro from TEN-T).	The additional time needed for a technical control for trains entering Italy at the Brennersee station at the Austrian-Italian border, because the Italian railway undertaking does not accept the technical control already carried out at the point of departure in München by its German counterpart.

(European Court of Auditors 2010c)

4.2 Just a question of money

The success of the EU budget cannot be measured by a high rate of expenditure implementation. This rate could represent a good indicator of "political efficiency" for the various levels of government concerned, showing how far their (often short-term) expectations have been fulfilled. However, a more adequate approach would require an examination of "policy efficiency" and, in particular, of the achievement of the declared objectives.

Things do not happen automatically just because there are funds and processes in place. The European added value of a policy is not only dependent on its stated objectives but also on its management system, funding tools and implementation. Policies that, at face value, appear to have a high added value can fail to deliver it in practice (Núñez Ferrer 2012, 10). Box 4-2 shows a key EU objective that might not be achieved due to an inadequate framework.

Box 4-2

Measures taken to date to reduce fishing overcapacity by adapting the fishing fleet to fishing resources have been unsuccessful. This is due in particular to important weaknesses in the framework, such as the existing definitions of fishing capacity did not adequately reflect the ability of vessels to catch fish; fleet capacity ceilings do not impose real restrictions on fishing fleet capacity; despite the key objective of aligning fishing capacity to fishing opportunities, fishing overcapacity has not been defined or quantified (European Court of Auditors 2011d).

4.3 Recovery procedures: a full damage waiver

EU rules allow the Commission to apply financial corrections in the case of irregularities in EU spending. In the Commission's view, these procedures permit the restoration of a situation where 100% of the EU expenditure complies with the applicable rules.[15] Yet, the effectiveness of ex-post clearance in both "cleaning" national expenditure and in representing

[15] Financial corrections are the main tool for the correction of errors and irregularities in the context of shared management. The final objective is to ensure that all expenditure declared by the member state (i.e., on the basis of which the EU contribution is paid) is regular (see the annual accounts of the European Union 2010, 61).

a deterrent against irregularities does not meet with unanimous agreement (Box 4-3).[16]

Three main factors weaken the actual impact of the financial correction mechanisms. First, financial corrections do not constitute genuine financial sanctions. Corrections are limited to a recovery of EU irregular expenditure from member states and the final recipient may feel no effect whatsoever. The same expenditure can still continue to be financed through national budgets and represent, in the end, a further contribution by taxpayers. Additionally, the practical possibility of imposing financial corrections is very much dependent on the necessarily reduced number of the Commission's controls. Second, as these corrections generally occur at the end of a programme, it is no longer possible to correct any fundamental system weaknesses and to re-direct the objectives to be achieved by the co-financed policies. Third, due to the "input" nature of EU expenditure, based on items of eligible spending, the extent to which the expected outputs, outcomes and impacts are achieved by the EU programmes is not the basis on which a financial correction is triggered.

The regular (and increasing) occurrence of financial corrections has made them an inevitable routine procedure, thus demonstrating the limited deterrence of this instrument and its reduced ability to effect structural repairs. The corrections can counteract the financial consequences of an "error", but not necessarily solve the problem at source.[17]

---

[16] Parliament has recently confirmed serious doubts on the effectiveness of financial corrections mechanisms (see European Parliament resolution of 10 May 2012 with observations forming an integral part of its Decisions on discharge in respect of the implementation of the European Union general budget for the financial year 2010, Section III – Commission and executive agencies, paras. 120–122).

[17] This situation, for example, occurs in the case for the non respect of procurement procedures, a key precondition for the implementation of the internal market but also a major source of infringements in the cohesion area. If public administrations and beneficiaries in the member states are unable to improve the implementation of the procurement rules, the cohesion policy would continue to be systematically affected.

Box 4-3

The likelihood of recovery of an undue payment made under the Common Agricultural Policy is affected by delays in the member states initiation of recovery procedures, shortcomings in their recovery actions, and their limited enforcement possibilities. During the period 2006–2008 around 90% of the amounts reported in the EU annual accounts as "recoveries of undue payments" were those made by the Commission through deductions from the member states and not actual recoveries of the unduly paid aid from beneficiaries. This undoubtedly protects the financial interests of the EU but without the full deterrent effect of a recovery made from an unduly paid beneficiary (European Court of Auditors 2011c).

For the cohesion policy, although the financial correction process is lengthy (30 months on average), the Commission took the appropriate actions and measures were properly applied in about two-thirds of the cases examined. However, there is a limited assurance that financial corrections mechanisms translate into lasting systems' improvements as to avoid errors uncovered to occur again. Only in 28% of the programmes the assurance was found to be high. This means that the Commission will have to take further corrective actions, entailing increasing resource and administrative costs. For half of the programmes examined member states were able to replace ineligible expenditure disallowed by new projects, thus off-setting the financial impact of the corrections. This is not without risks, since some of the deficiencies identified are systemic (e.g. incorrect application of procurement rules) and are therefore likely to apply also to new projects (European Court of Auditors 2012a).

Financial corrections are, above all, an indicator of whether a policy has been implemented according to the established rules. If EU money is invested to achieve some sensible results, it can then be said that the objectives have not been met. As a result, the higher the number of financial corrections, the higher the evidence of failure and missed opportunities.

5. Light and shadow

The EU budget's reputation is sometimes tainted by cases of waste and fraud, which can represent a temptation to question the budget's very existence. Yet, there is no evidence that, overall, the EU budget is performing worse than national expenditures. Actually, for the policies where the actions are co-financed (for example, cohesion), if infringements are established for the EU's expenditures, then the national spending is equally affected.

Box 4-4

The waste water and sewage sludge from urban agglomerations can affect the quality of Europe's lakes, rivers, coastal waters, soils and ground waters. As a result the EU has adopted a series of directives and has also co-financed the building of urban waste water treatment plants through the Cohesion Fund and the ERDF.

The EU funded infrastructures have contributed to a significant increase in the coverage rate of the urban population served. This is particularly marked in the four member states who received more than 50% of EU expenditure for implementing urban waste water treatment for the 2000–06 programme period. Of the treatment plants visited, 18 out of 26 were deemed to be operating satisfactorily with regard to capacity, having a utilization rate above 50%. In these cases, there was an adequate connection of households and industrial users to the treatment plant. A large majority of the treatment plants produced effluent meeting EU requirements.

However, six of the seven cases of underutilization resulted from problems in completing the network, with many households and industrial users remaining unconnected to the treatment plants despite the plants being five years or more in operation. As a result, not all of the waste water produced in the area was treated. Where the quality of the effluent did not meet EU requirements (nine cases) one of the problems noted was that some treatment plants were being operated by local authorities lacking adequate resources and expertise and with no mechanisms in place to be informed of best practice (European Court of Auditors 2009b).

As for the national budgets, the main issue is how to make the best use of the available funds. The following examples show that useful achievements are reached through EU spending, although this does not necessarily mean that these funds were used in the most effective way and that, compared to national spending, EU funding has resulted in a better added value (Box 4-4, Box 4-5).

Box 4-5

Investments in water supply address different needs, such as: increasing availability of water in response to increased demand; expanding geographical coverage; improving the quality of the water distributed; improving the efficiency of water supply systems and the quality of the service.

Structural measures spending has contributed to improving the supply of water for domestic use, either by increasing the available volume of water, extending the public network to areas which were previously not connected or improving water quality, network efficiency or service continuity.

However, better results could have been achieved at a lower cost. In particular, the focus is on building infrastructures to exploit new water sources and attention is rarely paid to other solutions, such as reducing water losses and using other nearby resources. This could have made it possible to build smaller capacity infrastructure. Also, some projects were not operational because of missing complementary infrastructure. When measured by the two main efficiency parameters (capacity utilisation rate and non-invoiced water), several projects were found to operate with limited efficiency (European Court of Auditors 2010e).

The question is, therefore, how to make the EU budget more effective. In this respect, there are some lessons learned, pointing to three issues in particular.

5.1 Institutional capacity

As noted by the European Court of Auditors (2011a, para. 22), adequate institutional capacity is necessary to ensure that the EU funds are correctly spent to support durable economic development. The effectiveness of national management and control systems should therefore be ensured from the start. Regulation alone is, however, not enough. In this respect, the day-to-day actions of the managers in the member states are key because the assurance at the EU level heavily relies on their systems.[18] Additionally, these bodies very often also manage

[18] For example, the Commission's analysis of errors in cohesion policy for the years 2006–09 points to weaknesses in the administrative capacity and the national management and control systems as the main factors explaining those errors (see European Commission, 2011c).

national funds. Here, the interest in getting things right is therefore common because there is a real win-win opportunity for both the EU and the member states and, ultimately, for the taxpayer.

It is unrealistic to believe that in the current governance framework, the Commission can alone ensure an adequate budget implementation. As long as the member states do not put in place more effective management structures and increase the possibility that the Commission can rely upon these structures, it will not be possible to reduce the frequent checks, remedial action plans, and financial corrections, which will not compensate for the missed opportunities.

Box 4-6

Limited value was added by the Commission and the member states' Managing Authorities' appraisal (European Court of Auditors 2010e).

The Commission does not make full use of the instrument's potential due to insufficient expertise in the priority areas related to the General Budget Support programmes' objectives and weaknesses in its management of the dialogue process (European Court of Auditors 2010g).

Education expertise is not optimally assigned and developed in Delegations. This deprives the Commission of a vital monitoring mechanism as well as of the best opportunities for effective influence on implementation (European Court of Auditors 2010h).

The Commission assessments and decisions for Major Projects and Cohesion Fund projects did not lead to action to remedy project weaknesses observed during the audit. The results and impact of the projects were not monitored and empty ports and unused seaport infrastructures were found. Monitoring Committees and the Managing Authorities focused on the rate of spending. Some regions retrospectively financed replacement projects to absorb the available allocated resources. However, two of the three replacement projects included in the sample did not attain their objectives (European Court of Auditors 2012b).

The European Court of Auditors has, for example, observed that for a significant number of the transactions affected by error, sufficient information was available for the member state authorities to have detected and corrected at least some of the errors prior to certifying the expenditure to the Commission (European Court of Auditors 2009a, para. 4.23; 2010d, para. 4.25). This fact shows the difficulty of applying the principle of partnership and common interest that underlies the "shared management" arrangements.

There is no "geography" of the good and bad administration; improvements are needed in all member states. Improvements are also needed within the Commission. As a consequence of the emphasis put on compliance and funds absorption, the institutional capacity has focused on processes rather than on the achievement of sensible objectives. The Commission should therefore improve its appraisal procedures, supervision, and the monitoring of achievements to make the best use of the funds. There is also a need to put the right skills in the right places. Some examples are provided below (Box 4-6).

5.2 Needs and objectives

The EU budget is not meant to replace the national budgets; it is meant to perform better than them. The "needs" are basically quantified by 1% of the member states' GDP, which reflects what the member states' governments consider to be an acceptable contribution, rather than the outcome of an EU added value driven analysis. Whether the 1% is too little or too much depends on what it is intended to achieve.

As observed by the European Court of Auditors, the EU objectives are too wide-ranging, unclear or somewhat conflicting; policy instruments and resources are insufficient to meet the set objectives; causal links between the funded activities and the desired outcomes are unclear; and there are deficiencies in the monitoring and evaluation arrangements (European Court of Auditors 2010a, para. 14). Some examples are indicated below (Box 4-7).

The EU's expenditure is 'input' oriented, based on items of eligible spending, as opposed to disbursements based on a set of concrete objectives and linked to the achievement of results. Additionally, "fair return" considerations invite member states to seek "acceptable" net balances rather than specific policy objectives, leading to an inevitable trade-off between the desired outcomes and the spending levels. The absorption of funds potentially becomes an objective in itself, encouraging the dispersion of resources in a multitude of small initiatives whose main characteristic is that they are easily implemented rather than that they have intrinsic added value. This situation introduces a tension with the aim of making efficient, effective and economic use of funding by pursuing specific policy objectives. In this way, the EU budget is adding "something" to a number of existing policies already financed by national budgets, with a result that the EU *de facto* makes no choices regarding purpose. Where "political efficiency" can be satisfied, "policy efficiency" is diminished.

Box 4-7

The usefulness of the programming work was reduced by insufficient clarity and prioritisation. Clarity was further reduced as the same priorities were reformulated and restructured from one document to the next. The lengthy programming and design process did not suit the fast changing and conflict-affected environment of the Southern Caucasus, endangering the relevance of the assistance. Programming and design of assistance were not sufficiently guided by a structured dialogue with the beneficiary countries (European Court of Auditors 2010i).

There was a lack of clarity as to what was to be achieved and how the success of the projects' activities could be assessed. This had negative consequences for the implementation of projects (European Court of Auditors 2011b).

Concerning the EU financial assistance for the decommissioning of eight non-upgradeable nuclear reactors, the Court found that 10 years after there is still no comprehensive needs-assessment, prioritization and setting of specific objectives (European Court of Auditors 2011e).

None of the regions visited had a long term port development plan for seaports' transport infrastructures. Needs assessments to support the selection of seaport infrastructure projects had not been carried out (European Court of Auditors 2012b).

In some cases, as shown below, the objectives of the programmes were eventually not achieved, also because they were found to be contradictory, such as in the sugar sector (Box 4-8).

Box 4-8

There is no rationale in initially making available additional quotas and later striving to reduce them. Moreover, in the case of additional isoglucose quota, undertakings were paid even when they renounced quotas which had just been granted for free. The costs involved amounting to around 97 million euro cannot be justified. If additional costs are taken into account, the overall cost to the EU budget after the reform for the period 2007-2013 is likely to be 1.2 billion euro higher than before the reform. EU dependence on imports has been increased and the reduction of the prices of sugar is unlikely to benefit to final consumers (European Court of Auditors 2010b).

Owing in particular to the low subsidy rate, the school milk scheme continues to be relatively unattractive and, as a result, generally has no more than a deadweight effect. In most cases, the products subsidised either would have been included in canteen meals anyway or would probably have been bought by the beneficiaries even without the subsidy. While the decision by certain member states to organise milk distribution free of charge has resulted in a more satisfactory impact, this form of distribution is at present covered by costly national schemes to which the Community budget makes only a marginal contribution. Both the School Milk and School Fruit Schemes allow only of a limited impact, especially as neither scheme has a mechanism for targeting priority needs (European Court of Auditors 2010f).

5.3 Results

One of the consequences of the often grand EU objectives, with no clear or specific expected achievements, is that very little is known about the achievements, especially their outcomes and impacts (Box 4-9). This opacity makes it extremely difficult to identify (and report on) the added-value that citizens get in return for their money. As the Court has observed, "[i]nsufficient information on results and outcomes also undermines accountability and transparency as well as decisions on the allocation of resources" (European Court of Auditors 2010a, para. 16).

The lack of selective and focused objectives is directly reflected in the difficulty in setting measurable indicators for the policies financed. This difficulty, in turn, undermines the role of the ex-post evaluation and the potential 'pedagogical' effects for future policies. For example, the ex-post Evaluation of Cohesion Policy Programmes 2000-06 shows that, although quantitative targets were often set and an indicator system established, in many cases they were not linked in a meaningful way to any ultimate policy objectives and determined in relation to the funding made available and what it could plausibly achieve. Accordingly, targets were either attained far too easily or were unattainable given the funds deployed (European Commission 2010b, 11).

Box 4-9

The objectives of the programmes tend to be formulated in too general terms which hinders the design of the various components of the programmes and makes it more difficult to hold the Commission accountable for their effectiveness. The Commission should be able to demonstrate that the amount of funds allocated is appropriate in view of the objectives as well as the framework for dealing with risks and benefits. It is often difficult to assess whether conditions have been met or not, particularly due to a lack of clarity over what constitutes satisfactory progress as well as weaknesses in the statistical systems used for assessing results (European Court of Auditors 2010g).

Due to the 'input' based design of the spending programmes, the focus of a significant number of the reporting documents provided by the national bodies and by the Commission rests on financial and physical implementation only. The Treaty of Lisbon has recently introduced an obligation for the Commission to establish "an evaluation report on the Union's finances based on the results achieved", in particular in relation to the indications given by the budgetary authorities (Art. 318 TFEU). The idea was that this evaluation would represent an assessment that goes further than the traditional record of budgetary implementation and rules compliance "so that the relation between the key performance indicators, their legal/political basis, the amount of expenditure and the results achieved is clear and transparent".[19] Yet, the first report falls short of this

[19] See European Parliament resolution of 10 May 2011 with observations forming an integral part of the Decisions on discharge in respect of the implementation of the general budget of the European Union for the financial year 2009, Section III, para. 200.

expectation.[20] This shortfall is primarily due to a lack of sufficient and reliable information on the results and impacts of the specific programmes (European Commission 2012).

This means that if the EU rules oblige spending to comply with "sound financial management",[21] there is not yet a framework for 'performance' accountability. It is therefore not possible to provide a conclusive answer concerning the use of funds and their impact, thus making the Commission's ultimate responsibility all the more fragile.

6. If not now, when?

The financial and economic crisis has put the spotlight on the member states' severe public deficits, requiring the adoption of rigorous measures to significantly curb public spending. Tougher budgetary discipline and rigour will also be an issue for the next EU multi-annual financial framework, currently under discussion. In particular, future spending is bound to meet the expectations raised by the EU budget review for a more targeted and results-driven expenditure. Faced with these significant issues, the EU's credibility in providing clear and visible benefits for the EU and its citizens that could not be achieved by spending only at the

---

[20] For example, the European Parliament considered that the coverage and the content of this first report is not in line with the Treaty requirements (see resolution of 10 May 2012 with observations forming an integral part of its Decisions on discharge in respect of the implementation of the European Union general budget for the financial year 2010, para. 99). The European Court of Auditors observed that the report is vague, short on substance and, consequently, adds limited value. However, it presents the Parliament, the Council and Commission with an opportunity to discuss and agree how the evaluation report can be made useful to the discharge authority (see European Court of Auditors 2012c).

[21] See Articles 310 (5) and 317 TFEU. The concept of 'sound financial management' is built around three principles. The principle of "economy" requires that the resources used shall be made available in due time, in appropriate quantities, of appropriate quality and at the best price. "Efficiency" is characteristically a managerial value consisting, in essence, of maintaining a good ratio between the resources employed and the results attained. A related value is "effectiveness", which basically consists of ensuring that the performance of public administration is successful in achieving the goals and solving the public problems set for it by law and government (see Sigma 1999, 13). These principles (known as the "three E's") are codified in the EU Financial Regulation under the concept of sound financial management (see Art. 27 of the Financial Regulation, Council Regulation (EC, Euratom) No. 1605/2002, op. cit.).

national, regional or local level, is ultimately at stake.[22] The current difficulties and the longstanding weaknesses require that a number of issues be addressed and that the necessary changes be put into place without delay.

Indeed, identifying the areas where the EU dimension can offer more than national spending is not, in itself, sufficient. Spending on the right policies is only worthwhile if it secures the desired results (European Commission 2010d, 5–6). It is inevitable that hard choices are needed. A catalytical effect from EU expenditure would require a sufficient critical mass to produce visible results, which is also a factor in any potential increase of the EU citizens' confidence. Given the present financial constraints and compared to the present framework, this requirement should mean more money for a "few" spending programmes, rather than less money for a plurality of programmes. Less funds from the EU budget does not necessarily mean less funds for a given policy, but rather the choice to have funding supplied by a different level of government.[23] This concept would also mean fewer and more precise objectives than currently exist, to be put in relation to the available funding. The EU budget should provide the "cake" rather than the "icing".

Almost any expenditure creates somewhere some type of growth because it boosts consumption and therefore economic activity. It is, however, important to distinguish between short-term and lasting growth.

[22] The conclusions of the Westendorp report are illuminating in this respect, stating already in 1995 that "the Union's principal internal challenge is to reconcile itself with its citizens. Therefore, enhancing its legitimacy in their eyes has to be the prime task of the coming reform. The achievement of this aim will depend on a clear definition of the Union's objectives, i.e., the joint goals sought, the credibility of common policies and the cooperation machinery designed to attain those objectives (or, to put it another way, the suitability of the instruments for the purpose of achieving the objectives set) and the preservation of the Union's internal cohesion" (Report by the Reflection Group: A Strategy for Europe, Brussels, 5 December 1995, part two, para. 10). The Reflection Group was established by the Corfu European Council of 24 and 25 June 1994 to examine the challenges to be addressed to bring the European Union up to date and to prepare it for the next enlargement.

[23] For example, as noted by Parliament, "a large proportion of the Union's objectives have been taken into account by the Member States in their national budgets" (see European Parliament 2009, para 18). Parliament also noted that because the EU budget is very limited compared to the national budgets, there is a need to create synergies between the EU budget and the national budgets to implement common EU strategies. It stressed that coherence gives European policies greater impact, achieving true European added value while supporting long-term policy objectives (see European Parliament 2010, para. 15).

Consistent with the definition of EU added value and taking account of the limited resources available, one would expect EU expenditure to aim at long-term "sustainable" results. One should note in this respect that one of the three priorities of the Europe 2020 growth strategy is precisely to achieve sustainable growth (European Commission 2010a, 10; 14–17). However, the fact that less than half of the EU annual budget is currently directed at financing initiatives that support the Europe 2020 strategy shows the long road still ahead of us (European Commission 2011a, 10).

The Commission's claim of a results-driven EU expenditure (European Commission 2010c, point 4; 2011b, points 1 and 5.2.2.) should materialise with a shift from the 'eligible' inputs for spending towards outputs and outcomes. Yet, for example, for the future cohesion scheme, the Commission has essentially proposed retaining the old input-based framework, though with a few performance-based exceptions. The same applies to the future agricultural policy scheme, which remains fundamentally input-based and therefore oriented more towards compliance than performance.

For EU expenditures to be measured in terms of real impact, rather than in terms of the inputs involved, there is a need to set meaningful indicators that are linked to realistic policy objectives and to evaluate at key intermediate points whether the defined objectives and intended impacts are likely to be achieved.

Processes and rules are not enough to deliver the expected results. There is a need for adequate governance. Because it is about placing public resources in common to achieve EU objectives, it is legitimate to expect that the management of the EU funds takes place through an effective EU-driven process, resulting in a full accountability at the EU level. This management should be the role of the Commission that is charged by the Treaty to promote in various ways the general interest of the Union: giving policy direction and coherence, initiating proposals for EU law, and acting as the guarantor of EU law and of a level playing field in Europe (European Commission 2008b, 2).[24] One of these roles is to "execute the budget and manage programmes" (Art. 17(1) TEU). As a result of an enhanced concept of EU added-value, the full responsibility for the Budget implementation should lay in the Commission's hands.

One precondition is the alignment of the Commission's tasks, powers and responsibilities. There should no longer be a segregation of functions between the EU and the national level, but a true "sharing" of roles under one single responsibility: national bodies handling EU funds should act on

---

[24] As pointed out by Ponzano (2009, 218), the general interest of the Union does not necessarily correspond to the addition of national interests, nor does it equate to the lowest common denominator of the different national stances.

behalf of the Commission. This responsibility would require some form of accreditation and "contract" based upon pre-specified output and performance targets and budgetary allocations consistent with the EU objectives selected.[25] The Commission should be prepared to directly endorse that, what is intended to be achieved, responds to the criteria of EU added-value. It is only if there is "one" implementation line (and not as many as there are national bodies), that the Commission's ultimate responsibility can be sustained.

The administrative structures at the national level should be assessed (at an operational level) by the Commission as being adequate to deliver the expected outcomes. The aim is to ascertain the structures' capacity to "absorb" funds effectively, by putting forward, managing and maintaining meaningful and sustainable projects consistent with the pre-agreed policy objectives. A "selective" process for the identification of national bodies for EU spending (a type of "Champions league") would introduce an element of "reward" and sound external pressure, which in the end should also benefit public spending at the national level.[26]

In a future perspective, where one might look more to results than to the inputs of spending, the Commission will have to demonstrate that it has done everything possible to achieve the intended results, 'making the difference' when compared to purely national actions and that it has learned from past experience what does and does not work. Indeed, the primary purpose of accountability is not to cast blame and to punish. Accountability should rather help to identify lessons for the future that make future approaches more relevant and effective.

The demonstration and acknowledgment that the EU's actions add value to national policies and address people's concerns more effectively than the "national" or "local" levels, potentially provides the grounds for a positive "Trojan Horse" impact on public spending in general. This effect occurs through identifying and promoting best practices in planning and

---

[25] In its conclusions on the EU budget review, the Commission proposes the idea of a 'Development and Investment Partnership Contract' between the Commission and the member states, setting out the objectives to be achieved, how the progress towards the achievement of these objectives will be quantified and measured and the allocation of national and EU resources among the priority areas and programmes. Also, the Commission identifies the institutional capacity at a national, regional and local level as the key for successful development, implementation and monitoring of the policies. The allocation of EU financial resources should therefore take account of the capacity to effectively utilise these resources (see European Commission 2010d, p. 14).

[26] This process should be effective, in particular, because of the national co-financing and/or because these bodies often manage other national funds.

managing by objectives, with managers held to account for the agreed expectations and the means used.

7. Conclusions

EU's actions represent a kind of 'Trojan Horse' to achieve specific objectives with better results than the member states could do by themselves. This is the basis of the EU added value concept which can be articulated around three main characteristics: *catalytic* (making something happen that would otherwise not happen or would happen more slowly); *targeted* (concentrating on the best added-value and the most effective results on the basis of evaluation and impact assessment); and *realistic* (objectives should be achievable).

To achieve EU objectives, EU spending is not necessarily required. For example, the strongest generators of economic expansion are most likely found in the regulatory sphere. In addition, spending is not by itself a sufficient condition for durable results. Finally, ineffective spending constitutes a missed opportunity that cannot be repaired *ex-post*.

Making the best use of the available funds requires paying due attention to three issues in particular: adequate institutional capacity to realise sensible projects, the identification of the needs and the establishment of realistic objectives consistent with the available funds, and the demonstration of the results achieved through meaningful indicators. This is equally important for both the EU and the national budgets also because very often the same bodies manage funds from both sources.

Consistent with the Europe 2020 growth strategy, the aim of EU spending should be to achieve sustainable growth. A distinction must be made between short-term and lasting growth. The requirement for a catalytic effect for EU expenditure would need to secure a sufficient critical mass to produce visible results. This concept should mean more money for a "few" spending programmes rather than less money for the approximately 70 current spending programmes. The EU budget should provide the "cake" rather than the "icing".

The natural outcome of a virtuous process where objectives are clear, agreed and realistic is an unequivocal ownership as a precondition for both achieving policy objectives and ensuring 'value for money'. Because the EU budget is about placing public resources in common to achieve common EU objectives, it is legitimate to expect the Commission, as the promoter of the general interest of the Union, to be fully accountable for the money spent. For this to happen, a precondition is the alignment of the

Commission's tasks, powers and responsibilities. An adequate accountability process for EU funds is not only instrumental in good management; it is also a critical condition of legitimacy for public authorities and therefore a factor in the potential increase of the EU citizens' confidence.

References

Barroso, J. M. 2008. Address to the conference on Reforming the Budget, Changing Europe. 12 November, Brussels.

Cipriani, G. 2007. "Rethinking the EU Budget: Three Unavoidable Reforms." *CEPS Paperback*. Brussels: Centre for European Policy Studies.

European Commission. 1978. "Global appraisal of the budgetary problems of the Community." COM (78) 64, 27 February.

—. 2001. "European governance." White paper. COM (2001) 428. 25 July.

—. 2002. "A project for the European Union." COM (2002) 247. 22 May.

—. 2004. "Financial Perspectives 2007-13." COM (2004) 487. 14 July.

—. 2008a. "EU Public Finance." http://ec.europa.eu/budget/library/biblio/publications/public_fin/EU_pub_fin_en.pdf

—. 2008b. "Acting now for a better Europe." COM (2008) 712. 5 November.

—. 2008c. "Reforming the Budget, Changing Europe." http://ec.europa.eu/budget/reform2008/index_en.htm

—. 2010a. "A strategy for smart, sustainable and inclusive growth." COM (2010) 2020. 3 March.

—. 2010b. "Ex-Post Evaluation of Cohesion Policy Programmes 2000–2006 financed by the European Regional Development Fund in Objective 1 and 2 Regions." Synthesis Report. April.

—. 2010c. "Proposal for a Regulation on the Financial Regulation applicable to the general budget of the European Union." COM (2010) 260, 28 May.

—. 2010d. "The EU Budget review." COM (2010) 700, 19 October.

—. 2011a. "A Budget for Europe 2020: The current system of funding, the challenges ahead, the results of stakeholders consultation and different options on the main horizontal and sectoral issues." Commission Staff Working Paper. SEC (2011) 868 final. 29 June.

—. 2011b. "Proposal for a Regulation laying down common provisions on the European Regional Development Fund, the European Social Fund, the Cohesion Fund, the European Agricultural Fund for Rural Development and the European Maritime and Fisheries Fund covered by the Common Strategic Framework and laying down general

provisions on the European Regional Development Fund, the European Social Fund and the Cohesion Fund and repealing Regulation (EC) No 1083/2006." COM (2011) 615, 6 October.
—. 2011c. "Analysis of errors in cohesion policy for the years 2006–2009 actions taken by the Commission and the way forward." Commission staff working paper. http://ec.europa.eu/internal_market/publicprocurement/docs/public_public_cooperation/sec2011_1169_en.pdf
—. 2012. "Report on the evaluation of the Union's finances based on the results achieved." COM (2012) 40. 17 February.
European Court of Auditors. 2009a. "Annual Report on the 2009 financial year."
—. 2009b. "The effectiveness of Structural Measures spending on waste water treatment for the 1994–99 and 2000–06 programme periods." Special Report no. 3/2009.
—. 2010a. "Improving the financial management of the European Union budget: Risks and challenges." Opinion no. 1/2010. 14 January.
—. 2010b. "Has the reform of the sugar market achieved its main objectives?" Special Report no. 6/2010.
—. 2010c. "Improving transport performance on Trans-European rail axes: Have EU rail infrastructure investments been effective?" Special Report no. 8/2010.
—. 2010d. "Annual Report on the 2010 financial year."
—. 2010e. "Is EU Structural Measures spending on the supply of water for domestic consumption used to best effect?" Special Report no. 9/2010.
—. 2010f. "Are the School Milk and School Fruit Schemes effective?" Special Report no. 10/2011.
—. 2010g. "The Commission's management of General Budget Support in ACP, Latin American and Asian Countries." Special Report no. 11/2010.
—. 2010h. "EU Development Assistance for Basic Education in Sub-Saharan Africa and South Asia." Special Report no. 12/2010.
—. 2010i. "Is the new European Neighbourhood and Partnership Instrument successfully launched and achieving results in the Southern Caucasus?" Special Report no. 13/2010.
—. 2011a. "On the proposal for a Regulation of the European Parliament and of the Council laying down common provisions on the European Regional Development Fund, the European Social Fund, the Cohesion Fund, the European Agricultural Fund for Rural Development and the European Maritime and Fisheries Fund covered by the Common Strategic Framework and laying down general provisions on the European Regional Development Fund, the European Social Fund and

the Cohesion Fund and repealing Regulation (EC) No 1083/2006." Opinion No 7/2011. 15 December.
—. 2011b. "The efficiency and effectiveness of EU contributions channelled through United Nations Organisations in conflict-affected countries." Special Report no. 3/2011.
—. 2011c. "Recovery of undue payments made under the Common Agricultural Policy." Special Report no. 8/2011.
—. 2011d. "Have EU measures contributed to adapting the capacity of the fishing fleets to available fishing opportunities?" Special Report no. 12/2011.
—. 2011e. "EU financial assistance for the decommissioning of nuclear plants in Bulgaria, Lithuania and Slovakia." Special Report no. 16/2011.
—. 2012a. "Did the Commission successfully deal with deficiencies identified in the Member States' management and control systems?" Special Report no. 3/2012.
—. 2012b. "Using Structural and Cohesion Funds to co-finance transport infrastructures in seaports: an effective investment?" Special Report no. 4/2012.
—. 2012c. "The Commission's evaluation report on the Union's finances based on results achieved established under Article 318 of the Treaty on the Functioning of the European Union." Opinion no. 4/2012. 14 May.
European Parliament. 2009. "Resolution on the Mid-Term Review of the 2007–2013 Financial Framework." 25 March.
—. 2010. "Resolution on the mandate for the trilogue on the 2011 draft budget." 15 June.
—. 2011. "Resolution on Investing in the future: a new Multiannual Financial Framework (MFF) for a competitive, sustainable and inclusive Europe." 8 June.
European Union. 2010. *Official Journal* C332 of 14 November 2011.
Gros, D. 2008. "How to Achieve a Better Budget for the European Union." Paper presented at the Conference on Public Finances in the EU, European Commission, Brussels, 3–4 April.
Hübner, D. 2007. "European Regional Policy: History, Achievements and Perspectives." Speech 07/542, Lunch Debate on the 50th Anniversary of the EU. Brussels. 17 September.
Ponzano, P. 2009. "Brèves considerations sur le rôle de la Commission européenne." *Revue du Droit de l'Union Européenne* 2.

Núñez Ferrer, J. 2012. "Investing where it matters, an EU budget for long-term growth." CEPS Task force report. Brussels: Centre for European Policy Studies.

Sigma, 1998. "Preparing public administrations for the European Administrative Space." Sigma Paper no. 23. Paris: OECD. May.

—. 1999. "European Principles For Public Administration." Sigma Paper no. 27. Paris: OECD. November.

Tarschys, D. 2005. "The Enigma of European Added Value: Setting Priorities for the European Union." SIEPS Report 2005. Stockholm: Swedish Institute for European Policy Studies.

Vergilius, P. M. *Aeneid, Book II*. Translated by John Dryden. http://ancienthistory.about.com/library/bl/bl_text_vergil_aeneid_ii.htm.

THE EURO CRISIS: TEN ROOTS BUT FEWER SOLUTIONS

ZSOLT DARVAS

1. Introduction

The euro faces an existential crisis. While shortly after the collapse of Lehman Brothers, which led to an unprecedented disruption in the functioning of the modern global financial system, the euro seemed to be a shelter for its members (Wyplosz 2009), attitudes regarding the euro changed completely following a series of events that began with the Greek fiscal crisis in early 2010. Despite a number of attempts by various European institutions, the crisis continues and the outlook is bleak. Why is it so difficult to resolve the euro-crisis?

The typical answers to this question are that the euro-area does not constitute an optimum currency area or that monetary unions were traditionally combined with fiscal and political unions. These generalisations of course have some validity, but given the status quo and the complexity of the euro-area's legal and institutional arrangements, they are not very helpful in providing solutions or determining the fate of the euro.

In this article we summarise ten major roots of the euro-crisis and assess the policy responses (if any) to these issues. This is followed by a more in-depth examination of the most pressing problem that also constitutes the most serious threat to the integrity of the euro-area: the dreary economic outlook of southern euro-area member states. We conclude that instead of exiting or breaking-up the euro, the common interest lies in discovering ways in which these countries can be offered improved prospects for the future. A great deal of homework needs to be accomplished in these countries, but other euro-area partners, as well as European institutions, will also have a decisive role to play in supporting the process. In the medium term, additional intuitional changes will be necessary to complement the currently planned overhaul of the euro-area's institutional framework.

2. Ten major reasons behind the euro-area crisis and the EU's policy responses to date

The euro-area has deep-rooted problems. We follow Darvas (2011c) in categorising ten important issues – the first four relate to pre-crisis developments, while the other six relate to issues highlighted by the crisis.

2.1 The failure of the Stability and Growth Pact

First, the rules-based Stability and Growth Pact (SGP), which was the cornerstone of fiscal prudence in the European Union, failed. In Darvas (2010b), we calculated the number of violations of the euro-entry criteria, which also include the two fiscal criteria of the SGP: the 3% of GDP budget deficit criterion and the 60% of GDP government debt criterion.[1] We found that between 2001 and 2006, i.e., after the euro was introduced but before the global financial crisis erupted in 2007, approximately one-third of euro-area member states had violated the SGP. Such violations have greatly diminished the trust in the effectiveness of European rules-based surveillance systems and resulted in high public debt, especially in Greece and Italy, at the start of the crisis.

A number of new agreements have been reached to strengthen the SGP. The new agreements include the so-called "Six-Pack" (five regulations and one directive approved by all 27 Member States and the European

---

[1] To be more precise, the exact definitions are as follows: (a) the budget deficit should not be larger than three per cent of GDP, unless "either the ratio has declined substantially and continuously and reached a level that comes close to the reference value, or, alternatively, the excess over the reference value is only exceptional and temporary and the ratio remains close to the reference value"; (b) government debt should not be greater than 60% of GDP, unless "the ratio is sufficiently diminishing and approaching the reference value at a satisfactory pace". To calculate the number of violations of these criteria in Darvas (2010b) we used the three per cent benchmark for the deficit and the following definition of meeting the general government debt criterion: a country is considered to meet the criterion if either the debt/GDP ratio is below 60% or, if it is above this figure, then projecting the average change in the debt/GDP ratio over the latest three years 20 years ahead will lead to a ratio below 60%. Note that the "Six-Pack" reforms adopted in 2011 operationalised this criterion exactly the same way (just the wording differs): the gap between the debt level and the 60% reference should be reduced by at least 1/20th annually (on average over three years); see European Commission (2011).

Parliament in October 2010), [2] the "Euro Plus Pact" (signed by 23 countries in March 2011), [3] the so-called "Fiscal Compact" (Treaty on Stability, Coordination and Governance in the EMU, signed by 25 countries in March 2012). [4] Furthermore, a new proposal called the "Two-Pack" drafted by the European Commission in November 2011 is currently under negotiation.[5] These new agreements fundamentally reform fiscal coordination, surveillance and enforcement in the EU, and in particular, in the euro-area. Fiscal rules will be stronger, they will be enshrined in national constitutions and non-compliance will be sanctioned in a quasi-automatic way. These agreements, if implemented and properly employed in practice, could help to sustain healthy fiscal positions once the current crisis is solved. However, they are less helpful in resolving the current fiscal crisis in the euro-area. Although the so-called structural budget balance (i.e., a budget that is balanced once the impact of the economic cycle and one-time expenditures and revenue measures are removed) will receive greater emphasis, the new agreements lead to a strong contractionary bias, i.e., pro-cyclical fiscal policy during the current downturn. Moreover, the current situation could only be made worse by forcing Spain to pay an immediate fine.

An alternative solution, a form of Eurobonds (i.e., pooled national debt issuances), is unfortunately not yet on the table. The proposal by Delpla and von Weizsäcker (2010) of splitting debt issuances into a senior component of up to 60% of a member state's GDP (called "Blue bonds", guaranteed by all participating countries) and a junior component above the 60% threshold ("Red bonds", guaranteed by the issuing country alone), would stabilise government financing (via the Blue bonds) but at the same time would expose governments to market discipline (via the Red bonds). At the current juncture, Blue bonds should be phased in through complete pooling of new issuances, in which a member state can participate until its share of the stock of Eurobonds reaches 60% of its GDP (Darvas 2011b). Such a phasing in would provide struggling countries with a long period of time to put their fiscal houses in order, while benefiting from a low interest rate. Unfortunately, talks for any sort of Eurobonds are not on the table, partly due to the mistrust between euro-area nations, and partly due to the very complex institutional framework that would be required to make the

[2] See European Commission (2011).

[3] See European Council (2011).

[4] See European Council (2012b).

[5] See European Commission (2012a) for a concise comparison of the "Six-Pack", the "Fiscal Compact" and the "Two-Pack".

common bond issuance function properly, in the absence of an adequate level of political and fiscal integration.

2.2 Neglect of private-sector vulnerabilities

Second, there was a sole focus on fiscal issues – and a consequent neglect of private-sector behaviour. This resulted in unsustainable credit and housing booms in countries such as Ireland and Spain (Ahearne et al. 2008) and the emergence of structural imbalances such as high current-account deficits and eroded competitiveness. Divergence within a monetary union, such as divergence in current account balances, is not necessarily a bad thing. Capital flows across regions and the ensuing current account deficits and surpluses may reflect the improved utilisation of resources when capital moves to fast-growing regions to the benefit of the entire monetary union. However, the booms and busts in the Irish and Spanish housing sectors (Ahearne et al. 2008) exemplify capital misallocation. Additionally the accumulation of "excessive" regional debt is undesirable, and there are good reasons to conclude that the external debt of Greece, Portugal and Spain became excessive (Darvas 2012b). Figure 5-1 depicts changes in current account balances in five main geographical regions of the EU since 1995 and the projections of the IMF until 2017. In southern European countries, the median current account balance exceeded ten per cent of GDP before the crisis and the pace of adjustment is slow, especially in comparison to the rapid adjustment in eastern European countries. While private capital inflows halted and even reversed both in southern and eastern Europe, in southern Europe banks received massive liquidity support from the European Central Bank (ECB), which has offset the sudden stop in private capital flows. Such support has contributed to financial stability, but at the same time, has made it possible for these countries to delay the adjustment, as noted by Sinn (2011).

The crisis was a bitter proof that not only fiscal issues matter. The "Six-Pack" and "Euro Plus Pact" also include regulations to prevent and correct of private sector imbalances, such as weak competitiveness positions and high private debt. A new procedure, the so-called Macroeconomic Imbalance Procedure (MIP), was introduced with the aim of assessing these private sector vulnerabilities and assisting countries in designing remedies (European Commission 2012b). Undoubtedly, this procedure is a major innovation in the EU's economic governance framework. However, their effectiveness needs to be tested, and in any case adjustment within the euro-area could take a long time and hence quick improvements are not expected.

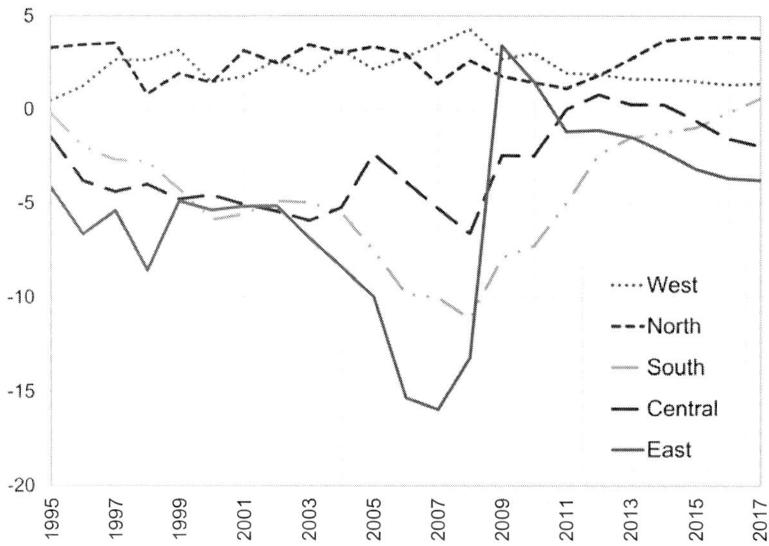

Fig. 5-1 Current account balances in main geographical groups of the EU (% of GDP), 1995–2017
Source: Author's calculations using data from IMF (2012) data
Note: median values are indicated for the groups, which have the following composition:
West: Austria, Belgium, France, Germany, and the Netherlands;
South: Greece, Italy, Portugal, and Spain;
North: Denmark, Finland, Sweden, Ireland, and the UK;
Central: the Czech Republic, Hungary, Poland, Slovakia, and Slovenia;
East: Estonia, Latvia, Lithuania, Bulgaria, and Romania.

2.3 Lack of structural adjustment

Third, there were no proper mechanisms to foster structural adjustment. Some countries, such as Germany, were able to adjust within the euro-area on their own (i.e., Germany's competitiveness improved considerably from the mid-1990s until the onset of the current crisis; see, e.g., Darvas 2012a), but others, such as Greece, Italy, Spain and Portugal, were not. While Germany, Italy and Portugal had the worst growth performance among euro-area member states before the crisis, Germany boosted its competitiveness during this period, but not Italy and Portugal.

Booming domestic demand contributed to rapid economic growth in Spain and Greece before the crisis, which obscured the more serious structural problems. Following IMF (2010) and Allard and Evaraert (2010), in Darvas and Pisani-Ferry (2011) we studied certain aspects of growth that could be improved with structural reforms. We found that southern European countries are severely lagging behind in all criteria.

Fostering structural adjustment is one of the aims of the MIP. The so-called "European Semester," a yearly cycle of mutual assessment of fiscal and structural issues was introduced in 2010, which encompasses all new instruments, including the MIP. This is also undoubtedly useful, yet the jury is still out on its effectiveness. By studying the first European Semester, Marzinotto et al. (2011) conclude that member states are only slowly internalising the new procedure and the Semester has thus far lacked legitimacy due to the minor role assigned to the European Parliament, the marginal involvement of national parliaments and the lack of transparency at some stages of the process.

2.4 Lack of a crisis-resolution mechanism

Fourth, there was no crisis-resolution mechanism for euro-area countries. The series of sovereign debt crises in the euro-area came as a surprise and euro-area policymakers had to improvise. It is important to highlight that in other federations, such as the US, there are no crisis-resolution mechanisms for sub-central governments either (Darvas 2010a). When studying the conditions required for a fiscal union to function smoothly and successfully, Bordo et al. (2011) conclude "The first and probably the most important condition is a credible commitment to a no-bailout rule." In the euro-area at present, the reluctance on the part of the citizens of economically stronger countries such as Germany, the Netherlands and Finland, to extend loans to economically weaker countries, such as Greece, highlight the validity of this conclusion. However, it also must be recognised that public debt levels in certain euro-area member states are much higher than sub-central government debt in other federations, and due to the reasons discussed in the next two sections, an uncontrolled default could be more harmful for the rest of the euro-area than a similar default of a sub-central government in other federations.[6]

---

[6] This conclusion remains valid even though a properly designed debt restructuring inside the euro-area should not cause a major contagion, as we argued in Darvas (2011a), and as the subsequent Greek experience has shown.

The lack of a sovereign debt crisis resolution mechanism was initially addressed through some temporary arrangements: bilateral lending from euro-area partners (in partnership with the IMF) to Greece in May 2010, and the establishment of two financing mechanisms, the EFSF (European Financial Stability Facility)[7] and the EFSM (European Financial Stability Mechanism)[8]. The European Stability Mechanism (ESM)[9], a permanent rescue fund with €500 billion in resources, will likely be introduced later in 2012. The resources, even if augmented with IMF lending, would not be sufficient if Italy were to require assistance. Moreover, it would be much more preferable to design an institutional framework in which member states did not have to lend money to each other.

2.5 Interdependence of banks and sovereigns

Fifth, the national bank resolution regimes and the large home country bias in banks' government bond holdings imply that there is a lethal correlation between banking and sovereign debt crises. When a government gets into trouble, so does the country's banking system (e.g., Greece), and vice versa (e.g., Ireland). Merler and Pisani-Ferry (2012a) demonstrated that most continental euro-area countries were characterised by the large size of their banks' portfolios of domestic government bonds, which were markedly larger than in the UK or the US. Moreover, during the crisis this vulnerability has increased, as all countries for which concerns about state solvency arose have observed a reversal in the previously steady increase of the share of government debt held by non-residents. Germany, by contrast, has seen an increase in the share held by non-residents.

The lethal correlation between banking and sovereign debt crises could be best addressed with a so-called "banking federation" or "banking union", whereby bank resolution and deposit guarantees would be centralised at the euro-area (or preferably the EU) level, which would also require the centralisation of regulation and supervision. This is because when bank resolution in a given country is not the responsibility of that country's government, but bank recapitalisation, when needed, would be financed using a common fund, then banking fragility would not lead directly to sovereign debt problems for that government. The opposite case, where the fragility of the government is transmitted to the banks of a given country, could also be better managed when regulation and

---

[7] See EFSF (2012).
[8] See EFSM (2012).
[9] See European Council (2012a).

supervision are centralised at the euro-area level. The notion of a banking union was not on the agenda until late spring 2012, despite numerous calls by economists (see, e.g., Véron 2011). However, the intensification of the euro crisis brought euro-area policymakers back to reality, and perhaps the call for a banking union seemed a politically more acceptable alternative compared to a more rapid move towards a full-fledged fiscal union. Consequently, the European Council on 28–29 June 2012 called for a banking union and the European Commission proposed its first element, a single supervisory mechanism for banks on 12 September 2012. It was agreed that once banks come under the control of the joint supervisor, the ESM would be able to recapitalise banks directly. The willingness of member states to relinquish national sovereignty over major banking issues is clearly an important development in crisis management. However, the formation of the banking union will be an extremely complex process, and many open issues need to be negotiated and agreed upon, as discussed by Pisani-Ferry et al. (2012), including the means of providing financing for the banking union, which is studied by Pisani-Ferry and Wolff (2012).

2.6 Interdependence between countries

Sixth, there is a strong interdependence between countries – much stronger than was generally perceived during the good years before the crisis. The collapse of a small country can create a contagion and the collapse of a large country would lead to a meltdown. Italy, for example, cannot be allowed to go bankrupt, as it would bankrupt the Italian banking system, which in turn would cause a meltdown throughout the rest of the euro-area banking system through high-level linkages and would also have disruptive effects outside the euro-area. This channel remains important even if financial integration were reversed to a significant extent, as argued by the ECB (2012a).

The strong interdependence between countries should primarily be addressed via limiting the scope of the fiscal and private sector vulnerabilities of member states. Once the crisis is over, the European Semester and all the instruments included in it could help in this regard – to the extent of course that the Semester will prove to be effective. A properly designed banking union as discussed above is the best means of addressing banking interdependence. Furthermore, a type of Eurobonds, such as the Blue bond discussed before, would help to limit the spread of a sovereign debt crisis from one country to another.

2.7 Lack of a lender of last resort for sovereigns

Seventh, the strict prohibition on the European Central Bank/Eurosystem providing monetary financing means that euro-area governments borrow as if they were borrowing in a "foreign" currency, as highlighted by De Grauwe (2011). This is because a central bank can in principle act as a lender of last resort for the sovereign, i.e., print money and buy government bonds (as the Federal Reserve, the Bank of England and the Bank of Japan did during the crisis). The lack of a lender of last resort for sovereigns of individual states of a monetary union is not a substantial problem when the level of debt is low. For example, in the US, the Federal Reserve does not buy the debt of states such as California or New York but only buys federal bonds. Although California has been in deep financial trouble since 2007, its eventual default would not cause a major disruption to the US banking system. The reasons are that the debt of the State of California is small, approximately 7% of California's GDP (the debt of local governments in California represents an additional 13% of the state's GDP); moreover, this debt is not held by banks, but mainly by individuals. However the default of Italy would be a game changer in Europe.

The lack of a lender of last resort for sovereigns could be remedied by establishing a stronger political and fiscal union that could provide the basis for changing the statutes of the ECB. Absent such a change, the ECB can act within its current mandate. The ECB has already purchased the sovereign bonds of member states under the so-called Securities Market Programme (SMP) beginning in May 2010, which was terminated on 6 September 2012, and a new programme called Outright Monetary Transactions (OMT) was introduced (ECB 2010, 2012b).

The SMP only had temporary effects on government bond yields for a number of reasons. First, the ECB itself communicated that these operations will remain limited, and even introduced a weekly cap. Second, the ECB claimed senior creditor status with respect to other bondholders, and therefore ECB purchases increased the eventual losses of other bondholders in the case of a default. Third, the modalities of the SMP were unclear: the ECB started and ended bond purchases without known guidelines. Fourth, in the case of Greece the SMP attempted to temper the government bond market in a country with a fundamentally unsustainable fiscal situation (Darvas et al. 2011). Finally, the SMP was subject to moral hazard, exemplified by the Italian government's backtracking on promised reforms in the summer of 2011, after the ECB began purchasing Italian bonds.

The new OMT differs from the SMP in major respects. First, it will be based on strong conditionality (i.e., compliance with a full or a precautionary macroeconomic adjustment programme by the EFSF or the ESM). ECB intervention will not be automatic, but the Governing Council will decide on a case-by-case basis when and to what extent it will intervene. Second, it will be unlimited in principle. Third, the ECB will be treated *pari passu* with other creditors, i.e. the ECB will not have any preferential treatment in the case of a credit event. Furthermore, transparency of OMT holdings will also be higher (the breakdown by country and the average duration of holdings will be published). Moreover, there is clarity on the maturity of eligible bonds, i.e. between one and three years, which is the relevant horizon for monetary transmission. These characteristics likely constitute the outer limit of what is feasible within the ECB's mandate.

The initial reactions in the markets (until the completion of the manuscript for this article in mid-September 2012) were positive. For example, the 2-year Spanish government bond yield fell from a 15-year record high of 6.9% in late July 2012 to below 3% in early September 2012. Longer maturity yields have also fallen somewhat.

It was wise for the ECB to introduce the OMT, as otherwise the euro crisis may have escalated in mid-2012. By preventing a self-fulfilling crisis, the OMT may help to reduce government bond yields, and thereby also lower private sector yields, which will help the economy. However, the OMT operations can only buy precious time, but cannot solve the euro crisis and cannot fully eliminate the risk of an eventual euro-area exit, as these are dependent on the answers given to the other more fundamental problems of the euro-area we discuss.[10]

2.8 Downward spiral and negative feedback between the crisis and growth

Eighth, there is a downward spiral in adjusting countries: i.e., fiscal adjustment leading to a weaker economy, thereby reducing public revenues and creating additional fiscal adjustment needs. It is extremely difficult to break this vicious circle in the absence of a stand-alone currency. In the US, automatic stabilisers, such as unemployment insurance, are operated by the federal government, which also invests more in distressed states – but in Europe such instruments do not exist. An economic stabilisation tool is badly needed for the euro-area, which should work as automatically as possible and be financed from a euro-area wide tax. It should be confined to economic stabilisation only, but not making a platform for permanent transfers between euro-area member states.

[10] See Darvas (2012c) for an assessment of the various criticisms of the OMT.

The negative feedback loop between the crisis and growth does not only exist in southern European adjusting countries, but in all euro-area countries. Uncertainty over the future of the euro, and the risk of economic hardship that an eventual break-up would bring, makes corporations and households more hesitant to invest and consume. Corporations in the economically stronger countries are also directly affected by the deteriorating situation in economically weaker countries through trade and financial links.

Furthermore, the funding constraints in the banking sector, the increasing credit risks for banks due to the weakening economic outlook, and the efforts to raise banks' capital ratios lead to a reduction in credit supply. Reduced credit availability further dampens economic growth. Without effective solutions to address the crisis, growth is unlikely to resume.

The EU did not have a powerful response to the growth crisis. The main goals of the "Compact for Growth and Jobs" agreed to at the 29 June 2012 summit (European Council 2012c), such as structural reforms, completing the restructuring of the banking sector, growth-friendly fiscal consolidations, addressing the social consequences of the crisis, and deepening the single market, are all correct. However, few new tools were mobilised to achieve these goals. Providing fresh capital to the European Investment Bank (EIB) in the amount of €10 billion (which would increase lending capacity by €60 billion) and launching a pilot phase for Project Bonds up to €4.5 billion are welcome, but these would have a limited impact on growth in the EU. Moreover, while mobilising idle structural funds, which was also agreed on at the summit, is also crucial, this does not constitute new funding.

2.9 Lack of a euro-area fiscal policy

Ninth, no institution is responsible for managing the overall fiscal stance of the euro-area. Member states implement the policy deemed appropriate for their own economies, subject to the constraints of the European fiscal governance framework. However, on aggregate, such decentralised fiscal policy is unlikely to produce optimal fiscal policy for the euro-area as a whole. For example, while the aggregate fiscal position of the euro-area is much better than that of the US (Figure 5-2), and while the economic outlook is arguably more fragile in the euro-area, there is a much stronger consolidation bias in the euro-area as a whole than in the US. Certainly, states in the US are also independent in setting state-level fiscal policies (all but one has a balanced-budget constitutional rule), and the second major conclusion of Bordo et al. (2011) concerning the conditions necessary for a fiscal union to function smoothly and successfully is "a degree of revenue and expenditure independence of the members of the fiscal union reflecting their preferences." However in the US the federal government dispenses approximately half of the total tax revenues and considers the US economy as a whole when setting fiscal policy targets (Darvas 2010a). In other federations, such as Canada or Switzerland, the circumstances are similar.

Unfortunately, the euro-area has not yet reached a point where a discussion can be begun on the overall fiscal stance of the euro-area and the way it could be aligned to the situation of the euro-area as a whole.

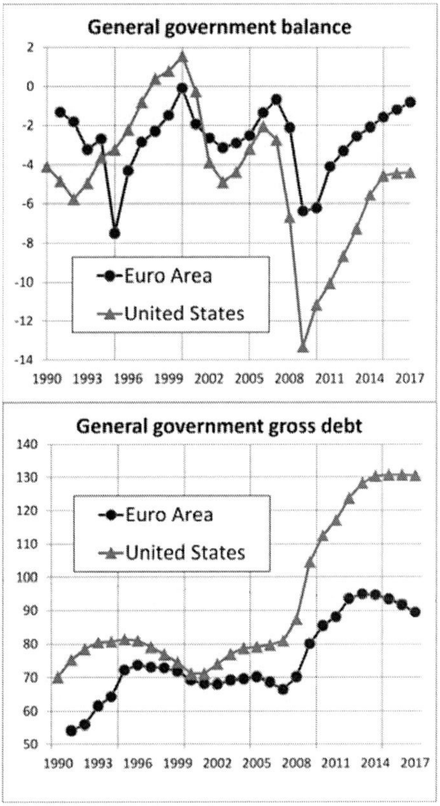

Fig. 5-2 The aggregate fiscal positions of the euro-area and the USA (% of GDP), 1990–2017
Sources: Euro-area balance and debt – IMF (2012); US balance – AMECO database up to 2000 and IMF (2012) for 2001–2017;

US debt: USGovernmentSpending.com (2012) up to 2012, for 2013–2017 we assumed that state and local government debt will remain at the 2012 value as a per cent of GDP and federal debt increases as projected by IMF (2012).
Note: US general government debt also includes the debt of states and local governments (IMF and European Commission data only report federal debt, even though they call it, erroneously, "general government gross debt").

2.10 Executive and democratic deficit

Tenth, the current crisis is not just a sovereign debt, banking and growth crisis, but is also a governance crisis. In most cases the response of European policymakers has been partial, inadequate and belated, and they have thereby lost trust in their ability to resolve the crisis. Some observers have concluded that agreeing on a comprehensive solution is technically and politically beyond reach. Compounded with the lack of democratic accountability of various European decision making bodies, Véron (2012) places the "executive and democratic deficit" at the centre of the lingering euro crisis and argues that some of the most important problems, such as Europe's banking crisis, the Greek sovereign debt saga, or the weak growth outlook of southern European member states, could have been addressed earlier and in a decisive way, had proper European decision making processes existed.

Regarding the political constraints, overcoming executive and democratic deficiencies is a truly fundamental issue. Nigel Lawson is most likely right when he claimed: "There is no wish among the people of Europe … for a full blooded United States of Europe political union".[11] Therefore, any progress towards a more effective and legitimate decision making and executive system will be, at best, piecemeal.

3. Southern Europe and the euro's future

The combined impact of all the factors discussed thus far drives down the economic outlook in the euro-area, and in particular, in Southern Europe. Figure 5-3 takes a historical perspective on changes in GDP per capita in the main geographical areas of the EU. After World War II, European countries embarked on a rapid convergence with the US in terms

---

[11] Nigel Lawson was the Chancellor of the Exchequer in the government of Margaret Thatcher during 1983–1989. He also claimed that "The whole thing [i.e. the euro] is a nonsense, and the sooner the whole thing can be dismantled in an orderly way, the better", with which I disagree. Source of the quotes: Mullholland (2011).

of GDP per capita, which was in part based on the rebuilding of the capital stock lost during the war, in part on technological catching-up and in part on economic integration efforts (Darvas and Pisani-Ferry 2011). By the late 1970s, however, convergence with the US had stopped in most countries of the "older" Europe – although with significant exceptions, such as Ireland. However, in the years ahead, according to the world economic outlook of the IMF, European countries are expected to fall behind, especially in southern Europe. Moreover, the IMF outlook must be interpreted as a baseline scenario and the risks are on the downside.

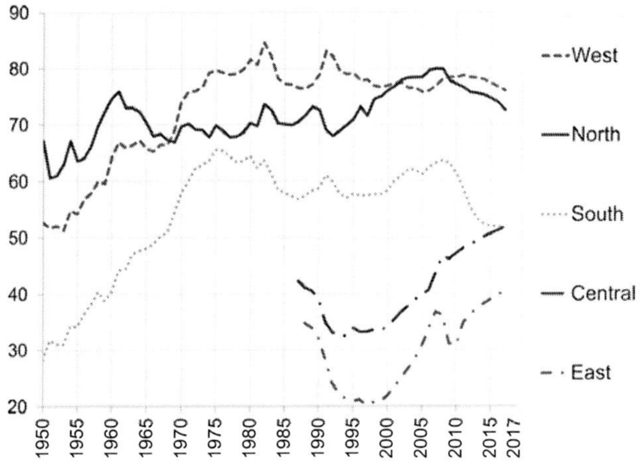

Fig. 5-3 GDP per capita in major geographical regions of the EU (USA = 100), 1950–2017
Source: Author's calculations using data from IMF (2012), PENN World Tables and EBRD
Note: GDP is based on purchasing power parity dollars; median values are shown for the country groups defined in the note to Figure 5-2.

The single most important threat to the integrity, and perhaps also the existence, of the euro is the bleak economic outlook for southern European member states. Without the problems of economically weaker countries in Southern Europe (for which western and northern members also bear responsibility), western and northern members would be able to overcome their baking woes, and the other issues we identified as the roots of the euro crisis would be much less relevant.

Economic growth in Southern Europe would gradually help to improve the unemployment situation and ease social tensions. It would help to improve public finances, thereby lessening the need for fiscal consolidation. It would help to stabilise asset prices, and in particular, housing prices, which in turn would improve the balance sheets of banks, thereby also reducing recapitalisation needs. Increased trust in banks and the hope of an economic recovery would slow or even reverse capital outflows from these counties. As a consequence, economic growth in Southern Europe would greatly diminish the exit risk facing some southern euro members.

But growth is not coming, and in fact the recession deepens. Several commentators concluded that southern euro members have no hope for growth inside the euro-area and an exit from the euro is the only viable option. While undoubtedly it would be much easier for southern euro members to solve their problems outside the euro-area, I disagree on both counts: there is some hope, at least in some southern members on the one hand, and on the other hand an exit would likely be so disastrous that it would take a very long time to recoup the output that would be lost during the exit process. An exit would cause devastating consequences for economically stronger countries as well, thereby creating existential risk for the euro, with severe implications for the EU as well.

- Hope: Since 2008, Spanish exports are performing the best among the EU-15 countries, i.e., the pre-2004 members of the EU (Darvas 2012a). Spain is followed by Germany, Ireland and Portugal. Spain and Portugal even outperform the UK and Sweden, two countries that benefitted from significant currency depreciation during the crisis.[12] While their tradable sectors remain small, solid export performance is an indication the tradable sector is able to expand. Additionally, the World Bank (2012) found that large and internationalised firms in Southern Europe are as productive as large firms in Western and Northern Europe, and the main issue is that there are far fewer large firms in Southern Europe, due to various barriers. Altomonte et al. (2012) arrived at a similar conclusion. This suggests that while the business conditions are unfavourable and there are barriers to firm growth, properly managed firms are able to achieve a high level of efficiency even in Southern Europe.
- Disastrous exit: It is impossible to provide an accurate estimate of the cost of an exit from the euro, but it would most likely be huge. UBS (2011) have concluded that an economically weak country leaving the euro-area would lose approximately one half of its GDP

[12] However, the export performance of Greece is very weak.

in the first year. If they are correct, it is unclear how many years it would take to compensate for the lost output, even if growth were to increase from this halved level of output. The huge decline in output would necessitate even harsher fiscal austerity, as it is not very likely that in the event of a messy exit from the euro other euro-area partners would be happy to lend to the country that left the euro – without such support, the government could spend only tax revenues, which would be dramatically reduced by the collapse of GDP. Moreover, there would also be longer term consequences, as the low credibility of the newly stand-alone central bank of the exiting country would likely lead to much higher real interest rates and a period of high inflation, which are bad for growth. Additionally, a euro exit may be accompanied by an EU exit and thereby the country would lose huge transfers form the EU. It is also in the best interest of euro-area partners to keep these countries in the union, and not just because of the direct losses that would arise from financial and trade relations with the exiting country. Even more importantly, the exit of a country would open Pandora's box: it would be very difficult to safeguard other economically weaker countries and a wave of exits would be even more disastrous for the economically stronger euro-area countries.[13]

However, the good news we highlighted and the fears of disaster do not guarantee that the deep economic slump in these countries will end anytime soon. If the recession continues to deepen, social tensions could escalate, which may lead to domestic political paralysis. Under such circumstances, cooperation between euro-area partners and the country in question, including financial assistance that has already been granted to some southern euro members, would halt, leading to an accelerated and possibly uncontrolled exit from the euro-area, with all the consequences we described above.

Therefore, ending the recession and offering improved economic prospects for southern euro members is pivotal, and actions will be required at both the national and European levels – well beyond the Compact for growth and jobs:

- The southern euro-countries should engage in a number of efforts: we have highlighted that they suffer from huge structural weaknesses, which are impediments to growth. Moreover, while

[13] And the euro is not just about economics but has major historical and political roots as well.

productivity has improved and unit labour costs have fallen, e.g., in Spain since 2008, this was mainly the consequence of reduced employment, which has adverse social consequences. Wages proved to be downwardly rigid (Darvas 2012a). Structural reforms to improve the functioning of labour markets are also inevitable, yet it will take a long time for these reforms to take effect.

- There is a strong case for calling for unit labour cost (ULC) increases in "western" and "northern" euro-area trading partners (see for example Wolff (2012) and Merler and Pisani-Ferry (2012b)). To some extent wages have begun to increase in Germany, but in any case this process will take a long time. Moreover, higher average inflation in the euro-area may also help to correct pre-crisis intra-euro divergences in prices and wages, but such a policy would be clearly unacceptable to the economically stronger countries of the euro-area.
- Fiscal expansion in northern members of the euro-area, or at least a significant slowdown in the pace of fiscal consolidation, would facilitate the economic adjustment of the southern members (Merler and Pisani-Ferry 2012b), but unfortunately, the relaxation of fiscal targets in Northern Europe does not seem to be on the agenda.
- A weaker euro would also greatly facilitate the adjustment of southern euro-area members (Darvas 2012b), which would be fostered by further interest rate cuts and quantitative easing by the European Central Bank. A weaker euro would help southern economies to improve their trade balances with non-euro countries and would also boost German exports. This in turn would help to address intra-euro imbalances, since increased exports would likely translate into greater wage increases in Germany, due to the country's tight labour market, but not in Spain, due to its high unemployment. Thus, Spain's competitiveness vis-à-vis Germany would also improve. Without a weaker euro, Spain would need to enter a deflationary period, which on the one hand is difficult to achieve and on the other would make debt sustainability even more difficult.
- Euro-area partners should also recognise that public debt at least in Greece is still too high. Even if the austerity programme is implemented as planned, it is very unlikely that Greece will be able to repay all of its public debt. Prolonging the recognition of this issue simply prolongs the uncertainty about Greece's future, thereby also negatively impacting the economy. However, as European partners have lent money to Greece to repay private

lenders and therefore 'socialised' Greek public debt, further significant public debt reduction cannot be accomplished without some involvement by the official sector. This is the price that euro-area partners have to pay for their mistakes in managing the Greek crisis in 2010 and 2011.

- Finally, to help break the downward economic spiral that southern euro-area member states face, a very significant European investments programme is needed for southern members. Note that investments are different from aid and lending.

4. Concluding remarks

The euro suffers from a large number of flaws, which were cast in stark relief during the crisis. For some of these flaws, solutions were provided, even if belatedly, and member states exhibited a willingness to improve the functioning of the euro by agreeing to relinquish national sovereignty in some important dimensions. However, the single most pressing issue, which threatens the integrity and perhaps the existence of the euro, is not yet well addressed: the deepening economic recession in southern member states. Most of the major policy measures that would help to stop the economic misery of these countries and offer the prospect for improved economic conditions are not yet on the agenda. Only time will tell the economic and political denouement of southern euro member and what progress will be made in addressing the ten main roots of the euro crisis that we have identified.

References

Ahearne, A. and Delgado, J. and von Weizsäcker, J. 2008. "A tail of two countries." *Bruegel Policy Brief* 2008/04, June. http://www.bruegel.org/download/parent/6-a-tail-of-two-countries /file/361-a-tail-of-two-countries-english/

Allard, C. and Everaert, L. 2010. "Lifting Euro-area Growth: Priorities for Structural Reforms and Governance." Staff Position Note 10/19, International Monetary Fund.

Altomonte, C. and Aquilante, T. and Ottaviano, G. 2012. "The triggers of competitiveness: The EFIGE cross-country report." *Bruegel Blueprint* 17, July. http://www.bruegel.org/download/parent/738-the-triggers-of-competitiveness-the-efige-cross-country-report/file/1600-the-triggers-of-competitiveness-the-efige-cross-country-report/

Bordo, M. D. and Markiewicz, A. and Jonung, L. 2011. "A Fiscal Union for the Euro: Some Lessons from History." NBER Working Paper 17380, September. http://www.nber.org/papers/w17380

Darvas, Zs. 2010a. "Fiscal federalism in crisis: lessons for Europe from the US." *Bruegel Policy Contribution* 2010/07. http://www.bruegel.org/download/parent/420-fiscal-federalism-in-crisis-lessons-for-europe-from-the-us/file/901-fiscal-federalism-in-crisis-lessons-for-europe-from-the-us-english

—. 2010b. "The Case for Reforming Euro-area Entry Criteria." *Society and Economy* 32, 2: 195-219, http://akkrt.metapress.com/content/f31518426t738884/fulltext.pdf

—. 2011a. "Debt restructuring in the euro-area: A necessary but manageable evil?" *Bruegel Policy Contribution* 2011/07, June. http://www.bruegel.org/download/parent/567-debt-restructuring-in-the-euro-area-a-necessary-but-manageable-evil/file/1422-debt-restructuring-in-the-euro-area-a-necessary-but-manageable-evil/

—. 2011b. "The euro's last-chance saloon." *Bruegel blog*, September. http://www.bruegel.org/blog/detail/article/162-the-euros-last-chance-saloon/

—. 2011c. "The Ten Roots of the Euro Crisis." *CESifo Forum* 2011/4, 3-4. http://www.bruegel.org/blog/detail/article/119-the-ten-roots-of-the-euro-crisis/

—. 2012a. "Compositional effects on productivity, labour cost and export adjustment." *Bruegel Policy Contribution* 2011/11, June. http://www.bruegel.org/download/parent/730-compositional-effects-on-productivity-labour-cost-and-export-adjustments/file/1594-compositional-effects-on-productivity-labour-cost-and-export-adjustments/

—. 2012b. "Intra-euro rebalancing is inevitable, but insufficient." *Bruegel Policy Contribution* 2012/15, August. http://www.bruegel.org/download/parent/747-intra-euro-rebalancing-is-inevitable-but-insufficient/file/1607-intra-euro-rebalancing-is-inevitable-but-insufficient/

—. 2012c. "The ECB's Magic Wand." *Intereconomics* 47, 4: 266–267. http://www.bruegel.org/nc/blog/detail/article/904-the-ecbs-magic-wand/

Darvas, Zs. and Pisani-Ferry, J. 2011. "Europe's growth emergency." *Bruegel Policy Contribution* 2011/13, October, http://www.bruegel.org/download/parent/623-europes-growth-emergency/file/1485-europes-growth-emergency/

Darvas, Zs. and Pisani-Ferry, J. and Sapir, A. 2011. "A comprehensive approach to the euro-area debt crisis." *Bruegel Policy Brief* 2011/02, February.
http://www.bruegel.org/download/parent/491-a-comprehensive-approach-to-the-euro-area-debt-crisis/file//988-a-comprehensive-approach-to-the-euro-area-debt-crisis/

De Grauwe, P. 2011. "The Governance of a Fragile Eurozone." CEPS Working Document 346, May.
http://www.ceps.eu/ceps/download/5523

Delpla, J. and von Weizsäcker, J. 2010. "The Blue Bond Proposal." *Bruegel Policy Brief* 2010/03, May.
http://www.bruegel.org/download/parent/403-the-blue-bond-proposal/file /885-the-blue-bond-proposal-english/

ECB. 2010. "Decision of the European Central Bank of 14 May 2010 establishing a securities markets programme."
http://www.ecb.int/ecb/legal/pdf/en_dec_2010_5__f_sign.pdf?254fd4539fb4248f368f12987016f26e

—. 2012a. "Financial integration in Europe." European Central Bank.
http://www.ecb.int/pub/pdf/other/financialintegrationineurope201204en.pdf

—. 2012b. "Technical features of Outright Monetary Transactions."
http://www.ecb.int/press/pr/date/2012/html/pr120906_1.en.html

EFSF. 2012. "European Financial Stabilisation Mechanism (EFSM)." European Commission. http://www.efsf.europa.eu/about/index.htm

EFSM. 2012. "European Financial Stabilisation Mechanism (EFSM)." European Commission.
http://ec.europa.eu/economy_finance/eu_borrower/efsm/index_en.htm

European Commission. 2011. "EU Economic governance "Six-Pack" enters into force." MEMO/11/898, December. http://europa.eu/rapid/pressReleasesAction.do?reference=MEMO/11/898

—. 2012a. "Six-pack? Two-pack? Fiscal compact? A short guide to the new EU fiscal governance." March,
http://ec.europa.eu/economy_finance/articles/governance/2012-03-14_six_pack_en.htm

—. 2012b. "Macroeconomic Imbalance Procedure." July.
http://ec.europa.eu/economy_finance/economic_governance/macroeconomic_imbalance_procedure/index_en.htm

European Council. 2011. "Conclusions of the European Council 24/25 March 2011." April,
http://www.consilium.europa.eu/uedocs/cms_data/docs/pressdata/en/ec/120296.pdf

—. 2012a. "European Stability Mechanism Treaty (ESM)." February. http://european-council.europa.eu/eurozone-governance/esm-treaty-signature?lang=en
—. 2012b. "Treaty on Stability, Coordination and Governance in the Economic and Monetary Union (TSCG)." March, http://european-council.europa.eu/eurozone-governance/treaty-on-stability
—. 2012c. "Conclusions of the European Council (28/29 June)." http://www.consilium.europa.eu/uedocs/cms_Data/docs/pressdata/en/ec/131388.pdf
IMF. 2010. "Cross-Cutting Themes in Employment Experiences during the Crisis." Strategy, Policy, and Review Department of the IMF, http://www.imf.org/external/pp/longres.aspx?id=4499
—. 2012. "World Economic Outlook", October.
Marzinotto, B. and Wolff, G. B. and Hallerberg, M. 2011. "How effective and legitimate is the European semester? Increasing role of the European parliament." Bruegel Working Paper 2011/09. http://www.bruegel.org/download/parent/612-how-effective-and-legitimate-is-the-european-semester-increasing-role-of-the-european-parliament/file/1472-how-effective-and-legitimate-is-the-european-semester-increasing-role-of-the-european-parliament/
Merler, S. and Pisani-Ferry, J. 2012a. "Who's afraid of sovereign bonds?" *Bruegel Policy Contribution* 2012/2, February. http://www.bruegel.org/download/parent/695-whos-afraid-of-sovereign-bonds/file//1551-whos-afraid-of-sovereign-bonds/
—. .2012b. "The simple macroeconomics of North and South in EMU." Bruegel Working Paper 2012/12. http://www.bruegel.org/download/parent/740-the-simple-macroeconomics-of-north-and-south-in-emu/file/1603-the-simple-macroeconomics-of-north-and-south-in-emu/
Mullholland, H. 2011. "Politics Live blog – Thursday 27 October 2011." Politics Live with Andrew Sparrow. http://www.guardian.co.uk/politics/2011/oct/27/politics-live-blog
Pisani-Ferry, J. and Wolff, G. B. 2012. "The fiscal implications of a banking union." *Bruegel Policy Brief* 2012/02, September. http://www.bruegel.org/download/parent/748-the-fiscal-implications-of-a-banking-union/file//1608-the-fiscal-implications-of-a-banking-union/
Pisani-Ferry, J. and Sapir, A. and Véron, N. and Wolff, G. B. 2012. "What kind of European banking union?" *Bruegel Policy Contribution* 2012/12, June. http://www.bruegel.org/download/parent/731-what-

kind-of-european-banking-union/file/1595-what-kind-of-european-banking-union/

Sinn, H.-W. 2011. "The ECB's stealth bailout." *VOXEU*, June. http://www.voxeu.org/article/ecb-s-stealth-bailout

UBS. 2011. "Euro break-up – the consequences." *Global Economic Perspectives*, UBS Investment Research, September. http://bruxelles.blogs.liberation.fr/UBS fin de l'euro.pdf

USGovernamentSpending.com. 2012. "US Federal State Local Debt As Percent Of GDP United States 1902-2012 - Federal State Local Data." http://www.usgovernmentspending.com/federal_state_local_debt_chart.html

Véron, N. 2011. "Euro-area banks must be freed from national capitals." *Bruegel blog*, September. http://www.bruegel.org/nc/blog/detail/article/151-euro-area-banks-must-be-freed-from-national-capitals/

—. 2012. "The challenges of Europe's fourfold union." *Bruegel Policy Contribution* 2012/12, August. http://www.bruegel.org/download/parent/741-the-challenges-of-europes-fourfold-union/file/1604-the-challenges-of-europes-fourfold-union/

Wolff, G. B. 2012. "Arithmetic is absolute: euro-area adjustment." *Bruegel Policy Contribution* 2012/09, May. http://www.bruegel.org/download/parent/724-arithmetic-is-absolute-euro-area-adjustment/file/1581-arithmetic-is-absolute-euroarea-adjustment/

World Bank. 2012. "Golden growth: Restoring the lustre of the European economic growth model" edited by Gill, I. S. and Raiser, M. http://siteresources.worldbank.org/INTECA/Resources/gg_overview.pdf

Wyplosz, C. 2009. "Viewpoint: The Euro's Finest Hour?" *Finance & Development*, IMF, June, 22–24. http://www.imf.org/external/pubs/ft/fandd/2009/06/pdf/wyplosz.pdf

THE SOVEREIGN DEBT CRISIS AND THE WEAKENING OF THE PILLARS OF THE ECONOMIC AND MONETARY UNION

MIKLÓS LOSONCZ

1. Introduction

The sovereign or government debt crisis that entails solvency risk on the part of sovereign debtors or governments began in November 2009 in the wake of the global financial and economic crisis. It brought the institutional weaknesses of the Economic and Monetary Union (EMU), established between 1999 and 2002, to the surface. Given the dysfunctional operation of its institutional and regulatory systems, perspectives emerged that questioned the long-term viability of the EMU and anticipating the exit of individual member states (particularly Greece) or its complete break-up.

This paper analyses the latest developments of the sovereign debt crisis by focusing on the relationship between the institutional system and the operation of the EMU on the one hand and the sovereign debt crisis on the other. The objective of the paper is to discuss the ways in which the sovereign debt crisis affected the pillars (no exits, no defaults and no bail-outs) of the EMU. It argues that they were softened to certain degrees, but because they form essential parts of the monetary integration they cannot be dismissed completely.

Before discussing the issue it should be underlined that the crisis has not primarily affected the euro's role as a common currency. Considering its internal and external purchasing power (its exchange rate to major currencies), the euro is relatively strong in spite of eventual short-term depreciations against major currencies. Its roles in international settlements and central bank reserves were not weakened significantly. In terms of purchasing power parity, the euro is still overvalued vis-à-vis a number of major currencies. The sovereign debt crisis did not have a negative impact on the stability and international position of the common currency. The crisis impacted the member states of the EMU both directly and through the regulatory mechanisms of the EMU. Thus, in this respect, the EMU also contributed to the sovereign debt crisis, as will be analysed below.

The first section of this report discusses the three prohibitions stipulated in the relevant EU treaty (no exits, no defaults and no bail-outs) that form the three pillars of the EMU, their consequences in the management of the crisis, and optimum currency area theory. The subsequent three sections focus on the softening of the pillars of the EMU. The fifth section provides an overview of the latest measures. The final section contains the summary and conclusions. The sovereign debt crisis in the EMU has yet to come to an end. This report relies on data and information that were available before 15 July 2012.

2. The three prohibitions and their consequences on managing the crisis

The legal regulation of the Economic and Monetary Union was originally based on *three prohibitions* or negations that are strongly interrelated and should be interpreted together.[1] Regarding the irrevocability of the EMU, *the first prohibition is that there be no exits*. The possibility of exit would weaken the credibility of the EMU and nurture speculation against weak member states. If exit were a real possibility, investors would purchase the high quality government securities of economically stable member states rather than those of weak ones predicted to leave the EMU. The absence of an exit clause indicates that the EMU is something more than a loose fixed exchange rate area or a group of countries using a common currency.

According to the second prohibition, government default is not possible in the EMU. Government default should be avoided and there are no institutions, legal rules or procedures to handle the default of member states.

The *third prohibition contains rules on the financing of general government deficits and government debts*. The major principle is that general government deficits and government debts have to be financed exclusively using the money and capital markets. Consequently, funding general government expenditures with central bank credits is prohibited, and EU institutions and member states are forbidden from providing the public sectors of troubled members with financial aid. The latter is the so-

---

[1] In the Hungarian economic literature, this topic was discussed by Benczes (2011).

called *no bail-out clause* that covers all EU member states rather than only those of the EMU. The set of rules included in the Treaty of Lisbon and reinforced by the Stability and Growth Pact and other documents are designed to avoid excessive general government deficits. *The independence of the European Central Bank* (ECB), which is considered an important value, is closely related to the no bail-out clause. The objective of the ECB's monetary policy is price stability; it does not have any other tasks, including fiscal ones.

Because of the no bail-out clause, EU member states facing financial difficulties may only turn to the International Monetary Fund (IMF) for assistance. In fact, the possibility of applying for loans to the IMF may have been a means of escape from the no bail-out clause. Member states are willing to avoid this mechanism because of reputational considerations. Nevertheless, the empirical evidence demonstrates that the IMF had to be involved in the management of the sovereign debt crisis in the EMU. However, the IMF has agreed that it will only begin negotiations regarding loans to EU member states with the consent of EU institutions. Thus, this theoretical legal escape clause was also restricted.

According to the founders, the three prohibitions were necessary to guarantee the credibility of the EMU. They also assumed that if the legal rules ensuring fiscal discipline were observed systematically, financial crises could be avoided.

The three prohibitions have further implications. A consequence of the *exit prohibition* is that an EMU member state using the common currency may not mitigate short-term disequilibria and competitiveness issues by devaluating their national currencies. Devaluations based on the discretionary decision of central banks would only be possible if member states were to exit the EMU, but this is not permitted.

With respect to adjustment mechanisms, the EMU is similar to the *gold standard* of the 19th century but without the use of gold. Historically, those countries that insisted on retaining the gold standard faced more substantial fiscal and political consequences during the Great Depression of 1929–1933 than those that eventually abandoned it. Analogously, under a fixed exchange rate regime in the EMU, competitiveness can be improved only by *internal devaluation*, i.e., by reducing wages (more precisely unit labour costs) and prices, which is a rather painful process; one that is more painful than external devaluation. Unlike the US, the EMU does not have a federal budget that makes it possible to bail out indebted member states facing financial tensions.

The prohibition on government default for individual member states is explained by the desire to inhibit the spill-over of its negative effects to the rest of the EMU. First, a government default would have a negative impact on *banks* with large proportions of the government securities of financially troubled member states in their portfolios. Thus, due to the strong ties between governments and banks, government defaults may also lead to bank defaults. Bank failures may have an adverse impact on financial stability.

Second, the *spill-over effects* may be quite significant. The default of a sovereign debtor in the EMU (at present that of Greece is the most probable) may well have repercussions on other countries (such as Spain, Portugal and Italy) that should also be taken into account. In this context, the first question is whether it is possible for governments to avoid default by exclusively relying on their own resources or if the financial support of other member states and international organisations is indispensable. The involvement of external sources calls the validity of the no bail-out clause into question. The second question is, if it proves unavoidable, whether government default should be disorderly or managed. The latter seems to be preferable because it entails lower expected costs.

The *no bail-out clause* is more than a limiting legal formula; it can be logically derived from the structure of the economic and monetary union. In a decentralised monetary union where no common fiscal policy exists and there are no cross-border transfers due to political reasons, the no bail-out clause is the essential guarantee of the functioning of the EMU.

The first *consequence* of the no bail-out clause was the rise in the default risks of sovereign debtors in the EMU. While this has long been a theoretical possibility, it was regarded as a very low probability event. However, with the expansion and deepening of the sovereign debt crisis, the probability of government defaults has increased. The *second consequence* of the no bail-out clause is that according to the provisions of EU law, the ECB may not assume the role of the lender of last resort for the banking system, a role that otherwise may be very useful in crisis situations. This is different from the status of central banks in non-EMU countries. The balance between solidarity and autonomy is not proportional in the EMU. In the case of complete solidarity, when government debts are fully guaranteed, free riders and moral hazard appear. In the absence of any guarantee, speculation may loom. Mutual guarantees are missing in the EMU. The EMU was established without any insurance mechanism, and it was assumed that a monetary union could be successful without a budgetary or fiscal union (De Grauwe 2010).

In spite of the structural problems, the lack of institutions, financial funds and crisis management mechanisms, the set of rules based on the three prohibitions did not inhibit the smooth functioning of the EMU in a period when the global economy developed without major issues and global liquidity was abundant, although prior to its establishment several experts voiced their doubts over the long-term viability of the EMU (see in retrospect e.g., Feldstein 2012). In the late 1990s, the extent to which the EMU would meet the criteria for an optimum currency area was not clear to experts who were critical of the then current form of monetary integration.

Optimum currency area theory focuses on the criteria that are essential for a country or group of countries to form an economic and monetary union. In an optimum currency area (a group of countries suitable for a monetary union), the following criteria are met:[2]

First, the markets for production factors (labour and capital) are flexible and function well, the production factors are mobile, and therefore their prices are able to adjust to external price changes.

Second, the area is internally homogeneous, implying that its member countries have similar economic structures and their business cycles are synchronised. The internal homogeneity of the area must have reached such a level that it is not threatened by asymmetric external shocks. The term asymmetric external shock means that countries forming the monetary union suffer shocks of different sizes from the same external event. The reason for this is that the commodity and geographical structures of their exports and imports, their reliance on imported energy and external finances, etc., are significantly different.

Third, budgetary transfers are also available to fend off various economic disturbances including asymmetric shocks.

The analysis of the applicability of these criteria to the EMU would go beyond the scope of this study. Nevertheless, it is worth mentioning that, first, the no bail-out clause excluded budgetary transfers in the EMU. The reason for this was that monetary integration was not accompanied with the creation of a fiscal union. Budgetary transfers would have implied a transfer union with permanent transfers from richer to poorer countries as is the case within individual countries. Second, the internal homogeneity of the EMU must have not yet reached a level at which it is exempt from asymmetric shocks. Third, doubts over the mobility of the labour force and the flexibility of the labour market may also be justified. All of these deficiencies are demonstrated by relevant research. These deficiencies

[2] The original concept of the optimal currency area was elaborated by Mundell (1961). The theory was amended and further developed by many scholars. The issue and other relevant problems are discussed in detail by, e.g., De Grauwe (2003).

mean that the criteria for an optimum currency area were not met from the outset.

Nevertheless, of the three criteria for an optimum currency area, only one can be directly associated with the three prohibitions, namely the no bail-out clause. The structural weaknesses of inflexible labour markets and differences in macroeconomic structures were *aggravated by deficiencies in the institutional and policy frameworks of the EMU*. One such weakness was the primacy of real interest rate effect over the real exchange rate effect (Tomaso Padoa-Schioppa Group 2012). The one-size-fits-all monetary policy of the ECB led to excessive cyclical divergences and imbalances. Real interest rates were negative in the dynamically growing peripheral countries of the EMU (Ireland and Southern Europe, including Greece, Portugal, Spain and Italy) that led to sharp price and wage increases and the subsequent deterioration of their relative international competitiveness resulting in a competitiveness crisis on one hand and credit and real estate bubbles and the accumulation of private and/or government debts on the other.

Furthermore, in the absence of flexible labour markets and official transfers in the EMU, huge *imbalances* accumulated in conjunction with substantial *current account surpluses* in the core economies (such as Germany, Austria and the Netherlands) and enormous *current account deficits* in the peripheral member states. They generated a balance of payments crisis (EEAG 2012). The EMU regulatory system did not include guarantees for financing international imbalances (current account surpluses and deficits), managing financial shocks or implementing adjustments to restore international competitiveness (for details see e.g., EuroMemorandum Group 2010). The sovereign debt crisis called into question prior assumptions that international disequilibria are not relevant.

In managing the sovereign debt crisis, rules based on the three prohibitions substantially impeded the ability to shift economic policy for both nation states and EU institutions. The constraints were particularly pronounced relative to the possible actions and economic policy tools of the EU's competitors. The relaxation of some of the prohibitions played an important role in managing the sovereign debt crisis.

3. Easing the exit from the EU

According to Article 50 of the Treaty on the European Union (TEU, the first part of the Treaty of Lisbon) that became effective as of 1 December 2009, any member state may quit the EU. If an EU member state is simultaneously an EMU member, it has to exit the latter as well.

The TEU makes no explicit mention of exiting the EMU. However, according to the relevant EU laws governing monetary integration (regulations concerning the introduction of the euro, the irrevocable fixing of the conversion rates of the national currencies against the euro, the irreversibility of the EMU, etc.) that are based on the basic treaties, member states are not allowed to leave the EMU. This implies that an EMU member state is barred from leaving the EMU while remaining in the EU. Because an exit from the EMU is unprecedented, there are no formal procedures or mechanisms for departing the EU in general and the EMU in particular.

EU law does not allow for the exclusion of any member state from the EU and the EMU. Although from the standpoint of the ECB, it may be feasible to exclude a member state from the EMU through indirect means, it is not possible through current legal provisions. An example of such indirect means would be the ECB refusing liquidity to member state banks that suffered runs on their deposits. This was a perceived danger in Greece in May 2012. The legal possibility of exclusion would undermine the Economic and Monetary Union by sending markets the message that the union is no more than an exchange rate mechanism, which individual countries may join or leave, depending on their actual economic situation (The Economist 2008).

The provisions concerning exit from the EU have nothing to do with the sovereign debt crisis and attempts to ameliorate it with economic policies. The elaboration of the Treaty of Lisbon began well before the outbreak of the sovereign debt crisis. However, the possibility of exiting the EU and the EMU has received a different interpretation in light of the crisis. The major reason for a member state to leave the EMU is to regain its independence in exchange rate policy. This would make it possible to remedy or at least mitigate the negative effects of the crisis by devaluing the national currency that would replace the euro at least in the short run.

From the *legal point of view*, an exit from the EMU *could be* feasible in two ways, at least in principle. First, the TEU and other relevant legal rules regarding the EMU and the euro could be explicitly modified to allow member states to leave the EMU and remain in the EU. Such a change in the basic treaty seems nearly out of the question under normal conditions. It is not realistic to assume that 27 EU member states could agree on a new treaty or the necessary modifications to the existing one at an intergovernmental conference within a reasonable timeframe. In addition, lengthy negotiations would also have an adverse impact on financial stability. The legal codification of exit criteria would also weaken the credibility of the EMU. This possibility could only become reality in a very severe crisis.

Second, apart from the rationality of such a decision, exiting the EMU is the *autonomous, independent decision of a member state*. To avoid or moderate capital flight, exit measures must to be taken on a single day or within a few days. In this sense, a managed exit based on negotiations with other member states and EU institutions would hardly be possible. Of course the detailed conditions for the exit would have to be clarified subsequently in long and complicated negotiations.

Assuming that a member state leaves the EMU and remains in the EU, it would face serious *legal problems*. In this case, EU law would remain effective in the departing member country. "If it abandoned the euro in all domestic contracts, but maintained it in all foreign contracts, the consequence would be a flood of well-founded lawsuits. Every citizen of the departing country would have a legal case against its own government – and possibly against the other member states as well. A euro zone exit would constitute discrimination on grounds of nationality – the biggest "no, no" under EU law" (Münchau 2012d).

If a member state exits both the EMU and the EU, it will be isolated in Europe. The EU would impose tariffs on its goods. The Schengen Agreement would be suspended with the direct consequence of the introduction of visas. To halt capital flight, the departing country would have to introduce restrictions on capital flows. The departing country would lose access to transfers from the structural funds and the Cohesion Fund.

In addition to legal factors, there are also *economic arguments* against the partial or complete break-up of the EMU. First, it would *trigger chaos or uncontrollable developments*. Second, it would entail *unbearable costs* on those concerned. According to model calculations, the direct losses from a break-up or the exit of strong and weak member states would amount to 20–50% of the GDPs of the countries concerned. Germany would suffer losses amounting to 20% of GDP and those of Greece would be 50%.[3] These are approximate figures. Modelling the consequences is difficult because the effects are unprecedented.

With respect to the most troubled countries, the most probable case may be that Greece would exit the EMU. Then it will have to balance its primary budget (deficit excluding interest payments) immediately, otherwise it would not be able to finance its deficit. As in the ensuing chaos, mass corporate and household defaults, increasing unemployment, recession, etc., general government revenues will decrease, a primary

[3] The figures come from an analysis by UBS. Source: The Economist (2011).

surplus should be achieved rather than a balanced budget. The Greek primary general government deficit amounted to 2.5% of GDP in 2011; it is expected to total 1% in 2012. This would necessitate a 20–30% wage reduction in the public sector. Under these circumstances, the collapse of the public sector would be unavoidable, and the government would not be able to rely on underpaid civil servants to maintain law and order. If the government were to default, Greek banks would be cut off from the liquidity facilities of the ECB. If the Bank of Greece did not comply with relevant EU rules, Greece could be excluded from the EMU's payment system and the government would be forced to reintroduce the drachma.

The new drachma[4] replacing euro would depreciate quickly (likely by 30–40%, but more pessimistic estimates place the decline at 80–90%), the subsequent inflation increase would improve the external competitiveness of Greece through the contraction of real wages. Nevertheless, this possibility could only be modestly exploited because manufacturing accounts for merely 7% of Greek GDP. The role of tourism could be more significant, as its share of GDP is 18% and that of maritime transport is another 12%. Given the relatively low importance of manufacturing, Greece is not integrated in the EU supplier network and German corporations within it. Consequently, the acceleration of GDP growth in the EU in general and Germany in particular would not provide a great deal of a boost to Greek manufacturing. In addition, the depreciation of the new drachma would trigger a strong inflationary spiral.

Devaluation and the subsequent increased inflation would lead to the loss of wealth due to plummeting real estate prices and the devaluation of financial assets. With the expected rapid devaluation of the new drachma, the costs of financing government debt denominated in euros would soar. The paradoxical feature of this strategy is that to avoid hyperinflation and restore international competitiveness, Greece has to pursue *prudent fiscal policy and accomplish structural reforms without external funding* that are similar to those requested by EU institutions and the IMF in exchange for the financial rescue packages (Münchau 2012a). However, the depreciation of the national currency may weaken the pressure for structural reforms faced by the government. In summary, an exit from the EMU would not solve the Greek economy's fundamental issues such as the limited export sector, the lack of competitiveness and substantial external imbalances.

---

[4] According to various sources, the Greek government would likely declare a bank holiday after announcing the country's exit from the EMU, and the euro banknotes held by the country's banks would be stamped to demonstrate the reintroduction of the drachma.

In the case of a Greek exit from the EMU, bank runs in other endangered countries (Portugal, Spain and perhaps Italy) are certain to occur, as economic actors would transfer their monetary holdings to safer EMU member states. To neutralise this threat, the ECB would have to provide additional liquidity to the banking systems of the countries endangered by the negative spill-over effects. It should be noted, however, that at present the major Greek political parties do not desire to quit the EMU. According to public opinion polls, the majority of the Greek population does not support an exit either.

Despite the severe negative effects, many experts argue that considering the existing set of rules governing the EMU, the most indebted member countries (Greece, Portugal and Spain) should quit the EMU (see, e.g., Arnab and Roubini 2012). They believe that the long term advantages created by such an exit will exceed short-term disadvantages. Apart from the fact that the author of this paper does not find these arguments convincing, a discussion of these views would go beyond the scope of this report. If Spain and Italy leave the EMU, they would likely default on their external debt. Such an act would probably lead to the collapse of the European financial system (Münchau 2012e). A Greek, Spanish or Italian exit would cause investors to perceive that EMU membership is reversible, implying the implicit reintroduction of currency risks (Kramer 2012).

In spite of the great uncertainty and enormous costs, *the partial or complete dissolution of the EMU cannot be excluded, but the probability of such events seems to be rather low*. Nevertheless, in the absence of counterbalancing forces, this probability may increase, particularly if the political, financial and economic tensions surrounding Greece or other troubled EU member countries intensify. Even a low probability of exit may create uncertainty among economic actors and bolster demand for the safest US and German government securities, increase capital outflows from the EMU, and weaken the euro's relative position against other major currencies. The Deutsche Bundesbank may have considered the exit of individual member states from the EMU when President Jens Weidemann proposed the securitisation of German surpluses valued at €500 billion that had been accumulated in the TARGET2 central payment system and which has managed settlements between the central banks of countries where euro is legal tender since 2007. By seeking insurance against the collapse of the euro, the Deutsche Bundesbank does not regard the dissolution of the EMU as a zero probability event (Münchau 2012b).

The insolvency of governments may also endanger the solvency of the debtor countries' central banks. This may impose substantial losses on the central banks of creditor member states that are likely to be covered by the taxpayers of the respective countries. This is a *disguised fiscal transfer* that cannot be sustained.

The major guarantee against the complete break-up of the EMU is of an *economic nature*, namely, the high cost of such an event. None of the member states would benefit from the partial or the complete break-up of the EMU. In spite of the sovereign debt crisis, the costs of maintaining the EMU are much lower than those of its break-up. There is broad recognition by the major political forces in the EU that member states have little future outside the EMU.[5] As the probability of a partial or complete break-up increases, exit costs may decrease. Discussions on managing the crisis focus on, first, the distribution of burdens across the remaining member states and economic actors rather than the question of whether the system is worth saving. The answer to the latter question is clear (The Economist 2012b). Second, the unwillingness of the governments of individual member states to abandon their sovereignty or at least parts of it inhibit a move towards stronger monetary and fiscal integration.

At first glance, the demise of the EMU would involve the cancellation of a number of obligations enshrined in the Treaty of Lisbon. Furthermore, the complete and disorderly break-up of the EMU would also lead to the collapse of the EU, including the single markets for goods, services, capital and labour. The benefits of European integration achieved over the past 55 years would disappear.

The other argument against the break-up is one of a *political nature*. Member states invested substantial political capital in the EMU over the past 10–15 years; they do not want to write it off. The political commitment to the euro is strong in a defensive sense but is not sufficient to support stronger financial integration.

Apart from the possibility of a partial or complete break-up, economic actors regard the elaboration of contingency scenarios for the EMU at both the macro- and microeconomic levels as necessary. Contingency scenarios were prepared, i.a., by British and US investment banks for their clients rather than by EU institutions for the general public. With the escalation of the crisis in Greece in May and June 2012, increasing numbers of such

---

[5] Of the $11 trillion worth of euro-area debt outstanding, $4 trillion must be regarded as at risk in the near term in a restructuring process. The capital markets of the EU, including that of $185 trillion in outstanding euro-denominated derivative contracts would be in turmoil, causing large-scale capital flight to the US and Asia (Vallée 2012). The general view among experts is that the disorderly break-up of the EMU would be a much greater shock than the default of Lehman Brothers in 2008.

contingency scenarios appeared that were elaborated by banks and large corporations.

It is difficult to judge whether discussions of contingency scenarios on the macro level would trigger market panic or help to reduce uncertainty.[6] Fearing panicked reactions, until recently EU institutions refrained from compiling contingency scenarios under the otherwise justifiable assumption that they cannot be kept secret. Such a worst case contingency scenario should discuss the ways in which financial assets and liabilities would be redenominated after the managed break-up of the EMU. This is particularly important if the EMU collapses with the demise of the euro. It should be noted, however, that the majority of assets and liabilities are subject to UK law rather than EU law. It is unclear how they can be redenominated. An interesting suggestion is that in the case of a break-up, the euro should be replaced by ECU-2 (European Currency Unit – ECU), similar to the original ECU (Nordvig 2012). The EMU and the euro have developed to a point where the return to individual member state currencies is unlikely, and the only future recourse would be the use of the ECU as a basket currency. Nevertheless, the tensions accumulated within the EMU can only be eased in the absence of its partial or complete break-up.

4. The softening of the prohibition on government default

It is worth considering the possibility of government default because it is *doubtful whether indebted countries* in general, and Greece in particular, *can repay their government debts*. In addition, large government debts could *stifle economic growth* for an extended period independent from the issue of repayment. It is assumed that the costs of avoiding a government default, in terms of external rescue packages, are smaller than those of the default itself, including its spill-over effects on the rest of the EMU.

Government *default* may take two forms. First, it could be *accompanied by an exit from the EMU* or, second, it could be accomplished *within the EMU*. The consequences of an exit have already been discussed. This implies at first glance that government default does not automatically imply that the defaulting countries would exit the EMU. Nevertheless, in

[6] In this context, the Wolfson prize should be mentioned. The British Tory offered GBP251 thousand to the authors of the best plan for the dismantling of the EMU (see, e.g., Rachman 2012). For some details of the proposal, see The Economist (2012c).

the case of Greece a government default would also result in the country exiting the EMU, as it would likely only be able to obtain financing by reintroducing a national currency. This also holds for Spain and other indebted member states.

Government defaults in the EMU can be either disorderly or managed. In a *disorderly default*, the government stops servicing its debt without consulting and cooperating with concerned parties including EU institutions, member states, banks and the private sector. The revenues of the Greek government are not sufficient to finance the public sector. Not only would public services collapse, but banks would as well, because they would be forced to write off the government securities they own. Following a disorderly government default, it would be difficult to find investors willing to finance the Greek government. A disorderly government default may easily lead to the country exiting the EMU, which would have negative implications for the rest of the EMU through contagion effects.

An *orderly or managed default* is based on negotiations between the parties concerned. This raises the issue of the creation of a European Crisis Resolution Mechanism, as proposed by Bruegel, based on two pillars (Gianviti et al. 2010). The first pillar is a procedure to initiate and conduct negotiations between a sovereign debtor with unsustainable levels of debt and its creditors resulting in an agreement. The second includes the provision of financial assistance to EMU member states in an effort to resolve the crisis.

A government default within the EMU would not improve the competitiveness of the Greek economy or any other defaulting member state. As devaluation is not allowed, the forces driving economic growth would likely be external, in the form of European investment programs. The precondition for this is the restoration of credibility and co-operation between the interested parties (Münchau 2012a). The probability of this scenario is very low.

The weaker form of government default, which can be considered an orderly or managed one, is the write-off of a certain portion of government debt. The dilemmas here are the following. 1) Do the advantages deriving from the decrease in government debt and related debt service burdens exceed the financial and economic losses that are associated with the decline in credibility (that may spill-over to the rest of the EMU)? 2) Are the costs of government default lower than those of a potential bail-out?

In Greece, 74% of government debt held by private investors was written off as losses in March 2012. The haircut of more than €100 billion was one of the largest in economic history. Representatives of EU institutions frequently underline the fact that the partial write-off of Greek government debt having only involved the private sector was an exceptional case; it cannot be regarded as a precedent and is not applicable to other EMU member states. This implies that these other states must employ all available measures to avoid government default. Nevertheless, after the Greek precedent, investors buying the government securities of indebted member states are likely to be more cautious, and this may make it more difficult to finance other troubled EMU member states. A sovereign debt default mechanism may have other negative effects; it may nurture moral hazard and speculation (De Grauwe 2010).

A Greek exit from the EMU or a government default would involve Greek debts worth €121 billion owed to official creditors, €27 billion owed to the IMF and €155 billion directly owed to the euro system (comprising the ECB and the 17 national central banks in the EMU). The last figure includes €110 billion provided directly to Greece through the TARGET2 payment system (Vallée 2012). These figures demonstrate that a Greek government default could have far-reaching consequences on the euro zone. If we consider the potential candidates for government default, according to estimates based on official data the claims of the euro system on troubled periphery countries amount to approximately €1.1 trillion, corresponding to 200% of the broadly defined capital of the euro zone (Vallée 2012). These figures indicate quite considerable risks for bank capital and taxpayers and represent a strong argument for avoiding government default in the EMU. The risk of the fear of contagion, including capital flight, cannot be quantified.

Because bank portfolios contain significant shares of government securities, the recapitalisation of banks in the EU and the EMU envisaged in mid-2012 by the European Council can be considered, inter alia, a precautionary move to dampen the effects of potential government defaults. The new idea of a banking union will be discussed below.

Despite the softening of the prohibition on government default, *the roll-over of government debt* is still more difficult in the EMU than outside it. Countries outside the EMU are less likely to be subject to liquidity crises than EMU member states because, first, the devaluation of the exchange rate will generate buyers for government securities, albeit presumably at a weak exchange rate and high yields. Second, the national central bank can assume the role of lender of last resort and inflate the debt by excessive money creation. In this way, a government default can be avoided. In the case of fixed exchange rates or a common currency and the absence of a national central bank, there may be no demand for government securities at high yields and the government may default. This may explain why Spain's rating is worse despite the lower level of government debt relative to GDP than that of the UK despite its higher level of indebtedness.[7] As a consequence, the indebtedness levels should be much lower in economic and monetary unions than outside them.

5. The modification of the no bail-out clause: financial rescue packages and bail-out funds

In the wake of the Greek sovereign debt crisis that began in autumn 2009, as well as the subsequent crises in Ireland and Portugal, the softening of the no bail-out clause in the Treaty on the European Union became necessary. According to an evaluation of EU institutions and the leaders of major EU member states, defaults on the part of the countries mentioned – including spill-over effects – would have entailed higher costs than bail-outs financed by credit.

With respect to the legal basis: "Member states referred to Article 122 of the Treaty on the Functioning of the European Union, according to which assistance by EU countries is allowed if member states are faced with difficulties that are beyond their control. Before the actual rescue packages this article was interpreted in such a way that it cannot be applied to the bailing out of debtor countries. Since the resolution of the European Council as of 8/9 May 2010, governments of EMU member states have based their bail-out actions on it by arguing that the sovereign debt crisis endangered the solvency of individual member states and posted a threat to the financial stability of the Economic and Monetary Union" (Sinn 2010, 5). Nevertheless, the Economic and Monetary Union has faced crises in specific indebted EMU member states rather than a systemic crisis since that time (Sinn 2010, 7). "The use of this provision to the legal justification of bail-outs may give ground to different interpretations by the constitutional courts of EMU member states. However, this seems to be a smaller risk for the time being than the rather complicated modification of the Treaty of Lisbon to provide a clear legal basis for bailing out troubled EMU member states. The legal basis of bail-outs is still rather shaky" (Sinn 2010, 7).

A European Council decision (European Council 2011) added the following paragraph to Article 136 of the Treaty on the Functioning of the European Union: "3. Member States whose currency is the euro may establish a stability mechanism to be activated if indispensable to safeguard the stability of the euro-area as a whole. The granting of any required financial assistance under the mechanism will be made subject to

[7] See details based on the explanation of Paul De Grauwe in Wolf (2011).

strict conditionality." As this mechanism is designed to safeguard the financial stability of the euro-area as a whole, Article 122(2) of the TFEU will no longer be needed for such purposes.

In light of the circumstances, *three funds* were established, which did not conform to the spirit of the original provisions of the Treaty of Lisbon, to bail out member states coping with funding difficulties. The first fund is the *European Financial Stabilisation Mechanism* with €60 billion that expired on 30 June 2012 and is designed to aid EU member states outside the EMU. The second is the *European Financial Stability Fund* (EFSF) with €440 billion in effective lending capacity that expires as of 30 June 2013. Its successor will be the third fund, called the *European Stability Mechanism (ESM)*, with €500 billion in effective lending capacity that will be operative as of June 30th 2013. The EFSF and the ESM are likely to work simultaneously until mid-2013. The combined lending capacity of the two funds will amount to €700 billion, out of which fresh money will total €500 billion, the remainder being parts of the on-going Greek, Portuguese and Irish programs. These efforts will be supported by a contingency reserve valued at €240 billion. The overall size of the funds will reach €940 billion. They are operated jointly by the European Commission, the European Central Bank and the International Monetary Fund. The difference between the EFSF and the ESM is that the loans of the ESM are senior to those of private investors, in other words, government defaults will be possible at rather limited risk to the budgets of lender countries. In the case of the EFSF, the lending member states are burdened with the costs of government default. The creation of bail-out funds can be considered an initial shift towards an optimum currency area where budgetary transfers are available to fend off various economic disturbances. The disputed issues include, first, the size of the funds required to match the potential risks and, second, the ways in which they are used, including conditionality.

Until recently, Greece, Ireland and Portugal have received financial packages. In June 2012, Spain was awarded €100 billion and Cyprus applied for assistance. The sizes of the funds fall short of the total needs of EMU member states endangered by potential government default. In principle, the optimal sources of the bail-out funds have to be sufficient to guarantee that new government securities can be issued to roll over the government debt of troubled sovereign debtors, such as Greece, Portugal, Ireland, Spain, Italy, France and Belgium, until the EU issues common euro bonds. According to the calculations of Bloomberg and the IMF, €2.5 trillion – €3 trillion would be necessary until 2015 (Bloomberg Business Week 2011). In addition, if temporary and transfer items are excluded, the actual amount of funds that can be used for bail-outs amounts to only €500 billion in the long run. This is significantly less than the amount necessary to guarantee the government debt of all of the member states potentially facing financial difficulties. However, the available money is sufficient to prevent government default in smaller countries (such as Greece, Portugal and Ireland), but it is insufficient to bail-out Spain.

On one hand, increased financing for the funds may have *psychological implications*. The larger the size of the funds, the more convincing the deterrence, and the lower the probability of their deployment. Therefore, the risk of political debates challenging solidarity within the EU diminishes (Editorial 2012). Another interesting psychological question is whether the interventions of the European Stability Mechanism avoid crises or, on the contrary, trigger them.

On the other hand, increasing the sizes of the funds is a *signal to the US, China and other non-EU member states* in general and those belonging to the G20 in particular that they, too, may wish to increase their contributions to the IMF's global crisis management funds that were promised in April 2012 in the amount of $430 million.

The further extension of the EFSF and ESM funds runs the risk that international rating agencies will *downgrade the best debtors* because both the EFSF and ESM raise funds in international money and capital markets. Another political obstacle to further increases in the funds is that an addition to German's existing €211 billion contribution is subject to parliamentary approval. Domestic political issues may make the approval of new sums uncertain. In addition, the simple fact that the German contribution temporarily exceeds the approved ceiling may provoke political disputes.

Furthermore, multilateral programs seem to approach their political limits. The liabilities faced by the individual member states are not sufficient to justify increasing the size of the bail-out funds. It is necessary to pool or share liability across the member states by issuing Eurobonds, etc. (Münchau 2012c). Nevertheless, the ESM can be perceived as a specific form of transfer mechanism among member states. Some experts regard its establishment as a further step towards a *transfer union*. Nonetheless, the bail-out packages and the EFSF and ESM shift risks from banks to taxpayers rather than improving the competitiveness of the beneficiary countries.

The provision of financial aid from the bail-out funds is tied to conditions designed to reduce general government spending by introducing, inter alia, austerity measures and structural reforms. Until recently, beneficiary member states attempted to meet stringent, self-imposed austerity conditions. Nevertheless, a new situation may emerge if a beneficiary country fails to comply with austerity and structural reform conditions wilfully and permanently. This risk is quite plausible in Greece, where the stringent measures implemented in previous years combined with the subsequent recession fuelled political and social resistance to further austerity. The Greek public opposes the program designed by the European Commission, the European Central Bank and the International Monetary Fund. The situation is similar in the other heavily indebted member states. If wilfully and permanently non-compliant program beneficiaries are denied further funding, the exit of the respective member state cannot be avoided, entailing the risk of spill-over and contagion effects for other endangered countries. If further funding is not denied, the result may be "the creation of an open-ended, uncapped transfer union without the surrender of national sovereignty to the supranational European level" (Buiter 2012).

6. The modification of the no bail-out clause: changes in the ECB's tasks

Faced with the financial and economic crisis, the European Central Bank also modified its views on bail-outs. First, *the ECB began to buy the government bonds* of EMU member states facing financial difficulties in 2009 *in the secondary market*. The purchases were beyond the size required for conducting its monetary policy operations. In the framework of its Securities Market Program, the ECB purchased government securities valued at more than €200 billion. Moreover, the ECB sold high-quality government bonds to neutralise the inflationary effects of these purchases. Although this type of operation stabilised the yields on sovereign debt, it drove banks to sell off the government bonds of weak EMU member states, which are hence being accumulated by the ECB. "Since the start of 2007, the ECB purchased financial assets totalling 1.7 trillion euros, expanding its portfolio from 13% to over 30% of the euro zone's GDP" (Mallaby 2012, 7). This figure represented more than eight years of Greek GDP.

Second, the ECB offered unlimited liquidity loans to banks at an auction held in June 2009 with one-year maturities. The amount totalled €442 billion. Through these operations, the ECB reduced short term interest rates to US and UK levels (The Economist 2012a).

Third, the threat of a new recession loomed, bank capitalisation reached critical levels and investors only purchased the safest government securities in December 2011. As a response, the ECB offered commercial banks *unlimited liquidity* loans for three years against any collateral at a 1% interest rate (Long-term Refinancing Operation – LTRO). The action was repeated in late February 2012. Commercial banks borrowed more than €1000 billion under this scheme, although the assets of the banking system grew by only €503 billion if expiring loans and deposits at the ECB are taken into account. These measures are similar to the quantitative easing practices of the US Fed and the Bank of England.

In this scheme, the ECB formally observed the no bail-out clause of the Treaty on the Functioning of the European Union. Nevertheless, the LTRO can be regarded as a disguised bail-out. In Germany the ECB was criticised for not fully respecting the provisions of the EU Treaty that prohibit monetary financing of government debts. The ECB circumvented the formal legal provisions of the EU Treaty because commercial banks were provided loans rather than the governments directly. As the ECB accepted government bonds deposited by banks as collateral, the LTRO is an indirect means of bailing out indebted governments. It should be noted that the ECB is legally allowed to accept government securities as collateral.

Although the motivations for their introduction were more diverse, the loans provided by the ECB under the LTRO framework amended or extended the financial sources of the rescue funds. However, decision making in the ECB is more rapid than in the EFSF and ESM, and the ECB is more credible than the bail-out fund institutions.

There is insufficient space in the present article to analyse the effects of the LTRO in detail. However, it should be mentioned briefly that the ECB's primary objective with the LTRO was to reduce the yields of government securities and other risky assets and thereby fend off liquidity crises in some indebted EMU member states (particularly in Spain and Italy). The LTRO also contributed to the recapitalisation of banks, thereby preventing an eventual banking crisis. The LTRO undoubtedly helped to ease liquidity tensions in the EMU, but it was not appropriate to improve solvency and reduce general government debt, let alone improve competitiveness in indebted EMU member states and dampen current account imbalances in the EMU.[8] The three-year maturity of the loans provided governments and banks with time to make adjustments and reforms.

---

[8] EU policies "have failed to recognise the possibility of insolvency and have addressed all crises as if they were pure liquidity crises; they have failed to address systematically the interdependence between banking and sovereign crises and cross-country interdependence; and they have been reactive rather than proactive, squandering credibility because of inadequate responses" (Darvas et al. 2011, 1).

The risks of the LTRO are rather diverse. First, commercial banks may face difficulties in December 2014 and February 2015 in raising the amounts needed to repay the loans (Jenkins 2012). In addition, the three-year maturity is rather short for many banks.

Second, commercial banks may become too dependent on the ECB's inexpensive loans. If they buy government securities using these loans (this is a carry trade, and governments are prone to encourage it), the relationships between banks and governments may intensify. The relationship between the sovereign debt of financially troubled countries and the actual state of the banking sector will be reinforced (The Economist 2012b). With government securities in their portfolios, banks may be more vulnerable during difficult periods of the sovereign debt crisis. Therefore, sovereign debt crises may easily lead to bank crises.

Third, inexpensive loans may foster money and capital market bubbles similar to those that preceded the global financial and economic crisis, but with sovereign debt securities being purchased in this case. With the LTRO, the ECB may be unwillingly sowing the seeds of the next crisis (Milne and Watkins 2012).

Fourth, the central banks in the US and UK purchased government securities. In other words, sovereign risk was transferred from the public sector to the central bank. In the EMU, sovereign risk is still being carried by the private sector, namely the ECB shifted it to the balance sheets of undercapitalised commercial banks. In the US, the Fed directly provides loans to banks with a wide range of control mechanisms. In the EMU, the ECB offers banks refinancing, therefore its monetary policy is less predictable than that of the Fed. To add insult to injury, ECB monetary policy remains tight; there is room for a further reduction in its reference rate, although it was reduced from 1% to 0.75% in July 2012.

Fifth, there is no guarantee that the commercial banks that borrowed from the ECB are willing to buy the government securities of EMU member states with high yields and high risks or that increased liquidity can be channelled to the real economy.

Sixth, it is difficult to assess how long the ECB's last two liquidity injections through the LTRO will last. There are signs that their effects tend to fade away slowly.

Finally, the inexpensive loans provided by the ECB have reduced the pressure on both governments and commercial banks to implement reforms. For governments, the unconditional and unlimited purchase of government securities also leads to moral hazard problems.

By providing commercial banks with unlimited loans against government bonds (as collateral at specific LTRO auctions) the ECB essentially assumed the de facto role of the banking system's lender of last resort with some limitations (although the scheme cannot be considered a European Monetary Fund at present). However, this has yet to be declared officially, causing uncertainty among economic actors to remain. Germany opposes this mainly because of its inflationary impact in the long run. Nevertheless, in sharp crisis situations the benefits of crisis prevention outweigh the long-term costs in terms of inflation.

7. Measures aiming at the overhaul of the institutional system

The objective of softening the three prohibitions was to gain the time needed to take further measures at both the EU and the EMU levels to correct institutional deficiencies. They included the improvement of economic governance (the Stability and Growth Pact, Euro Pact, Six Pack, Treaty on Stability, Co-ordination and Governance in the Economic and Monetary Union, etc.), prevention (Excessive Imbalance Procedure), etc. The common objective of these legal rules is to reinforce fiscal discipline and thus somehow compensate for the lack of a fiscal union. The analysis of these measures is beyond the scope of this paper.

The most important proposals concerning the future of the EMU were submitted to the European Council in late June 2012. They contained, inter alia, an *integrated financial framework* including *integrated supervision* to ensure the effective application of prudential rules, risk control and crisis prevention throughout the EU; a *European deposit insurance scheme* to strengthen the credibility of the existing arrangements and secure eligible deposits at all credit institutions; and a European bank resolution scheme funded by contributions from financial institutions to provide assistance to banks (Rompuy 2012). This issue was also addressed previously by the Tommaso Padoa-Schioppa Group.

The concept is referred to as a *banking union* and it should be elaborated in detail. Based on the available information, the banking union should comprise all 27 member states of the EU to avoid the fragmentation of the single market for financial services.

Banking supervision would be delegated to the ECB. *Bail-out funds* could go directly to banks (the ESM will be allowed to recapitalise banks directly) rather than to governments, therefore they would not increase the government debts of the member states involved. This rule has already been applied to Spain. In addition, the ESM will be allowed to buy government bonds in secondary markets and thereby stabilise the market.

The common deposit insurance system could reduce the risk of bank runs in vulnerable member states. If a country is likely to leave the EMU and deposits are guaranteed in euros, people may borrow heavily in their local markets and deposit the money in their bank accounts. Their debts would be redenominated while their savings would be protected. This could be considered a direct transfer from the rest of the euro zone to the periphery (The Economist 2012d).

According to calculations by Barclays, an insurance fund would have to cover €11 trillion in deposits. For the banking industry to raise an amount worth 1.4% of assets, EMU banks would have to be taxed a fifth of their annual earnings for five years. According to more conservative calculations, more than €100 billion would have to be raised (The Economist 2012d).

The banking union could dismantle the link between governments and banks, creating a more stable financial environment in the EU. It can be considered a first step towards a fiscal union, although common responsibility and liability are rather limited.

8. Summary and conclusions

The sovereign debt crisis that evolved in the Economic and Monetary Union was fundamentally the result of economic policies in general and unsustainable fiscal policies in particular, pursued by member states, rather than the introduction of the *common currency*. The external and the internal stability of the euro have yet to be challenged. During the global financial and economic crisis, the *euro provided EMU member states with protection* against internal exchange rate shocks. After its introduction, conversion costs, exchange rate risks and uncertainties disappeared and, as a result, transaction costs decreased in intra-EMU trade, which also boosted GDP growth.

Nevertheless, the *basic legal rules* governing the EMU combined with some specific features of member states have long mitigated or even hidden economic disequilibria and tensions that developed both within and among member states for a long time. They were primarily the consequences of the fact that, first, the EMU was not an optimum currency area; second, EU legal rules were not efficient enough to enforce fiscal discipline and inhibit the accumulation of private sector debts in member states. The absence of the first two preconditions for an optimum currency area (flexible factor markets and internal homogeneity) was of minor importance in contrast to critiques written prior to the establishment of the EMU; whereas the third criterion (the availability of budgetary transfers) was not compatible with the notion of a monetary union in the absence of a fiscal one. Under the given circumstances, *exchange rate and liquidity crises were avoided.*

However, the economic disequilibria and tensions that had accumulated as a consequence of the global financial and economic crisis, the lack of an optimum currency area and the inadequate policies pursued by member states since the launch of the EMU in 1999 led to a sovereign debt crisis to *which the institutional and regulatory framework of the Economic and Monetary Union* also contributed. In addition, with the establishment of the EMU, its member states lost the majority of the traditional, national crisis management tools, which were replaced by very weak tools and mechanisms and funds that were endowed with limited financial resources at the level of economic integration.

The sovereign debt crisis challenged the three pillars of the Economic and Monetary Union. The three prohibitions (no exits, no defaults and no bail-outs) were originally incorporated in the Treaty of Maastricht and secondary EU legislation to ensure the credibility of monetary integration. They did not constrain economic development and economic policy in the period of excessive global liquidity, but they did restrain the EMU member states' manoeuvrability during the sovereign debt crisis. With the softening of two of the three prohibitions (no government defaults and no bail-outs), the economic policy tools and crisis management mechanisms in the EMU became more similar but far from identical to those prevailing in countries outside the EMU.

As far as the *first pillar* is concerned, the Treaty on the European Union (the first part of the Treaty of Lisbon) allows any member state to exit the EMU if it simultaneously leaves the EU. This is independent of the sovereign debt crisis. The exit of a member state, be it a strong or weak one, from the EMU would pose insurmountable legal difficulties and would constitute economic suicide due to the costs, despite the arguments of economists stressing the presumed advantages of such a move. The major guarantees for the EMU are the enormous cost of its dissolution, the fear of the collapse of the EU and the loss of the tremendous amount of political capital invested in it over the past 10–15 years. Therefore, assuming rational behaviour on the part of governments, no member state is likely to make use of the legal possibility of exiting the EU. Despite the great uncertainty and enormous costs, the partial or complete dissolution of the EMU cannot be excluded, but its probability is relatively low under more or less "normal" circumstances. Nevertheless, contingency scenarios for the break-up of the EMU may be justified.

In the EMU, where their debts are issued in a currency over which they do not have full control, member states *cannot rely on devaluation* as a means of managing the crisis and restoring international competitiveness. Therefore, the likelihood of default is rather high. Devaluation could only be an option if member states leave the EMU. Therefore, the means of making adjustments and restoring international competitiveness include the consolidation of the general government through fiscal austerity, structural reforms and *internal devaluation*, in terms of reducing prices and unit labour costs, which are rather painful and may have adverse effects on GDP growth.

The prohibition on *government default* was only partially softened because, regarding economic actors on the one hand, it was limited to the write-off of government debts held by private investors (the weak form of government default) and, on the other, in geographical terms to Greece, establishing a precedent. Because of its limited scope and size (in terms of the exclusion of public debt), its impact on easing debt's drag on Greek economic growth is likely to remain modest.

The *softening of the no bail-out clause* included establishing rescue funds, the ECB's purchases of government bonds in secondary markets and the indirect involvement of the ECB in the purchase of government bonds through the provision of loans to commercial banks against government bond collateral, based on an innovative interpretation of existing basic EU legal rules. The legal basis for the softening of the no bail-out clause is rather uncertain. In addition, the rescue funds and ECB loans assist in the creation of conditions necessary for the member states to make adjustments rather than substituting for policy measures to be taken by the EU and the individual member states.

It is also theoretically possible for the ECB to assume the role of lender of last resort should the necessity arise, although this is not included in its statute and opposition to this remains rather strong, mainly because of the inflationary risks perceived by some member states, particularly Germany. Nevertheless, it seems most likely that in serious crisis situations, the European Central Bank would provide member states with unlimited liquidity.

The softening of the prohibitions on government defaults and bail-outs was a necessary but insufficient precondition for the management of the crisis. It was sufficient to prevent financial and economic disaster (bank crises and sovereign defaults) in the short-term, but it did not properly address the core issues related to the limited compliances of the EMU with respect to the criteria for an optimum currency area.

In addition, it involved undesired negative side-effects. First, the EMU has faced solvency problems rather than liquidity problems, while the rescue funds were designed to ease the liquidity problems of indebted member states. Second, the softening of the non-default assumption and the no bail-out clause had nothing to do with long-term issues, such as the core problems of the Economic and Monetary Union including the restoration of competitiveness in the peripheral member states, the reduction of external imbalances (huge current account surpluses in the core economies and equally large deficits in the periphery) and the stimulation of economic growth. The changes to the pillars of the EMU provided EU institutions, member states and economic actors with the time to implement structural reforms, undertake measures to transition towards a genuine optimum currency area (not discussed in this report) and promote economic growth. However, the increased flexibility created by the softening of the prohibitions on government defaults and bail-outs may mitigate the pressure weighing on national governments and EU institutions to introduce reforms. Given the specific features of the monetary union, including the impossibility of devaluation, crisis management is more difficult, and the requirements for implementing structural reforms and improving competitiveness are more difficult in the EMU than outside it.

Concerning future prospects, the possibility of moving towards an optimum currency area is limited. Such a move would only be feasible with the exclusion of the southern European member states (Greece, Portugal, Spain and Italy) from the EMU, which is neither a realistic assumption nor feasible. In addition, transitioning the EMU towards an optimum currency area would not be sufficient to solve the underlying institutional and governance problems.

The most desirable development in the EMU would be progress *towards a genuine monetary union combined with some forms of a fiscal union* based on the mutualisation of debts with more common responsibilities. A first step in this direction could be a banking union. This scenario would be most appropriate for overcoming the institutional weaknesses of the present Economic and Monetary Union. The probability of this development is rather low because of the diverging interests of the member states. Germany has opposed proposals aimed at a shift towards fiscal union because of fears of free riding and moral hazard. The probability of a painful *scenario based on internal devaluation* is also low. Considering the political constraints, the most probable scenario is that as a result of the softening of the no bail-out clause, *government debts will be inflated* with the help of the ECB's indirect quantitative (hopefully with strict conditionality) easing in the long run (there is no imminent inflationary danger in the EMU), particularly if no solutions are found to the structural weaknesses of the EMU.

References

Arnab, D. and Roubini, N. 2012. "A blueprint for an amicable divorce settlement." *Financial Times*, April 3: 9.

Benczes, I. 2011. "Az európai kormányzás előtt álló kihívások. A hármas tagadás lehetetlensége" [Challenges facing European governance. The impossibility of the three negations]. *Közgazdasági Szemle* [Economic Review] 57, 9: 759–774.

Bloomberg Business Week. 2011. "A Powell Doctrine for Europe on Debt." October 24–October 30: 10.

Buiter, W. 2012. "Race to save euro will follow 'Grexit'." *Financial Times*, June 21.

Darvas, Zs. and Pisani-Ferry, J. and Sapir, A. 2011. "A comprehensive approach to the euro-area debt crisis." *Bruegel Policy Brief*, January.

De Grauwe, P. 2003. *Economics of Monetary Union*, 5th edition. Oxford University Press.

—. 2010. "A Mechanism of Self-destruction of the Eurozone." *Intereconomics*, 45, 6: 343–346.

Editorial. 2012. "Euro fireproofs itself on cheap." *Financial Times*, March 30: 10.

EEAG. 2012. "The European balance of payments Problem." *The EEAG Report on the European Economy*, Munich: CESifo. 57–81.

EuroMemorandum Group. 2010. *Europe in Crisis: A Critique of the EU's Failure to Respond and Alternative Proposals in Times of Crisis.* http://www.lwbooks.co.uk/ebooks /EUROMEMORANDUM%202009-2010.pdf

European Council. 2011. "Decision of 25 March 2011 amending Article 136 of the Treaty on the functioning of the European Union with regard to a stability mechanism for Member States whose currency is the euro (2011/199/EU)."

Feldstein, M. 2012. "The failure of the euro. The Little Currency that Couldn't." *Foreign Affairs* 91, 1, January/February 2012: 105–106.

Gianviti, F. and Krueger, A.O. and Pisani-Ferry, J. and Sapir, A. and Hagen, J. 2010: "A European mechanism for sovereign debt crisis resolution: a proposal." *Bruegel Blueprint* 10, Brussels.

Jenkins, P. 2012. "Banks must beware the side-effects of ECB magic medicine." *Financial Times*, March 6: 14.

Kramer, M. 2012. "Beware the consequences of an accidental exit by Greece." *Financial Times*, June 13: 26.

Mallaby, S. 2012. "Europe's Optional Catastrophe. The Future of Monetary Union Lies in Germany's hands." *Foreign Affairs 91*, 4.

Milne, R. and Watkins, M. 2012. "The leaning tower of perils." *Financial Times*, March 28: 7.

Mundell, R. 1961. "A theory of optimum currency areas." *American Economic Review* 51, 4: 657–665.

Münchau, W. 2012a. "Greece needs another year to prepare for a total debt default." *Financial Times*, February 27: 9.

—. 2012b. "The Bundesbank has no fight at all to be baffled." *Financial Times*, March 5: 9.

—. 2012c. "Europe's bailout bazooka is proving a toy gun." *Financial Times*, March 26: 13.

—. 2012d. "The Wolfson prize for European Political illiteracy." *Financial Times*, April 9: 7

—. 2012e. "What happens if Angela Merkel does get her way." *Financial Times*, June 18: 9.

Nordvig, J. 2012. "Planning for the worst is the best way to save the eurozone." *Financial Times*, January 13: 9.

Rachman, G. 2012. "The euro is a time bomb that no one can defuse." *Financial Times*, April 3: 9.

Rompuy, H.V. 2012. "Towards a Genuine Economic and Monetary Union." European Council. The President. 26 June, Brussels: EUCO 120/12 Presse 296, PR PCE 102.

Sinn, H-W. 2010. "Rescuing Europe." CESifo Forum, Special Issue, Volume 2010, August: 5.

The Economist. 2008. "Redesigning global finance." November 15: 13.

—. 2011. "After the fall. The costs of break-up." September 17.

—. 2012a. "The silent bazooka." February 4: 64.

—. 2012b. "A firewall full of holes." March 3: 65

—. 2012c. "Currency disunion. Why Europe's leaders should think the unthinkable." April 7: 33.

—. 2012d. "Bankers of the euro-area, unite!" June 30: 72.

Tomaso Padoa-Schioppa Group. 2012. "Completing the Euro. A road map towards fiscal union in Europe." Paris: Notre Europe, June: 68.

Vallée, L. 2012. "How Europe Will disintegrate." *The Sceptical Market Observer*, June 6, http://scepticalmarketobserver.blogspot.hu/2012/06/how-europe-will-disintegrate.html

Wolf, M. 2011. "Managing the Eurozone's fragility." *Financial Times*, May 4: 9.

CHAPTER THREE

COPING WITH THE CRISIS IN THE EUROPEAN COHESION COUNTRIES

THE CRISIS AS A TURNING POINT IN THE EUROPEAN CONVERGENCE MODEL

BEÁTA FARKAS

1. Introduction

The impact of the economic crisis was dramatic in certain European Union member states; as early as 2008, Hungary and Latvia received combined rescue packages from the International Monetary Fund (IMF), the World Bank and the European Union. Romania turned to the IMF in 2009 and again in 2011. In 2010, Greece, as a member of the euro-area, received loans from the EU and the IMF. In the same year, a financial aid package was approved for Ireland, followed by one for Portugal in 2011. Spain requested financial assistance for the recapitalisation of its financial institutions in 2012.

This trend begs the question of whether it was really an accident that the most vulnerable countries were all old and new, so-called cohesion countries of the EU that received support from the Cohesion Fund.[1] In the media, as well as among experts, discussing the EU member states in terms of core and peripheral countries rapidly became commonplace and generally accepted. Should the crisis end one day, will this period have consequences, and will the countries return to the promising track they followed during their 5–25 year EU memberships? These questions are fundamentally important because one of the fundamental goals of European integration is to provide an opportunity to less-developed member states for convergence and to strengthen economic and social cohesion. The significance of convergence is also expressed in a European cohesion policy. The grave problems of old cohesion countries represent a particularly unexpected shock to integration, as their adaptation is usually considered a closed and completed process. Accordingly, all EU analyses

[1] The old cohesion countries are Ireland, Greece, Portugal and Spain, the new ones are Bulgaria, Cyprus, the Czech Republic, Estonia, Hungary, Latvia, Lithuania, Malta, Poland, Romania, Slovakia and Slovenia.

and studies examine old cohesion countries as a part of the EU-15, i.e., the old member states, and only separately consider the new member states.

In the fourth year of the crisis, it seems increasingly obvious that the cohesion countries cannot follow the same development trajectory as they did prior to the crisis. Our study will review how the crisis has affected the convergence results and how future perspectives can be appraised based on the evolution of the crisis to date. An investigation of the European convergence model reveals that it has vulnerabilities and limits that have not been revealed in the analyses of EU or World Bank experts. After studying these interpretations of convergence, we outline some necessary changes to the concept of European integration.

2. Threatened results of convergence

The convergence in terms of GDP per capita at purchasing power parity was impressive before the crisis. In 1995, the contraction resulting from the economic transition came to an end in the post-socialist countries. Choosing this year as a basis for comparison, all of the cohesion countries were catching up with the EU-27 average, although to different degrees. Ireland, the poorest Baltic states, Slovakia and Poland made the greatest progress (Figure 7-1).[2]

GDP per capita does not express the growth in a population's welfare that is central to the meaning of convergence. Another indicator, actual individual final consumption (including expenditures on the consumption of goods and services by households and non-profit institutions serving households and in-kind social transfers) is more appropriate for this purpose. The general picture is similar, but the positioning of the countries is different; in the case of Ireland, the difference between the two indicators is striking (Figure 7-2).

Summarising figures 7-1 and 7-2, we highlight that the crisis has injured the cohesion countries' convergence towards the EU-27 average (with the exception of Poland and Slovakia); however, these countries were able to preserve the bulk of their convergence results to date (Table 7-1). In most cases, the loss in the final consumption values is greater than in GDP per capita. This means that in the countries that were severely hit by the crisis, there were changes in consumption in response to the recession and austerity measures.

---

[2] To present the data in a clear and comprehensible manner, we omit the statistical data on the new member states Cyprus and Malta, as they are island states that do not share the common past and history of the Eastern and Central European region.

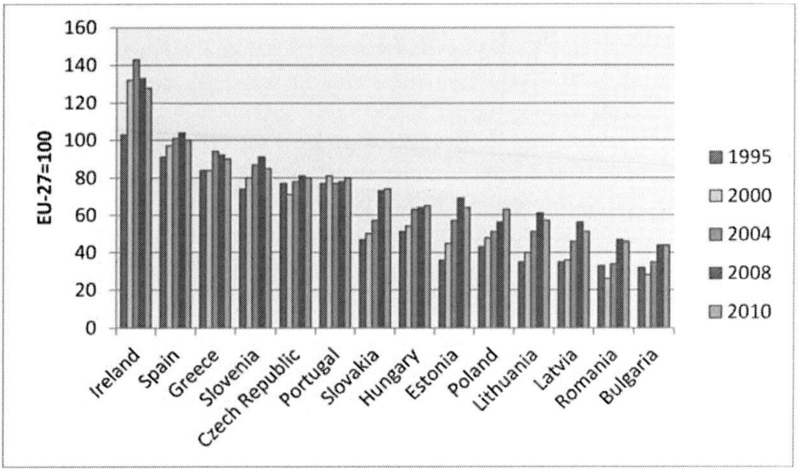

Fig. 7-1 The development of per capita GDP at purchasing power parity in the old and new cohesion countries compared to the EU-27 average
Source: Eurostat

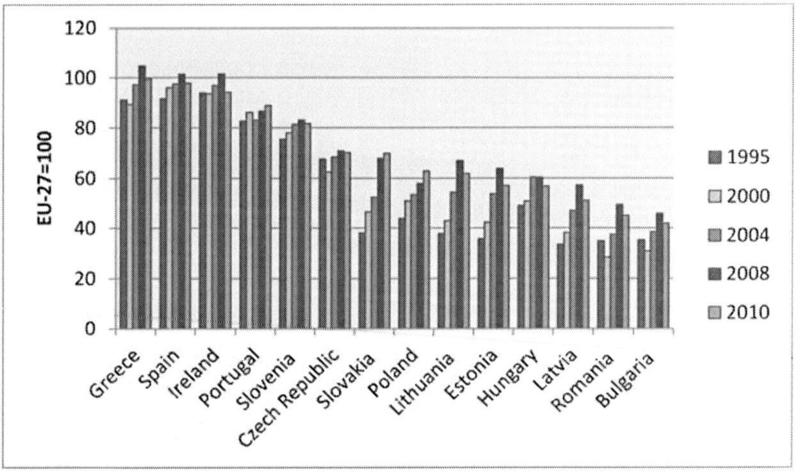

Fig. 7-2 The development of per capita actual individual final consumption at purchasing power parity in the old and new cohesion countries compared to the EU-27 average
Source: Author's calculation based on AMECO database

Table 7-1 Catching-up in the actual individual final consumption of households and in GDP per capita with the EU-27 average compared to 1995 levels in percentage points

	Actual individual final consumption		GDP per capita	
	2008	2010	2008	2010
Slovakia	30	32	26	27
Lithuania	29	24	26	22
Estonia	28	21	33	28
Poland	14	19	13	20
Latvia	24	18	21	16
Romania	14	10	14	13
Greece	14	8	8	6
Hungary	11	8	13	14
Bulgaria	11	7	12	12
Spain	10	6	13	9
Portugal	4	6	1	3
Slovenia	8	6	17	11
Czech Republic	3	3	4	3
Ireland	8	0	30	25

Source: Author's calculation based on Eurostat and AMECO database

The economic and financial crises in the cohesion countries have been thoroughly analysed (e.g., Becker et al. 2010, European Commission 2009c, European Commission 2010b, Gardó and Martin 2010, Gligorov et al. 2012). These studies came to similar conclusions with respect to the "anatomy" of the crisis. Here, we do not provide a reconstruction of the crisis; rather, we focus only on the processes that severely affected the European convergence model.

The crisis highlighted that the European Union has a unique growth model that makes it possible for relatively low-income countries to catch up rapidly with their richer neighbours. This model is based on foreign capital inflows. Europe is the only region where the different forms of private capital – both foreign direct investment (FDI) and portfolio funds –

flow downhill from richer to poorer countries and from low-growth to high-growth countries (Becker et al. 2010, Gill and Raiser 2012).

At its outset, the crisis affected the Central and Eastern European countries (CEEC) and Mediterranean countries differently. In 2009, the rate of decline exceeded the EU average – with the exception of Poland – in every new member state, with the Baltic states suffering extremely large losses. In contrast, of the old cohesion countries, only Ireland experienced an immediate, strong recession; the others faced smaller scale, but prolonged, downturns. However, it has subsequently become increasingly clear that there is a common element in their situations: the previously advantageous growth model made them particularly vulnerable during the crisis when capital inflows fell. Despite the differences between the countries, the foreign capital-based convergence combined with low saving rates is a distinctive feature of catching-up in both the old and new cohesion countries.

Scrutinising these countries, the severity of the recession unambiguously depended on the degree of pre-crisis economic imbalances. This is not surprising, but it seems to determine their development paths at least in the medium-term. The differences among the countries are instructive from the perspective of the convergence model.

Three Central European countries, the Czech Republic, Poland and Slovakia, did not accumulate notable disequilibria prior to the crisis. In the CEEC (including Hungary and Slovenia), growth was accompanied by small and improving trade imbalances, as a reflection of reindustrialisation after the economic transition that followed the fall of the socialist system. These five countries had little or no problems with respect to their competitiveness in their tradable sectors. Despite the favourable conditions in manufacturing, in Hungary, the initial levels of both private and public debt were high at the beginning of the crisis; the Slovenian economy was overheated (characterised by full capacity utilisation and inflation pressure) when the crisis broke out, and the private sector (mainly corporate) debt position increased (Farkas 2012, Tajnikar et al. 2011). Of the old cohesion countries, Ireland also coped with debt- rather than competitiveness-related problems.

In the Mediterranean cohesion countries, the three Baltic states, Bulgaria, and Romania, growth in the period preceding the crisis was driven by domestic demand, whereas the contribution of net exports to growth was negative (European Commission 2009b, 2009c). In this second group, the current account balance deteriorated sharply, and these countries were on an unsustainable development path, even before the crisis. The underlying issue is that these economies suffer from competitiveness issues in their tradable sectors, although Spain shows better results. The percentage of medium- and high-technology product exports as a percentage of total product exports demonstrates these differences (Figure 7-3).

The division between Central European countries, Ireland and the others concerning competitive tradable sectors may be surprising because the forms of capital inflows differ between the old and new cohesion countries. In the new cohesion countries, the main form of foreign capital was FDI, while the old Mediterranean cohesion countries attracted portfolio and other capital inflows (Figure 7-4). However, the Central European countries were the primary beneficiaries of rapid technology transfer, where the FDI flowed into manufacturing, which is a tradable sector. (Slovenia is a special case where FDI stock remained low.) In the Baltic states, Bulgaria and Romania, the FDI was biased in favour of banking, real estate and other non-tradable sectors. Unfortunately, the FDI thereby fuelled an unsustainable boom and contributed to the development of housing bubbles (Becker et al. 2010, European Commission 2010a).

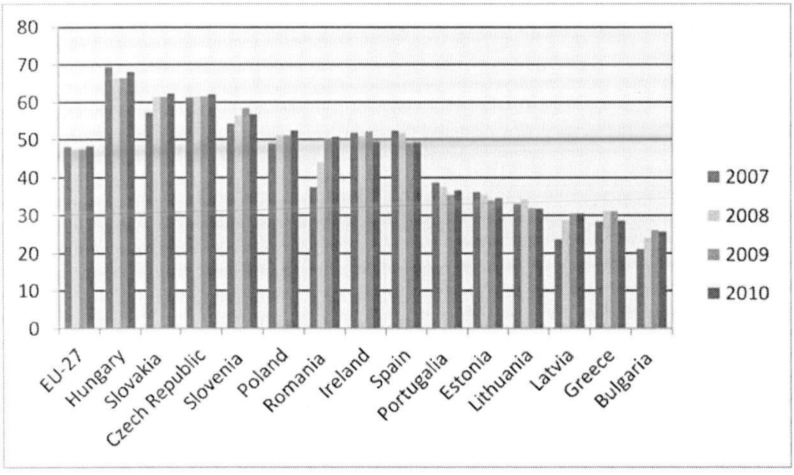

Fig. 7-3 Medium- and high-technology product exports as a percentage of total product exports in the cohesion countries, 2007–2010
Source: Author's compilation from European Commission (2011a, 2012) and UNU-MERIT (2009, 2010) data

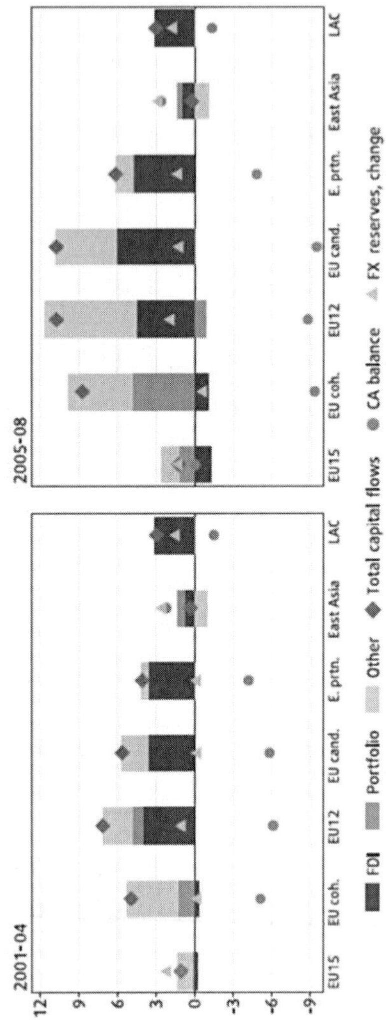

Fig. 7-4 Capital flows in emerging countries, 2001–2004; 2005–2008
Source: Gill and Raiser (2012, 134)
Note: "EU coh." refers to the EU old cohesion countries, "EU cand." refers to EU candidate countries, "E. prtn." refers to EU eastern partnership countries and "LAC" refers to the Latin America and the Caribbean region. CA stands for current account and FX is foreign exchange.

The different compositions of foreign capital can also be observed in the banking sector. In the new cohesion countries, banking instruments were 60–90% foreign-owned, whereas the same ratio for the EU-15 was between 10–50% (European Central Bank 2010). Despite this difference, due to financial integration, external vulnerability reached critical levels in both groups. In the Mediterranean countries, net foreign liabilities were approximately 80–100% of GDP at the start of the crisis (European Commission 2010b). The average for the new member states was over 60%, and in the case of Bulgaria and Hungary, exceeded 100% (Jevčák et al. 2010). Of the old cohesion countries, Ireland and Spain were engaged in disciplined fiscal policy before the crisis, but real estate bubbles developed in both countries, and the bursting of these bubbles led to a crisis in the banking system that was transformed into a public debt crisis. This was particularly tragic for Ireland because, relative to its GDP, its banking sector was the largest in Europe (Kinsella 2011, Kovács and Halmosi 2012, OECD 2009, Udvari 2012).

In Greece and Portugal, in addition to external disequilibrium, the fiscal policies followed by these countries also exhibited certain disciplinary problems after the introduction of the euro. Twin deficits developed, and Portugal stepped off the convergence path at the beginning of the 2000s. All three Mediterranean countries were characterised by stagnating productivity starting in the beginning of the 2000s. Greece, in particular, was characterised by a distinct drop in productivity (Mitsopoulos and Pelagidis 2011, Royo 2010).

Apart from Hungary, in the new cohesion countries, public debt remained under the 60% rate stipulated by the Maastricht Treaty, but with the exception of Estonia and Bulgaria, public debt rates began to increase significantly during the crisis.

In the non-euro-zone countries, the exchange-rate regimes had a clear influence on the composition of capital inflows and the accumulation of a vulnerable external debt position. The Central European countries where the FDI went to the manufacturing sector, opted for more or less flexible exchange rates (Slovakia until mid-2008). Slovenia, with its peg or crawling peg system connected to the euro, was also an exception in this field. In fixed exchange-rate regimes (in the Baltic states and Bulgaria), it was the use of capital in the form of foreign loans rather than FDI that was preferable, especially in the banking and real-estate sectors. Taking domestic inflation into account, fixed currencies meant significant negative real interest rates for domestic borrowers. Credit supplying foreign banks did not need to rely on local markets for raising funds, and nominal interest rates were attractive. The fixed exchange-rate policy was not changed during the crisis, and these countries could adjust their imbalances via internal devaluation, that is, domestic price and wage cuts (Becker et al. 2010).

Although the growth rates in the majority of the new cohesion countries were again higher than the EU-15 or EU-27 average after the first wave of the crisis, these rates are high enough to ensure the mathematical convergence, but not sufficient enough to provide convergences that are perceptible for households in these countries, with the exemption of Poland and Slovakia (Table 7-2). (In the Baltic states and Romania, the higher rates compensate for the large GDP loss in 2009.) There is a danger that this situation is not temporary but the beginning of a medium-term or even longer trend.

Table 7-2 Real GDP growth rates in the cohesion countries, 2011–2013

	2011	2012*	2013*
EU-27	1.5	0	1.3
EU-15	1.4	-0.2	1.2
Bulgaria	1.7	0.5	1.9
Czech Republic	1.7	0	1.5
Estonia	7.6	1.6	3.8
Ireland	0.7	0.5	1.9
Greece	-6.9	-4.7	0
Spain	0.7	-1.8	-0.3
Latvia	5.5	2.2	3.6
Lithuania	5.9	2.4	3.5
Hungary	1.6	-0.3	1
Poland	4.3	2.7	2.6
Portugal	-1.6	-3.3	0.3
Romania	2.5	1.4	2.9
Slovenia	-0.2	-1.4	0.7
Slovakia	3.3	1.8	2.9

Source: Eurostat
Note: * = forecast.

The external conditions have been changing unfavourably for a longer time. The contracted markets of the economies in the European Union do not promote export-led growth in the cohesion countries, and the management of European debt crisis and stricter financial regulation decrease the capital available to the cohesion countries. FDI and cross-border production networks cannot play as dynamic a role in the convergence as they did before the crisis. Financial markets' risk evaluations may remain higher, even for those cohesion countries that are not affected by more severe financial difficulties. Due to the indebtedness of households and governments in the majority of the cohesion countries, the diminishing external resources and markets cannot substitute for domestic ones.

Demographic processes are another factor that seemed to endanger convergence even before the crisis. By the mandate of the ECFIN Council, a group of experts investigates the age-related expenditures in the EU member states to 2060 regularly. This "Ageing Report 2009" had already indicated in 2009 that more rapid population declines in the new member states will slow the convergence process (European Commission 2009a). In the "Ageing Report 2012", the population loss combined with the effect of the crisis resulted in diminishing productivity presented even gloomier prospects for the majority of the cohesion countries (European Commission 2011b). The population census that was conducted in most of the European countries in 2011 and 2012 indicates that the average population decline in the ten new member states almost doubled over the past decade, according to preliminary data. Approximately half of the reduction from 2000 to 2011 is due to net migration and the other half to a natural decrease. A more striking figure is that the population aged 0 to 14 shrank by almost 25% (whereas the corresponding figure for the EU-15 is approximately 1%) (Gligorov et al. 2012).

3. Interpretation of the European convergence

The slowdown of convergence in European integration is a substantial challenge because the achievement of the European Union in this field is one of the main bases for legitimating the existence of integration, and, for the populations of the cohesion countries, it is the most convincing and attractive element of the EU membership. The Treaty on the European Union declares the EU's aims, one of which is that the EU "shall promote economic, social and territorial cohesion, and solidarity among member states" (Art. 3(3) TEU).

The crisis has highlighted the vulnerability of the European convergence model with respect to its dependence on foreign capital. However, if we study the assessments of European convergence carefully, we find other problems that are not explicitly revealed. We select two very thorough and influential analyses to show how these issues can affect the future of integration. One of the analyses is the report on the "Five years of an enlarged EU" that resulted from the collaboration of several Commission services of the EU and it only investigates the new member states (European Commission 2009b). The other work is a book by the World Bank's experts on "Golden Growth. Restoring the Lustre of the European Economic Model" (Gill and Raiser 2012), which scrutinises the entire European Union. It is remarkable that both follow the same logic in assessing the European convergence model. Gill and Raiser (2012) contrast the economic achievements of the new and old cohesion countries; they interpret the convergence of the former group of countries as a success story and the old Mediterranean cohesion countries' performances by and large as a failure.

In both analyses, the main arguments of the advantages of the European convergence model are the growth performances of the lagging countries and their capital-intensive export structures. They regard trade openness, FDI inflows and institutional improvements resulting from EU accession as the key drivers of growth. The EU report estimates that "each year during the period 2000–2008 accession gave the new member states an extra growth boost of approximately 1¾% on average… Model simulations suggest that…the new member states enjoy 50–100 basis points advantage relative to other emerging countries with comparable fundamentals" (European Commission 2009b, 17).

Both analyses agree that foreign capital inflows made it possible to overcome the lack of savings in the cohesion countries. Gill and Raiser (2012) emphasise that Europe is the only region where capital flows in the "right" direction, that is, towards poorer, high-growth countries. The EU report highlights that this catching-up model prompted current account deficits and the appreciation of real exchange rates. It supposes that, as a result of the global crisis, the slowdown of capital inflows will lead to significant contractions in economic activity, and in some of the new member states the income gap with richer EU countries will widen, at least temporarily. Gill and Raiser (2012) also call for prudence when financing is plentiful.

According to both investigations, FDI played a prominent role in the productivity growth in emerging Europe directly (investment) and indirectly (spill-over effects). The EU report provides a detailed overview on the knowledge spill-over effects of FDI in the empirical literature, which has contradictory results but the EU report regards the positive effects as decisive.

FDI is also closely connected with the other advantage of the European convergence model, the increased technological content and quality of the export basket. Both analyses underline, based on statistical data, that new member states' trade is becoming sophisticated and they have become even more specialised in capital-intensive goods.

This picture on the European convergence model would be convincing and unambiguous. However, both documents contain further elements that make their interpretation inconsistent. They also highlight the convergence model from the perspective of the non-cohesion countries. The EU report refutes the danger of the relocation of production and jobs. This occurs rather in the case of the efficiency-seeking manufacturing sector, but 70% of outward direct investment from the old to the new member states is in the services sector and of a market-seeking type, thus limiting the job losses. In some sectors where changes in competitive position lead to relocation, it helps to maintain competitiveness for corporations that maintain their more skilled-based units of production, technology development and ownership in mature economies (that is in the non-cohesion countries). Labour-intensive elements of production and routine tasks are located in the new member states.

Gill and Raiser (2012) also explain the success of convergence through reconfiguration of the value chain in Continental and Northern European based companies after the collapse of communism. They located their assembly activities in Central and Eastern Europe, and due to lower wages they could strengthen their competitiveness through their flexibility in offshoring. Central and Eastern Europe could integrate not only within the EU but also within the world economy through increased productivity. According to the authors, the reason for the difficult situation in Southern Europe is that these countries did not participate in these processes and they have few global companies. The EU can be described as a three-speed union with the Continental and Northern leaders, the Central and Eastern chasers and Southern laggards.

Gill and Raiser (2012) address innovation in a separate chapter. They define innovation as a source of long-term growth differentials. They note that "Europe's east is catching up in productivity, but remains far behind in innovation. For these countries, sustaining productivity growth is what matters, but the innovation gap so far has not been a binding constraint" (Gill and Raiser 2012, 256). Therefore, their policy recommendation is that countries in Central and Eastern Europe need not invest much more in

R&D and knowledge production. They should adopt existing technologies via FDI and trade links.

Neither assessment raises the questions that resulted from their analyses. Both accept convergence as a fundamental goal, but they do not address the issue of whether this model is appropriate to reach this goal or it has limits.

The above-mentioned expert group of "Ageing Report 2012" has already confronted the catching-up problem. They had to decide whether they assume convergence in either GDP level or GDP growth rate over the long-term projection exercise. Some exercises were run in the expert group that showed some convergence in GDP levels in past periods, but the growth rate needed to allow for this convergence in the projections (to 2060!) would not be plausible in the short- and medium-term. Thus, the expert group decided to assume that there would be convergence in growth rates in the long run (European Commission 2011b).

The limits of convergence can be derived not only from econometric projections but also from the EU report (European Commission 2009b) and Gill and Raiser (2012). Their analyses outline a division of labour and production between the north-western countries and the new member states. Although there are possibilities of upgrading along the value chain, there is no reason to assume that foreign companies will abandon their key positions in innovation, technology development and strategic decision-making. It seems to be much more likely that the current labour and production division will essentially be reproduced. Another possibility could be that spill-over effects help the domestic companies to foster internationally competitive economies that are able to accelerate and to complete the catching-up process. The literature on FDI spill-overs shows unambiguous positive productivity effects in the case of vertical, backward linkages. Domestic firms occupy the dependent position in these relationships. The horizontal spill-over effects seem to be weak in the overwhelming majority of empirical investigations (Gorodnichenko et al. 2007, Hanousek et al. 2010).[3] The third means of economic development would be to strengthen domestic capital accumulation. As we have seen, the cohesion countries have high levels of FDI inflows coupled with low savings rates. Therefore, domestic investment was not a decisive factor in this model, in contrast to some Asian countries.

Due to the low initial GDP levels in the cohesion countries, the above-outlined contradictions and the limits of the European convergence model could be disregarded; it provided sufficient space for the cohesion

---

[3] Both studies provide a comprehensive overview of the literature concerning spill-over effects in emerging Europe.

countries to develop. However, it is remarkable that the Czech Republic, which had one of the highest initial GDP levels in Central and Eastern Europe and is one of the "best pupils" in following the European convergence model, has made very moderate progress in catching-up (Table 7-1). Slovenia, with its higher initial GDP level, has achieved greater convergence but has always chosen different means, focusing on domestic economy and had already accumulated imbalances prior to the crisis.

In sum, it is questionable whether the European convergence model is appropriate for the long run catching-up of those countries that are already close to the efficiency/technical frontier. If the crisis had not occurred, the poorer countries could have further developed within the framework of the European convergence model, even if the development would have been concentrated in the areas that had attracted foreign capital (typically the capitals and their agglomerations) accompanied by increasing regional inequalities.

4. Conclusions

Assuming that the foreign capital inflows would return to the cohesion countries to their status prior to the crisis, the European convergence model could be restored despite its limits. The actors would be aware of the larger vulnerability of cohesion countries' economies, and European economic governance, e.g. in the form of the excessive imbalances procedure could help to avoid similar difficulties.

However, the only certainty in the current crisis is that things will not get back on track. The above-mentioned EU report (European Commission 2009b) did not address this problem at the beginning of the crisis; it simply referred to growth slowdowns and the new member states having a long way to go to full convergence. Gill and Raiser (2012) raise a question regarding the future of the European convergence model. They are very optimistic: "Restarting the convergence machine will not be difficult" (Gill and Raiser 2012, 10). The task is very simple; a single market for services should be completed. Although market liberalisation in services would be advantageous for the cohesion countries, it is difficult to imagine that it could compensate for the diminishing external and internal sources that we have already outlined.

In their common studies, experts at Bruegel, a European think tank, and the Vienna Institute for International Economic Studies, an independent research institute, made more sophisticated policy suggestions to reorient the European convergence model. Their starting point is that the reduction in the private sector savings-investment gap is unavoidable. In the medium-term this leads to the problem of dampened domestic demand. A sustained re-launch of growth requires a more efficient use of savings than in the past. They list a range of policies (human capital, technology, industrial and regional) that should be employed to improve the competitiveness of tradable sectors (Becker et al. 2010).

We can draw two conclusions independently from the ultimate outcome of the global crisis:

- Even if the economic actors in a country, including the government, adjust their behaviour and economic policies successfully, we cannot assume a return to the speed of convergence prior to the crisis.
- The reorientation of the growth model requires very professional government activities to promote the competitiveness of the tradable sector. It is difficult to believe that all of the governments in the cohesion countries will be able to exhibit high levels of administrative performance.

These consequences of the global crisis make some changes in the concept of integration necessary. As we have seen, the degree and speed of convergence between countries has played a central role in assessments regarding the effectiveness and legitimacy of European integration in recent decades. If the necessary adjustments to the post-crisis reality are not carried out at the conceptual level of European integration, the legitimacy of integration will be jeopardised. The Union's raison d'être in the next decade will be tied to the fact that without integration, European countries would not be considered global economic players. If, however, the speed of convergence remains a measure of the success of integration, the EU will doom itself.

One of the most important lessons from the last two decades is that the positive FDI spill-over effects are limited in market transactions. If foreign capital becomes scarcer, it will be even more important to promote the positive spill-over effects through economic policy. Even if there are numerous studies on the channels of spill-over effects and other measures of local economic development, the problems of a dual economy and the development of an internationally competitive domestic economy are missing from EU policies (e.g., cohesion, innovation). Failing to bridge the productivity gap between foreign and domestic companies makes catching-up impossible. However, the policy measures to develop a competitive domestic economy are essentially in the hands of national governments. The EU's cohesion policy only has a significant impact if the national economic policy creates the appropriate environment. In addition, the success of economic policy depends on not only the government but also on the state of social capital and other social and institutional conditions.

Despite these difficulties, efforts must be taken to maintain cohesion at the level of relevant policies because a certain degree of inequality leads to disintegration. Cohesion policy must remain an important tool to this end, a tool that reinforces a common European identity and a palpable manifestation of solidarity for the populations of cohesion countries that are already experiencing difficult times. Cohesion assistance should not be expected to be able to do anything more than dampen the effects of the unfavourable tendencies described above; it would be unrealistic to expect such assistance to bring about a reversal of these effects.

The content of cohesion policy should be revised. At present, it focuses on the support of SMEs, although the real problem in the cohesion countries is the productivity gap between foreign and domestic companies that cannot be addressed with the division of companies into large firms and SMEs.[4]

Considering all of these aspects, we cannot count on an economically and socially homogeneous area in the foreseeable future as the current integration concept does. To maintain a multi-speed integration will be the most important challenge for European integration.

Acknowledgement

The study was created within the framework of project No. TÁMOP-4.2.1/B-09/1/KONV-2010-0005 "Establishment of a Research University Centre of Excellence at the University of Szeged" supported by the European Union and co-financed by the European Social Fund.

---

[4] Gill and Raiser (2012) demonstrate how damaging it is for the Mediterranean economies that the business environment discourages their SMEs to grow. Mihályi's study in this volume analyses the reasons why the Hungarian micro- and small enterprises are not able and/or are uninterested in becoming middle-size or large firms, which is one of the most important reasons for the deteriorating Hungarian economic performance over the last decade.

References

Becker, T. and Daianu, D. and Darvas, Zs. and Gligorov, V. and Landesmann, M. and Petrovic, P. and Pisani-Ferry, J. and Rosati, D. and Sapir, A. and Weder Di Mauro, B. 2010. "Whither growth in central and eastern Europe? Policy lessons for an integrated Europe." *Bruegel Blueprint Series* 11. Brussels: Bruegel.

European Central Bank. 2010. "EU Banking Structures". Frankfurt am Main: European Central Bank.

European Commission. 2009a. "Ageing Report: Economic and budgetary. projections for the EU-27 Member States (2008-2060)." *European Economy* 2009, 2.

—. 2009b. "Five years of enlarged Europe." *European Economy* 2009, 1.

—. 2009c. "Economic Crisis in Europe." *European Economy* 2009, 7.

—. 2010a. "Cross-country study. Economic policy challenges in the Baltics." *European Economy. Occasional Papers* 58.

—. 2010b. "Surveillance of Intra-Euro-Area Competitiveness and Imbalances." *European Economy* 2010, 1.

—. 2011a. "Innovation Union Scoreboard 2010." Research and Innovation Union scoreboard.

—. 2011b. "The 2012 Ageing Report: Underlying Assumptions and Projection Methodologies." *European Economy* 2011, 4.

—. 2012. "Innovation Union Scoreboard 2012." The Innovation Union's performance scoreboard.

Gardó, S. and Martin, R. 2010. "The Impact of the Global Economic and Financial Crisis on Central, Eastern and South Eastern Europe. A Stock-taking Excercise." *European Central Bank, Occasional Paper Series* 114.

Farkas, B. 2012. "The Impact of the Global Economic Crisis in the Old and New Cohesion Member States of the European Union." *Public Finance Quarterly* 57, 1: 53–70.

Gligorov, V. and Holzner, M. and Landesmann, M. and Leitner, S. and Pindyuk, O. and Vidovic, H. et al. 2012. *New Divide(s) in Europe?* Wein: Wiener Institute für Internationale Wirtschaftsvergleiche.

Gill, I. and Raiser, M. 2012. *Golden Growth. Restoring the Lustre of the European Economic Model*. Washington: The World Bank.

Gorodnichenko, Y. and Svejnar, J. and Terrell, K. 2007. "When Does FDI Have Positive Spillovers? Evidence from 17 Emerging Market Economies." Institute for the Study of Labor (IZA), Bonn, IZA DP no. 3079, September.

Hanousek, J. and Kočenda, E. and Maurek, M. 2010. "Direct and Indirect Effects of FDI in Emerging European Markets: A Survey and Meta-analysis." The William Davidson Institute, University of Michigan, WP no. 976, March.

Jevčák, A. and Setzer, R. and Suardi, M. 2010. "Determinants of Capital Flows to the New EU Member States Before and During the Financial Crisis." *European Economy. Economic Papers* 425.

Kinsella, S. 2011. "Is Ireland really the role model for austerity?" University College Dublin, Geary WP2011/22.

Kovács, Á. and Halmosi, P. 2012. "Similarities and Differences in European Crisis Management." *Public Finance Quarterly,* 57, 1: 9–27.

Mitsopoulos, M. and Pelagidis, T. 2011. *Understanding the Crisis in Greece. From Boom to Bust.* Hampshire-New York: Palgrave Macmillan.

OECD. 2009. *OECD Economic Surveys: Ireland*. Paris: OECD.

Royo, S. 2010. "Portugal and Spain in the EU: paths of economic divergence (2000–2007)." *Análise Social* 45: 209–254.

UNU-MERIT (United Nations University – Maastricht Economic and Social Research and Training Centre on Innovation and Technology). 2009. *European Innovation Scoreboard 2008.* http://www.proinno-europe.eu/page/european-innovation-scoreboard-2008

—. 2010. *European Innovation Scoreboard 2009.* http://www.proinno-europe.eu/page /european-innovation-scoreboard-2009

Tajnikar, M. and Došenovič Bonča, P. and Ponikvar, N. and Pušnik, K. 2011. *Economic Crisis Exit by a Small EU Country. Challenges of Europe: Growth and Competitiveness – Reversing the Trends.* University of Split, Split-Bol, 26–28th May, Conference Proceedings.

Udvari, B. 2012. "A kelta tigris bukása: okok és következmények" [Fall of the Celtic Tiger – reasons and consequences]. In *Válság és* válságkezelés *az Európai Unió kohéziós országaiban* [Crisis and crisis management in the EU Cohesion Countries] edited by Farkas, B. and Voszka, É. and Mező, J., 9–24. Szeged: University of Szeged, Faculty of Economics and Business Administration, Discussion Papers MT-PNGKI – 2012/1.

Crisis Management Similarities and Differences in the Newly Accessed Central and Eastern European Countries

Árpád Kovács

1. Introduction

One of the cornerstones of the analysis of the economic crisis that began in 2008 is the analysis and evaluation of the different crisis management methods employed by the Central and Eastern European countries. Several researchers have been addressing the problems of the crisis.[1] However, most of these analyses are focusing on the antecedents and symptoms of the crisis, on the ways out via individual economic policies.[2] Focusing on *budgets and public finances*, the present monograph examines the similarities and differences of the crisis management practices employed by those Central and Eastern European countries that accessed the European Union between 2004 and 2007 and that were formerly "socialist" with a so-called planned economy (the EU-10) in comparison to each other and to the European "core-countries." We are

---

[1] This monograph is focusing on these countries because the historical and economic positions of the two Mediterranean countries that accessed the EU at the same time belong to different geopolitical groups – according to the categorisation used in the EU – when compared to Bulgaria, the Czech Republic, Estonia, Hungary, Latvia, Lithuania, Poland, Slovakia and Slovenia that, after World War II, belonged to the same political and economic block and shared a similar fate; despite a number of similarities, Slovenia can be put into the category of the "socialist block", with certain distinctions regarding its development course and inherited traditions.

[2] Lehman Brothers Holdings Inc. announced the greatest bankruptcy of economic history on September 15, 2008. Usually, this date is considered as the eruption of the crisis of the financial mediator systems.

presenting the *fiscal policy* steps that governments took by sorting them into so-called "action matrices."[3]

The "matrices" that sum up the characteristics of measures introduced at the eruption of the 2008 crisis and in 2010 and 2011 make the life cycles of the various measures traceable, whereas the analysis of the "condensation" of identities and differences helps to identify the characteristics of the different socio-economic traditions, public finance policies and governance models.

Our attempt is not merely to present the trends of the identities and differences of the crisis management by using the methods referred to in the literature review and sorted according to EU categorisations; we also attempt to analyse to what extent the crisis management of the Central and Eastern European countries that accessed the EU later,

- had a solid, theoretical grounding;
- proved to be pro-active and preventive;
- assisted in the re-structuring of social and economic services and the efficient operation of the large entitlement systems; and
- provided a solid, harmonised regulatory and governance framework.

In our conclusions, we are seeking to answer how, to what extent, and how separately, the crisis management by the Central and Eastern European countries has contributed to the stability of public finances, and whether the chosen solutions will be able to offer a sustainable, new development perspective by vitalising the economy or whether they will merely offer short-term relief. We tried to answer the question whether the crisis-related problems, by causing serious instability in certain countries, will deepen to the extent that they might endanger the sustainability of the European integration.

2. The trend in public debt in the EU countries and in the EU-10

The literature review on the topic shows that researchers agree that the financial crisis and the contraction of the economic performance have created a difficult situation regarding the sustainability of fiscal policies in every country of the European Union. Additionally, to a different extent in the different countries, new problems have emerged that can be traced

[3] We are only summarising literature from the second half of 2011, ignoring the tabular, comparative summary of the measures taken (European Institute 2011).

back to the persistent imbalance of performance and consumption, the issues that have not been addressed for a long time, and structural deficiencies. With the crisis, these issues have become more exposed, and they show the constraints of public financing.[4]

The performance of the economy and the extent of public financing, namely its functioning and *the efficiency of the allocation of coherent expenditures and their structure will, always and in every country, mutually determine each other*. Figures 8-1/a/b/c and 8-2 show the proportions and trends of the given years.

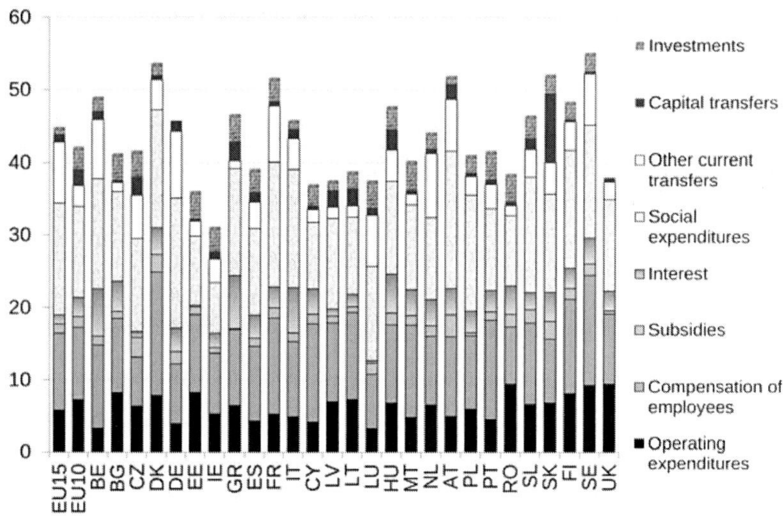

Fig. 8-1/a The amount and internal distribution of public expenditures in 2000 by country and EU-15 and EU-10 average, gross sum, in % of the GDP
Source: Eurostat

[4] Naturally, the articulation of the individual measures required simplifications and contractions that are based on focal points from the literature review. We are also aware that even a classification that considers most factors can only be accidental and that assigning other limits or categorisation would also be possible; it is also possible to believe that certain measures ("packages") are "independent" from the crisis and "merely" reflect the "general" modernisation intention prevailing within public finance.

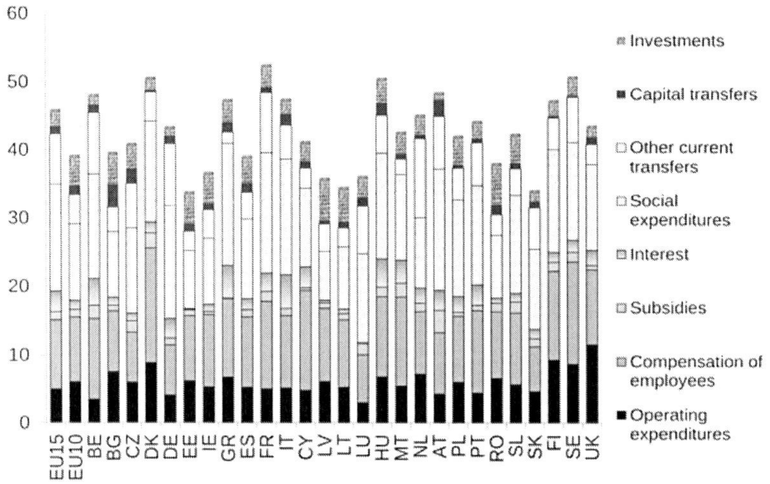

Fig. 8-1/b The amount and internal distribution of public expenditures in 2007 by country and EU-15 and EU-10 average, in % of the GDP
Source: Eurostat

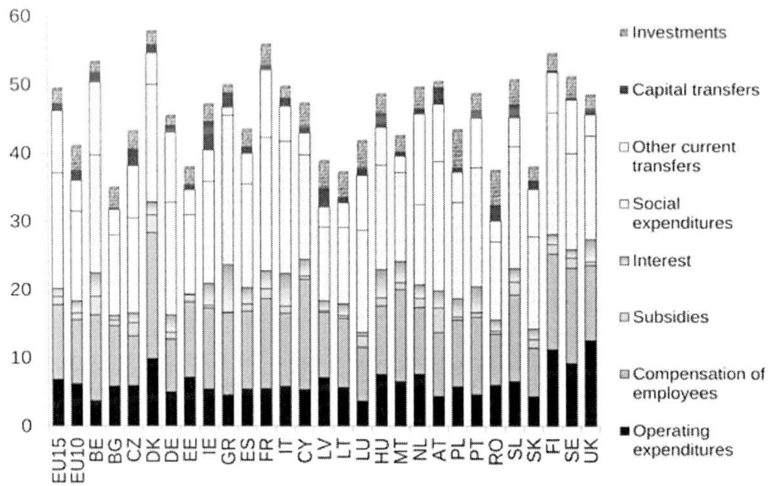

Fig. 8-1/c The amount and internal distribution of public expenditures in 2011 by country and EU-15 and EU-10 average, expenditure gross sum in % of the GDP
Source: Eurostat

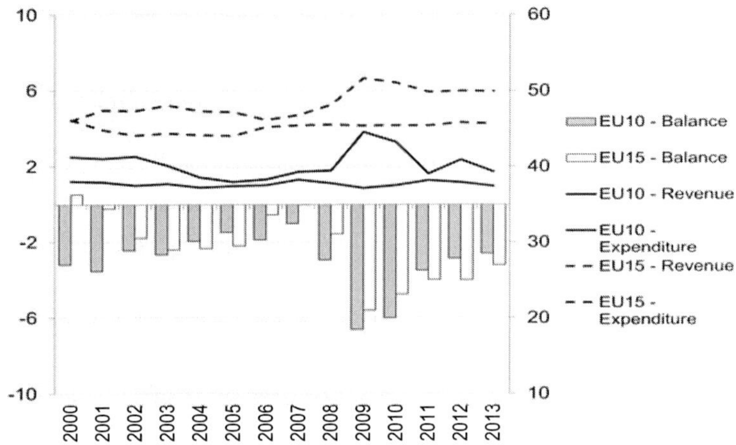

Fig. 8-2 Public revenues, expenditures, and deficit trends in the EU-15 and EU-10 countries, in % of the GDP
Source: Eurostat

As shown in Figure 8-2, the countries most affected by the crisis, the outdated structure of public expenditures and, most importantly, their unsustainable growth, played significant roles in the escalation of financial problems and the debt crisis (OECD 2010 and Inotai 2011). The transformation endeavours (modernisation, efficiency improvements) and the structural reforms that occurred in various short or long-term national government programmes have not resulted in radical changes. The ensuing and mostly campaign-like steps led to only a few and very different results in the different countries. However, it is worth analysing the reasons for the lack of significant results in more detail.

When comparing the average financing ratios of Bulgaria, the Czech Republic, Estonia, Hungary, Latvia, Lithuania, Poland, Romania, Slovenia and Slovakia (EU-10) with those of the EU-15 group consisting of the former EU, it is notable that there are no significant differences in the various public finance structures that would determine the sustainability of the financing. Additionally, we should note that the sustainability of the more developed, yet similarly outdated social entitlement systems of the Baltic states, Bulgaria, Poland, Romania and Slovakia, i.e., the majority of the later accessing European countries, requires less sacrifices than in the Czech Republic, Hungary and Slovenia. The public finance structure in the examined EU-10 group, partly due to the entitlements from the "socialistic" heritage, is rather rigid, and changing it significantly would require an emergency situation or the support of the society. The public finance structure has advanced, or rather inched forward, by changes affecting the total functioning of the state. In turn, social demand tends to result in over-consumption, inefficient but "familiar" social services, and qualitative improvements, not paying attention to the fact that the outdated financing system is leading to a path of deficits (Fig. 8-2); prior to the crisis, the individual countries have followed this path that they were unable to stray from, even at the price of heavy sacrifices.

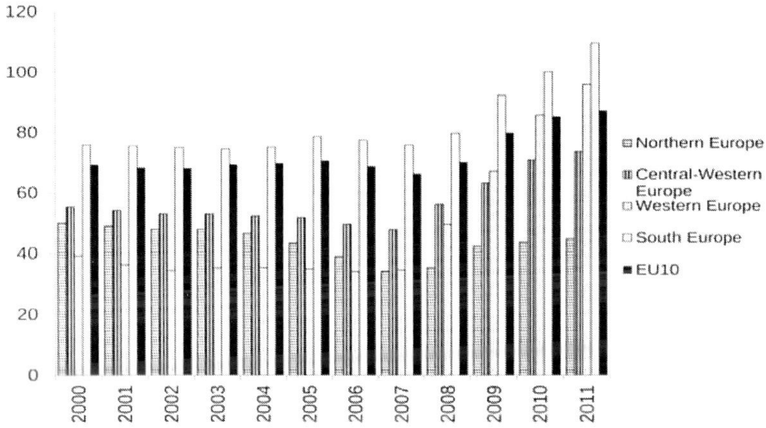

Fig. 8-3 Trend of indebtedness in proportion to the GDP in the EU-10 and Northern, Western and Southern European countries (2000–2011)
Source: Eurostat

Due to the earlier evolving and deepening "financing gap," the crisis affected the Central and Eastern European countries at the peripheries much more than the countries of Northern and Western Europe. In the first phase of the crisis, the situations of the EU-10 countries were in many aspects similar, as shown in Figure 8-3, before a relative improvement of the positions started. However, there were stability problems in the EU-10 as well as in the Southern European countries, where governments have been financing social services that lagged far behind the performance of the real economy in respect to their structure, scope and quality (Csaba 2010). According to different authors, the present Euro crisis is first of all a budgetary and public debt crisis or, in other words, a *sovereign debt crisis*, but one that affects only certain (southern) countries of the euro zone (Carmoy and Combes 2011 and Palánkai 2011).

From the above, it can be concluded that, as a consequence of the convergence[5] of basic social rights and demands, the welfare systems and institutional and entitlement models of the European Union countries are showing a number of similarities. At the same time, regarding the financing of these similar solutions, the differences were significant even prior to the crisis. Now, in light of the crisis – as we will show when discussing the crisis management measures – *the different approaches that were directly related to the size of public finance, the structure of services financed by the public finance, the technical implementation of the entitlements and their sustainable financing and, thus, a given country's inclination for crisis*[6] are called into question (Kovács 2011a and Muraközi 2012).

When comparing the GDP proportionate budget deficit of the EU-27 in 2009 to the pre-crisis years, it has nearly tripled to 6.8%, and the same development occurred in the Euro zone: the GDP proportionate budget deficit reached 6.3%. Budget surpluses disappeared in all countries, and only Denmark, Estonia, Finland, Germany, Luxemburg and Sweden performed below the 3% deficit threshold. The deficit level was approximately average in countries such as France, Italy, the Netherlands,

---

[5] In the second decade of the 21st century there are four interlinked and consequential challenges seeking answers (Muraközy 2012). Namely:

1. the lack of optimal-sized and affordable public services may result in losses that could
2. make it difficult to keep up in the competition of social models and the global economy. This challenge, in the coming decades, will be coupled with
3. changing demographic situations and, in a number of European countries, including Hungary, borrowing as a result of the postponement of reforms; social consumption that could not be financed from domestic resources and that was in no relation to the economic performance of the country resulted in the ensuing, differentiated
4. debt crisis that caused serious burdens making recovery difficult not only among those countries directly affected, but also within the risk-sharing community of the European Union (Cipriani 2010).

Among those challenges, in the coming decades, the management of the crisis and the challenges caused by demographic trends will receive most attention. Thus, it is not possible to employ action scenarios reflecting the traditional economic literature that emphasises economic development while maintaining social cohesion.

[6] Here we can refer to various norms, guidelines, and charters, but also to the fact that the Union identifies itself as a market economy, which is reflected, in different forms or wording, in the fundamental laws of the individual countries.

Poland, Slovenia and Slovakia. With a 4.4% deficit, Hungary's situation can be considered better than average.[7] By 2009, the budget deficit of several countries was near to or even higher than 10%, which can be considered a crisis level. Among the Euro zone countries, Greece, with a deficit of 15.4%, Ireland (14.4%), Spain (11.1%) and Portugal (9.2%) were in such a crisis situation. Similarly, high deficits were observed in the United Kingdom (11.4%) and, among the examined Central and Eastern European countries, in Lithuania (10.2%), Latvia (9.2%) and Romania (8.6%).

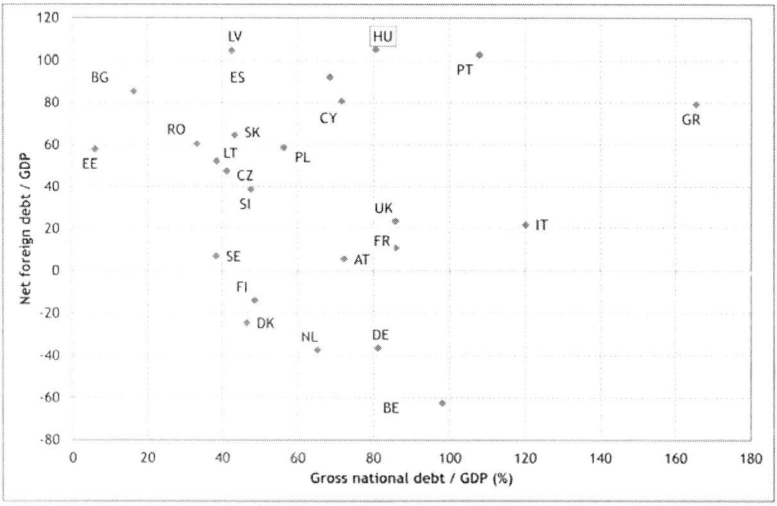

Fig. 8-4 Debt map of the European Union
Source: MNB data

The budget crisis continued in 2010–2011, and the average deficit of the EU-27 kept rising to 7.2%. In 2011, it was solely Sweden that produced a budget surplus (0.9%). The success of public finance stabilisation in seven countries, including three of the group of examined countries (Bulgaria, Germany and Hungary), that were able to reduce or stabilise their respective deficits in 2011 is conspicuous. Portugal (5.9%) as well as France, Poland and Slovenia (all 5.8%) had significant deficits.

[7] Obviously, maintaining welfare and education systems with identical efficiency, scope, quality and availability essentially requires identical expenditures, whether they are financed by taxes, centralised redistribution or citizen's income. Real differences are extorted by the differences of the economic performance.

Ireland (10.5%), Greece (9.5%), the United Kingdom (8.6%) and Spain (6.3%) were facing a grave situation.

According to forecasts, the majority of the EU countries will be successful in significantly decreasing their budget deficits. Among the Central and Eastern European countries, a deficit surpassing the 3% limit can be expected in Poland and Slovakia. Their trends, however, indicate that the stabilisation results will approach those of the so-called core countries of the euro zone. None of the EU-10 countries belongs to the lagging Mediterranean group, although, concerning the sustainability of stability, as can be seen in the trend prognosis of economic growth and investments in Figure 8-5/a-b, they are in different positions. The level of their respective deficits can be attributed to one-time effects (e.g., in Hungary), to the curtailment of services without structural transformation (e.g., in Romania), or to the invariability of the inherited low level (e.g., Slovakia, the Baltic states, Romania).

When searching for the causes of the growing national debt in the period of 2007–2011 (Fig. 8-6), concerning the EU-10, we can find several reasons. In the case of Romania and Poland, the 14.8% growth of national debt compared to the GDP can be explained entirely by the deterioration of the primary balance of the central budget, whereas, in the case of the Czech Republic, 13.7% of the 14.6% growth can be explained via that same reason. In the case of Lithuania, approximately half of the national debt deterioration can be explained by the deterioration of the primary balance. At the same time, in Hungary, the significant deterioration of the interest rate conditions for financing, the drop in the economic performance and the lagging speed of cost cuts[8] were also responsible for the growing national debt. In the remaining countries, a variety of other causes for debt deterioration were found. All these causes show that without a transformation of public finance structures, it would be difficult to achieve sustainable financing. However, as shown in Figures 8-1/a-c, only moderate results were achieved in this field.

---

[8] Most scholars accepted the favourable Hungarian deficit indicators because they were realised by using the share of the private pension fund above HUF 500 billion and by using other, non-recurring measures. At present, there are no rules concerning the structural balance. The Maastricht criteria merely state that the deficit cannot be higher than 3% of the GDP. There is a significant difference between the Maastricht deficit and a "structural deficit." Namely, the latter has to be adjusted by the so-called cyclical and non-recurring items; in our case, this would mean a 6–7% deficit.

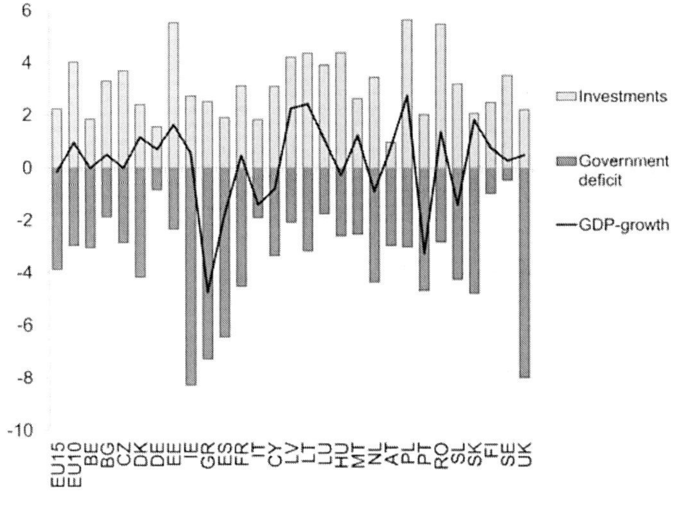

Fig. 8-5/a Expected trend of GDP growth, investments and budget deficits in 2012
Source: European Commission (2011)

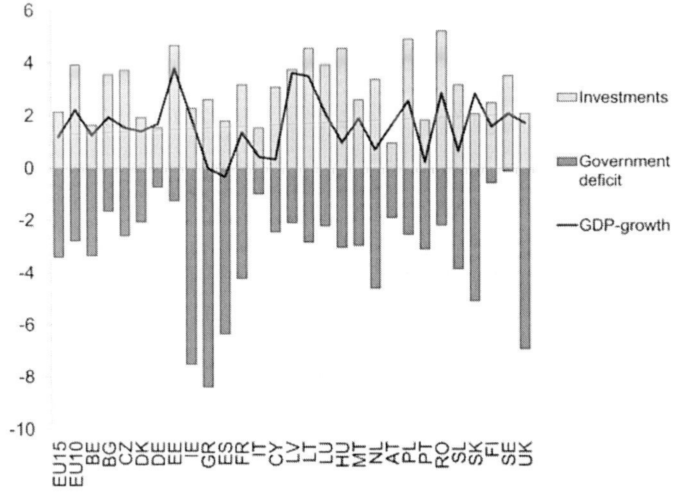

Fig. 8-5/b Forecast of the GDP growth, investments and budget deficits in 2013, in % of the GDP
Source: European Commission (2011)

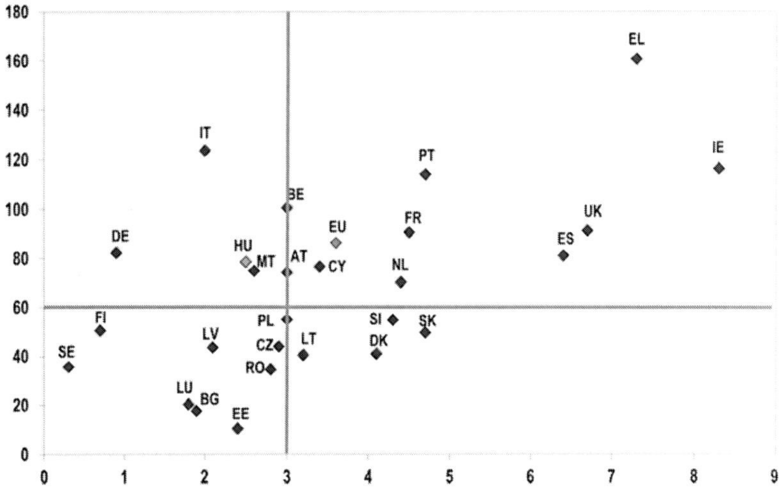

Fig. 8-6 Public finance deficit and public debt in the EU in 2012[9], in % of the GDP
Source: European Commission (2011) and GKI Economic Research Co.
Note: The lines within the diagram show the so-called Maastricht criteria.

Declining investments observed in indebted countries lead to a lasting decline in growth, which also cannot be compensated by the low level of domestic demand. The chances of recovery from the crisis look particularly gloomy in countries where the debt service for the previously accumulated deficit, despite some successful corrections and even with a positive budget, is so high that following the implementation of current financing restrictions, there is not enough money, and investments in infrastructure developments keep being postponed (see, for example, Hungary). This development, in turn, will reduce the chances for growth, even in the short run.

---

[9] "Reflexivity" is a concept promoted by George Soros. In his opinion, the balance of the market is the result of the continuous interaction of the subjective decisions by the actors of the market and the fundamentals of the market; thus, he rejects the theoretical principle that had been tacitly accepted in the course of the governance of the international financial system, according to which money markets are always aiming at a balanced position. During the crisis, investors and market analysers have exposed themselves as commentators serving their own interests and striving for influence in the processes. The world economy has been drifting and cannot provide an answer to the emerging social issues yet. At the same time, the whole European economy governing system is quietly moving towards centralisation and protection under the slogan of "let's save what can be saved."

Financing is influenced by the bankruptcy risk rating of the given country and by the costs of the external borrowing operations, the so-called credit default swap (CDS) premiums.[10] CDS premiums prevail via the strong fluctuation of securities market yields, and deviations are a sign of the fluctuating level of trust in the government policy of the given country. Figure 8-7 shows the aggregated, mutual effects of the securities market yields and political events[11] (European Commission 2011 and European Parliament 2011).

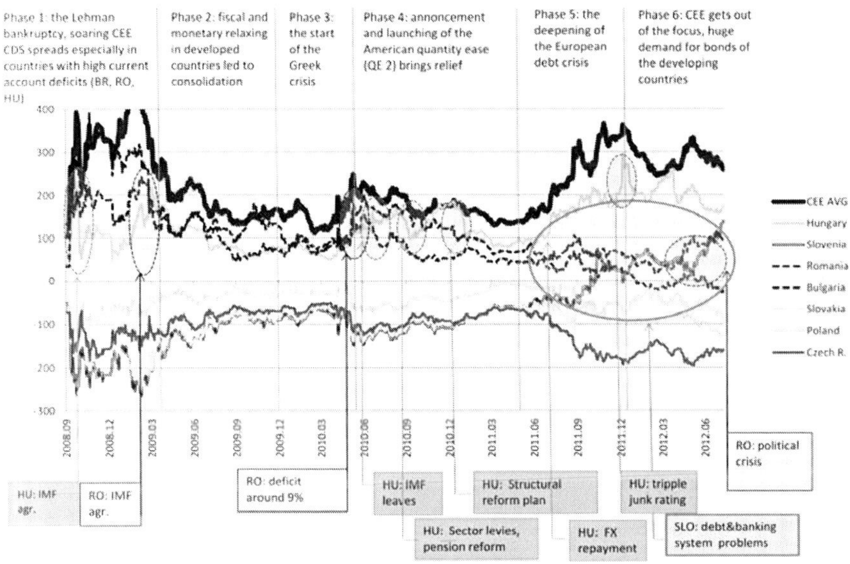

Fig. 8-7 Security markets yields of the EU-10 countries and decisive political events and economic initiatives
Source: Eurostat, OTP, own compilation

[10] Naturally, even the possibilities of decreasing expenditures cannot be final, and the transformation of the public finance structure, in the beginning, tends to show growing expenditures. An analysis of these social connections (action brakes in governance), and budgetary policy is beyond the scope of this article.

[11] At the beginning of January 2012, the Hungarian Credit Default Swap (CDS) rate was 670 basis points, compared to 255 at the beginning of summer in 2011. In March 2009, at the time of the expansion of the global financial crisis following the collapse of the large American bank Lehman Brothers in the fall of 2008, and when Hungary was near bankruptcy, the CDS rate was 630 basis points.

3. Matrices of fiscal interventions and the ensuing consequences

Shortly after the eruption of the Greek crisis, a number of leading economists called attention to the lack of economic policy harmonisation and the "softness" of the Stability and Growth Pact (Boefinger and Ried 2010). This situation implied that the member states would manage the effects of the economic crisis individually, which is what actually happened. Obviously, this led to a "mix of action scenarios" marked by significant randomness, instead of a scenario built on economic, social and political research. However, this approach also included some decisive elements that are prevailing in the long run.

The employed solutions included a mixture of taxations, cost reductions, service cuts, restrictions, consumption reductions and economic stimulus. However, the proportions, timing or dosage were different, depending on the size of the given country, its economic strength, indebtedness, social traditions, feasibility or the preferences of the respective government. Obviously, the results were also different. The same solutions, for example the introduction of a modest income tax, in some countries led to an increase in domestic savings, whereas in other countries those were depleted or transferred abroad (Haan et al. 2002).

The time that has passed since the eruption of the crisis can be divided into two phases: From 2008-2010, the first economic and political reactions indicated fundamentally similar situations in the individual countries. Regarding crisis management, maintaining the viability of the financial intermediary system was considered most important, followed by preventing economic decline. To this end, governments, if there was money for such measures, also tried to use appropriated stimulus funds. The EU-10 countries, however, did not have resources for the broad implementation of such solutions.

The deepening of the crisis from 2010 onward led to the renewal of crisis management strategies, including the employed solutions. Trying to identify the fundamental, stable characteristics of the EU-27 crisis management and the differences of the two crisis phases, we can find them in the following 7 areas:

- the prevailing reduction of public finance expenditures (restrictions) *in both phases* (in 2008–2010 and in 2011);
- the general growth of taxes, duties and levies of contributions that can be found *in both phases* (2008–2010 and 2011);

- the interventions into the economy, primarily into the labour market, that prevailed *in both phases* (2008–2010 and 2011);
- the selective reduction of taxes, duties and levies of contributions targeted at specific fields, characteristic primarily *in the first phase* (2008–2010);
- individual bank rescue operations *in the first phase* (2008–2010);
- changes to the operational rules, institutional systems and structures of public finance *that generally prevailed in the first phase*[12] (2008–2010), and
- special taxes targeted at the financial sector, *characteristic in the second phase of crisis management* (2011).

---

[12] A survey conducted by the European Committee in 2009 and encompassing 21 member states emphasised the following (European Commission 2010b):

- Among the countries that responded to the questionnaire, 19 often resorted to employing budgetary procedures as fiscal means that included the general curtailment of expenditures, building up bigger reserves and differentiated structural transformations.
- 13 countries introduced new, numeric fiscal rules; 13 countries reported new fiscal frameworks.
- In the given period, increasing transparency and the employment of the programs and the transformation of the budget process were characteristic.
- Strengthening fiscal discipline (e.g., budget centralisation, top-down budget) scarcely emerged.
- From among the 21 countries that responded, 19 introduced new fiscal rules, whereas 2 transformed the existing rules.
- 8 new regulations were dealing with restricting the growth of expenditures, 6 were dealing with balanced budgets, and 5 focused on the debt level.
- In the field of medium-term financial planning, ten countries witnessed both the transformation of the existing rules and the introduction of new regulations.
- 3 countries introduced as a first step medium-term financial planning systems as means of emerging from the crisis; therefore, 25 EU member states have such systems.
- Although several countries introduced new fiscal rules, the Council's recommendations have not been largely reflected yet; progress has been reported only in 7 cases.

Regarding this issue, the opinion of the European Committee is that additional/complementary fiscal incentives and initiatives are necessary. Fiscal regulations appeared strong enough only in 5 countries, which could lead to the conclusion that as long as the old structure can be financed, countries keep postponing the structural reform of public finance.

Additional measures are showing a rather mixed picture. The concerned countries regarded strengthening the monitoring of financial and economic processes, establishing supranational controlling and coordinating institutions, and the operation of these institutions as part of an early warning system as the best tools to prevent unexpected situations. The establishment of such a system, however, has been proceeding slowly and accompanied by debates (Moser 2011). At the same time, new advisory institutions with a specific control function have been formed, such as fiscal councils. By 2008, no such institution had been established among the EU-10 countries, but Hungary and Slovenia in 2009, Romania in 2010, and Slovakia in 2012 set up independent fiscal councils.

With the exception of Hungary, the intensive phase of crisis management in the EU-10 countries, not unlike in the Northern and Western parts of the EU, occurred in the years 2008–2009. In the Mediterranean countries, the indecisiveness concerning interventions resulted in the escalation of the crisis.

Considering the reasons and the feasibility of the intermediary "solutions" included in the "action scenario matrices," they are related to the public finance balance, the production and welfare systems and the size of the challenge. Obviously, governmental action is more "activist", both in terms of measure and expansion, in situations where the structural transformation of the welfare system made the decrease of public finance expenditures and their structural transformation more urgent.

Naturally, the conditionalities (e.g., social, stability, political, economic, public administration) of similar mixes of action scenarios differ; thus, the mechanisms are also different from country to country. In other words, identical or very similar prescriptions and "dosages" of solutions or techniques might lead to different results.[13] As such, it is difficult to draw generalised conclusions. However, even within the outlined limits, we can note that regarding the depth of the problems and crisis management activities *it would be impossible to state that there is a significant relationship between a country's size of public finance, its financing, and the inclination for a crisis*. Considering the successful crisis management,

---

[13] Answering these questions, namely why similar public finance governing and crisis solutions lead to different results in different EU countries, is beyond the limits of the present study; identifying the limits of creating a model in this respect would require additional research, involving many aspects of social studies such as the history of law, traditions, analysis of political, governance and management traditions as well as national characters.

or rather the absence of a crisis, in Slovenia,[14] the Northern European countries and the examined Central and Eastern European block of countries and considering the significant expansion of these countries' social services, we can conclude that *the question is not in what model (type of state participation) entitlement systems can function, but whether they are functioning efficiently and whether their financing is in harmony with the performance of the economy.*

Comparing the matrices, it was clear that tax reductions were implemented as a stimulus for certain productive industries. Also, special taxes were introduced as part of a general increase in tax burdens. The introduction of special taxes (solidarity taxes) and tax exemptions in Hungary has not been a unique phenomenon in the course of crisis management. The extent (e.g., the significant reduction of personal income taxes and corporate taxes), the broad variety of implementation tools, and the fragmented nature of the tax system itself, were significantly different and more complicated.[15] Regarding bank taxes, it is important to note that the concept itself has been used not only in countries belonging to the euro zone (Austria, France, Germany), but also in Hungary, Sweden, and the United Kingdom. At the same time, regarding the performance of the banking system, size indicators and the *gross sum of revenues* of the public finances of the countries that reported a resource surplus (and partial correction of the division of burdens) to ensure a balanced budget, *the solution employed in Hungary was incomparably more radical then the measures introduced in other countries and of a magnitude that might endanger the financing activity of the banking system and, also, economic growth.*[16]

---

[14] Contradictory information has been published about Slovenia recently, stating that it had accumulated many problems, that the economy was overheated prior to the crisis and that the current correction is belated; this information might imply the revaluation of the country's role as a "star pupil."

[15] Now, by making the conditionality of collection even harder, the trend of budgetary revenues is becoming disadvantageous, whereas leaving more income with the targeted section of the population – the so-called middle-class – did not result in significant saving surpluses, partly due to the decreasing of heavy indebtedness, partly due to lack of trust.

[16] In the period of 2008-2011 – with the exception of bank consolidating actions – Hungary tried almost every step of fiscal policy, which, in some cases, represented the opposite of existing policies, administering major changes that resulted in shocks to the system. It was also obvious that, especially in an unstable environment, repeatedly opting for creative, non-orthodox solutions that had not been tried before and that were scarcely paying attention to the harmonisation of different interests had a higher risk of achieving the desired results. First, because

4. First phase of crisis management in the EU-10 countries: 2008–2010

Looking at the reaction to activities during the first phase, we can see that government rhetoric was emphasising the decreasing of the burdens of the real economy as well as the launching of economic development in the EU-10 countries (Table 8-1). However, the actions themselves were not consistent, partly due to a lack of resources and due to political fluctuations. Revenue concentration generally became more moderate. The dynamics of the welfare expenses of public finance have generally dwindled; occasionally, countries spent less on such expenses, also in absolute numbers. The general assumption was that even with an increase – in contrast to a selective reduction – of corporate taxes, more would remain for development and to support innovations indispensable for growth. However, this assumption applied only to the Baltic States and Poland, who are closest to the group of the Northern countries.[17]

It is understandable that in every crisis where jobs are eliminated, the state tries actively to boost employment and offers support and training; thus, various labour-market programmes could be observed. One of the significant steps of the crisis management was a major decrease in, or even the elimination of, such "benefits" due to their welfare character, which lowered the labour-market participation of individuals. However, in 2009

---

the institutional system was bearing the burden and the responsibility of the international crisis management fearing the possible spreading of such "innovations" that might tear up cooperation, it was distrustful and ready to implement sanctions. Second, the rapidly changing conditions themselves pose a risk to feasibility. Creative ideas, if not tested for feasibility, sooner or later might become counter-productive and (might) lead to a diversion from the chosen scenario or make the goal unachievable, together with all the social and economic consequences.

[17] When experiencing the first signs of the crisis, the government of Lithuania made several, impressive promises, which included a whole range of measures: decreasing the salaries of senior officials and public servants, with the exception of teachers, increasing the value added tax, launching of employment protection programmes, and more (Hawkesworth et al. 2010). The government used the majority of the saved money for innovations and education because it considered these fields to be one of the most important engines of growth. As a counterexample, we can mention the case of the Czech Republic where, despite the increase of certain tax revenues (VAT, consumption taxes), the government did not pay much attention to supporting innovations and education; on the contrary, the amount of money spent on such purposes has decreased significantly (Hrdlicka et al. 2010).

Table 8-1 Characteristic crisis management steps in the years 2008–2009

Country	Measures taken												
	Significant curtailment of public finance expenditures	Raising taxes, duties, contributions	Decreasing taxes, duties, affixes	Significant money market borrowing for current financing	Borrowing from organisations, due to the pressures of the crisis	Introduction of solidarity tax for the banks	Solidarity taxes targeted at the servicing sectors	Specific bank saving actions	New governing and/or control organisations in public finance management	Transformation of the operational rules of public finance	Other, individual steps (e.g., privatisation, use of private pension fund assets)	Economy (consumption) stimulus programmes	Labour market interventions
EU-10													
Bulgaria	X	X	X		X					X			X
Czech Republic	X		X							X			X
Estonia		X								X			X
Hungary	X	X	X	X	X				X	X		X	X
Poland		X	X		X					X			X
Latvia		X	X							X			X
Lithuania	X	X	X							X			X
Romania	X	X		X	X				X	X			X
Slovakia		X	X							X			X
Slovenia		X	X						X	X			X

Source: OECD (2011) and European Commission (2010b), own compilation and 2010, the incentive programmes started to get "exhausted" as a consequence of the restrictions of the fiscal leeway (European Commission 2010a). The ineffective labour-market interventions, however, have not adequately recognised the dynamics of the deepening crisis and its effects on the structural transformation of the labour market. However, short-term governmental interests in maintaining social peace have also contributed to the contradictory character of the activities.[18]

5. Characteristics of the second phase of crisis management

The analysis showed that in the gripping global crisis, due to a lack of balance in world markets, earlier stimulus activities were not able to generate substantive growth. Thus, the effects of implemented measures have usually "lagged" behind the events, and stimulating the economy with public finance resources has also resulted in a transfer of market risks to the public sector. Therefore, after a certain period, when governments kept balancing public finances with new restrictions, the lessening of the burdens of the real sector was not able to boost growth in the real economy. Most countries that implemented economic stimulus measures saw their GDP deficit grow by 0.1-0.5%, which explains the complete disappearance of this solution from the crisis management toolbox (European Commission 2010a, 2010b, 2010c, 2011).

---

[18] Decreasing the various burdens of employees and employers represents an important measure to protect jobs. We find frequent examples illustrating this statement in the crisis management strategies of the countries addressed earlier: the wide-range measures taken in Slovakia included the partial or full overtaking of health insurance and pension contributions, the support of flexible working hours, the supervision of laws governing employment, and the saving of building construction jobs by government orders (Bucek 2010). In a similar way, Slovenia also spent a significant amount on protecting work places, on mitigating the effects of the crisis on businesses, as well as on increasing innovation and education expenses, similar to the above-mentioned case of the Baltic states (Beynet and Leibfritz 2009). In this respect, Poland has not been an exception either; as in the years prior to the crisis, it worked toward sustaining the domestic market and supporting the significant entrepreneurial layer of the society. This effort was manifested in the support of flexible working hours or the partial or full taking over of various contributions (Reichardt 2011). Drawing EU support in euros offered partial coverage to facilitate these actions; the favourably low exchange rate of the national currency as well as revenues from an increasing VAT have also served these purposes (Csomós 2011).

Within the EU member states, with the exception of Romania, Hungary and the Mediterranean countries that had been unable to solve the crisis, the crisis management in the period of 2010–2011 moved away from wide-range activities and indirect interventions targeted at public finance towards more reserved governmental activities.

The EU-10 countries were also able to consolidate their situations; contrary to earlier steps, they employed mostly 2–3 crisis management measures that typically have been restricted to the field of energy or general consumption taxes. At the same time, budgetary austerity measures and the protection of the labour market invariably prevailed. Estonia introduced exemplary restrictions as a result of its rapid growth after 2010.

The characteristic feature of the EU-10 crisis management was that, although with a delay compared to the Northern and Western countries of the EU, it also resorted to deficit reduction. Among the latter group of countries, this approach was more characteristic in the first period of the crisis, and both the efficiency and magnitude have been more favourable. However, while savings and restrictive measures contribute to the reduction of national debt, without additional, balancing steps such measures involved the risk of entering a downward spiral of increasing recession.

Budgetary measures impact fiscal sustainability through several channels: primarily, they affect the balance, followed by growth effects and long-term growth effects resulting from the increased trust of investors. In this respect, the ability to reach a consensus to introduce measures, and the consistency and predictability of these measures are important. In this respect, the Central and Eastern European countries followed a course that reflected a rather mixed picture, and the governments considered a lack of trust mostly as their heritage (Table 8-2).

Table 8-2 Characteristic steps employed in crisis management in the years 2010–2011

	Measures taken												
Country	Significant curtailment of public finance expenditures	Raising taxes, duties, contributions	Raising taxes, duties, contributions	Significant money market borrowing for current financing	Borrowing from organisations, due to the pressures of the crisis	Introduction of solidarity tax for the banks	Solidarity taxes targeted at the servicing sectors	Specific bank saving actions	New governing and/or controlling organisations in public finance management	Labour market interventions	Economy (consumption) stimulus programmes	Other, individual steps (e.g., privatisation, use of private pension fund assets)	Transformation of the operational rules of public finance
EU-10													
Bulgaria	X	X								X			
Czech Republic	X	X	X							X			
Estonia	X									X			
Hungary	X	X	X	X	X	X	X		X	X	X	x	X
Poland	X	X								X			
Latvia	X				X					X			
Lithuania	X	X								X			
Romania	X	X		X	X				X	X			
Slovakia	X	X								X			
Slovenia	No substantive measures that would be related to crisis management								X	X			

Source: OECD (2010) and European Commission (2010b) analyses, own compilation

6. Conclusions

The present crisis is a mix of problems with global, regional and national origins, reflecting that all three components can be attributed to the fact that institutional systems were not able to keep up with the changes in the economy. The multifaceted character of the European Union, mostly as a result of the expansion of the organisation to the South and the East, has become more pronounced. This fact is expressed in differences such as level of development, economic and social structures, traditions and values, which are all connected to the present European crisis by intricate links; therefore, the solution to the crisis does not depend solely on new institutions and policies (Kiss 2011).

Regarding the question of whether identities or differences were more dominant, we can state that *with respect to the employed solutions, identities were more dominant than differences, also in the case of the later accessed Central and Eastern European countries*. Differences have been present mostly around measures of interventions, the number of intervention areas, methods resorting to more "activist" interventions, individual solutions or more normative, careful approaches.

At the eruption of the crisis in 2008 and in 2009, EU countries with reserves and resources opted for Keynesian, demand-oriented, anti-cyclical economic policies that contributed to the growth of indebtedness, made debt financing more expensive, and resulted in growing budget shortfalls.

One consensus on the issue is that inadequate management was one of the major reasons for the deepening of the crisis. These days, it seems that decision-making based on socio-economic research is absent at the level of governmental, global and regional institutions. The conceptual and strategic handling of the problems is missing in the "Mediterranean" and "Continental" group of EU member states.[19] Mutually exclusive steps can often be observed, but such solutions reinforce rather than solve the crisis in the long run. Sustainable growth and monetary stability is not possible without the coherent implementation of reforms concerning the structure of public finance (Kovács 2011b). The definition of public tasks is a fundamental and conceptual issue, which is necessary on both national and EU levels. Budgetary savings should also be "sustainable" and have long-term effects.

---

[19] "Public finance expenditure overruns" is a relative concept: it shows to what extent governance is able to continuously maintain harmony between the available sources and the financed services to ensure the prevailing of social cohesion, either by meeting the growing social demand or not.

EU membership offered a certain (limited) protection against the direct, short-term consequences of the crisis. The imperfection of the integration framework has negatively influenced crisis management, which was not institutionalised (Carmoy and Combes 2011). The EU-27 countries and the EU itself, as observed, have not been able to employ a preventive, proactive and theoretically well-founded crisis management. However, by 2012, the EU was mostly able to stabilise its position and, for the time being, show solidarity with countries that are in trouble and unable to renew their social and economic models or that are still struggling with the debt trap.[20] The measures taken served the sustainability of the social and economic functioning on the EU level, and the chance remained that efficiency improvements and new growth would become reality, not only for certain groups of EU members but also for the whole union.

Instead of welfare redistribution, sharing of risks and burdens were the characteristic features. Today, regarding the EU countries – with significant simplifications – two groups can be observed: one group consists of those countries that had been able to stabilise their respective positions with the help of strict restrictions, whereas the other group contains those countries that are either bankrupt or on the brink of bankruptcy due to the late introduction of correction measures or the lack of social-political conditions for the implementation of restrictions.

The examined EU-10 countries belong more to the former group of countries that were able to stabilise their situations by resorting to strict fiscal restrictions, even though to a different degree and with different chances; they showed specific reactions related to government changes, followed occasional detours and used action scenario mixes that, in some cases, contained counterproductive elements. The chances of the EU-10 regarding catching up have improved. The crisis had painted a gloomy picture, based on earlier experiences, in respect to the "outer circle" or a

[20] The countries that received assistance were, in turn, former members of the EU. Unfortunately, there is little literature on what roles the dictate of political and economic interests have played in the enforcement of the common risks or to what extent considerations that focused on the development of the EU have influenced the decisions. Under these circumstances, it is a significant result that – for the time being – none of the new member states received assistance; although, this could also be explained by the relative low level of social services. In the case of Latvia and Romania, a financial safety net worth €1.7, respectively €12 billion was set up in 2009. Besides Hungary, Romania is currently also negotiating with international financial institutions and organisations on setting up a similar safety net worth €15 billion. In exchange, it will likely commit to the establishment of a system of responsible and sustainable budgetary processes (IMF 2009a, 2009b).

two-speed development (Farkas 2009). This group of countries has integrated more into the "core Europe" and the internal markets of the EU. The work force in those countries is well trained, and the legal environment for investments is mostly adequate. Poland, the Baltic States, Slovenia and, partly, due to geo-political reasons, the Czech Republic and Slovakia are closer to the core; Hungary, due to the market integration and, lately, the reduction and maintenance of a lower budget shortfall, belongs also to the circle of the "Northern and Western Group" of the EU. Hungary, however, has not yet entered the road to consolidation regarding the predictability and functioning of its institutional systems or the steady financing of the public finance system. Regarding investments with a significant effect on growth, Hungary is lagging behind. As a consequence, the chance of Hungary catching up is closer to Romania and Bulgaria, which are two countries with very favourable indebtedness indicators.

The conditions of the crisis made it obvious that maintaining public finance stability, boosting the economy and achieving sustainable development do not depend on the "appropriate mix or dosage" of economic rationalisations, which includes not only the taxation of restrictive and "relaxing" measures but also external and internal social adaptabilities, so-called quality adaptabilities, that cannot be quantified. Great self-discipline, restraint, patience and consensus seeking are required to ensure that endeavours to adjust to the changes are not distracted by the reflex to intervene immediately, resulting in improvised solutions. It is impossible to realise sound objectives if the tools are inappropriate, contradict each other, are unacceptable in the given socio-economic environment, or do not reflect economic realities. At the same time, the decision on what is unfeasible, futile and destabilising, and what is right, will improve safety, and create sustainable value, is impacted by constant changes and balance-related problems, which, in today's Europe, represent the greatest challenge.

Acknowledgement

The study was created within the framework of project No. TÁMOP-4.2.1/B-09/1/KONV-2010-0005 "Establishment of a Research University Centre of Excellence at the University of Szeged" supported by the European Union and co-financed by the European Social Fund.

References

Beynet, P. and Liebfritz, W. 2009. "Keeping Slovenian Public Finances on a Sustainable Path." Working paper No. 734, OECD Economics Department.

Boefinger, P. and Ried, S. 2010. "A New Framework for Fiscal Policy Consolidation in Europe." Working Paper 03/2010, German Council of Economic Experts.

Bucek, J. 2010. "The financial and economic crisis in Slovakia …– its spatial aspects and policy responses." In *Financial Crisis in Central and Eastern Europe: From Similarity to Diversity*, edited by Grzegorz Gorzelak and Chor-Ching Goh, 190–208. EUROREG, Centre for European Regional and Local Studies, University of Warsaw, World Bank.

Carmoy, H. D. and Combes, P. 2011. *Dealing with the next phase of financial crisis*. Hague: Trilateral Commission.

Cipriani, G. 2010. *European Budget, Responsibility without Accountability?* Brussels: Centre for European Policy Studies.

Csaba, L. 2010. "Paradigmaváltás az európai gazdaságpolitikában?" [Changing Paradigms in the European Economic Policy?] In *Válságban és válság nélkül (A gazdaságpolitika rétegei)* [In crisis and without crisis (Layers of Economic Policy)], edited by László Muraközi. Budapest: Akadémiai Kiadó.

Csomós D. 2011. "Eagles in the storm – The Sub-prime mortgage crisis in the United States and Poland." Debrecen: DEENK.

European Commission. 2010a. "European Economy 6/2010: Monitoring tax revenues and tax reforms in EU member states."

—. 2010b. "National fiscal governance reforms across EU member states." European Economy. Occasional Papers 67.

—. 2010c. "Public finances in the EMU." European Economy 4/2010.

—. 2011. "European Economic Forecast 2011 Spring."

European Institute. 2011. "Austerity measures in the EU – A country by country table". http://www.europeaninstitute.org/Special-G-20-Issue-on-Financial-Reform/austerity-measures-in-the-eu.html

European Parliament. 2011. "Eurobarometer on Europeans and the crisis." European Parliament Eurobarometer (EB Parlemeter, 76.1) Summary.

Farkas, B. 2009. "Perspectives of Convergence in the European Economic Performance and Institutional Systems." In Vol. 2 of *7th International Conference*, 103–109. Miskolc-Lillafüred: University of Miskolc, Faculty of Economics.

De Haan, J. and Inklaar, R. and Sleijpen, O. 2002. "Have Business Cycles Become More Synchronized?" Journal of Common Market Studies 40: 23–42.

IMF (International Monetary Fund) 2009a. "Republic of Latvia: Request for Stand-By Arrangement." Staff Report. Washington DC: International Monetary Fund.

— 2009b. "Romania: Request for Stand-By Arrangement." Staff Report. Washington DC: International Monetary Fund

Inotai, A. 2011. "Válság után?" [After the Crisis?]. *Pénzügyi Szemle* [Financial Review] 56, 3: 352–368.

Hawkesworth, I. and Emery, R. and Wehner, J., and Saegert, J. (2010): "Budgeting in Lithuania." *OECD Journal on Budgeting* 10, 3: 79–114.

Hrdlicka, Z. and Morgan, M. and Prušvic, D. and Tompson, W. and Vartia1, L. 2010. "Further Advancing Pro-growth Tax and Benefit Reform in the Czech Republic." Working Paper No. 758, OECD Economics Department.

Kiss, K. 2011. *A közgazdaságtan esendősége (és mihaszna a válság idején)* [The Frailty of Economics (and what is its use in crisis)]. Budapest: Stratégiakutató Intézet [Strategic Research Institute].

Kovács, Á. 2011a. "Az állam szerepe a versenyképesség fejlesztésében." [The role of the State in Developing Competitiveness] In *Vállalati versenyképesség és az állam szerepe, Tanulmányok 9.* [Company Competitiveness and the Role of the State, Monographies 9] edited by Klára Katona, 13–24. Szent István Társulat/PPKE JÁK.

— 2011b. "An outline of the determinations of the past two decades of Hungarian public Finance", In *Studies in International Economics and Finance*, edited by Beáta Farkas, 105–124. Szeged: JATEPress.

Moser, J. 2011. "The fallout of the Global Financial crisis – Lessons arising for government agencies and SAIs." Vienna: INTOSAI/ACA document.

Muraközy, L. 2012. *Államok kora*. [Age of States.]. Budapest: Akadémiai Kiadó [Academy Publishing House].

OECD 2010. Fiscal consolidation: requirements, timing, instruments and institutional arrangements. OECD Economic Outlook 2010/2.

Palánkai, T. 2011. Megmenthető-e az euró-övezet? [Can the Euro Zone be Saved? MKT Conference] Paper presented at the Conference of the Hungarian Economists' Association, Budapest, December 16.

Reichardt, A. 2011. "Poland and the Global Economic Crisis: Observations and Reflections on the Public Sector." *Journal of Finance and Management in Public Service*. Brentwood: Earlybrave Publications.

THE ADEQUACY OF INFLATION-TARGETING MONETARY POLICY AND EURO ZONE PARTICIPATION FOR THE CENTRAL-EAST EUROPEAN COUNTRIES

GÁBOR DÁVID KISS
AND ANDREÁSZ KOSZTOPULOSZ

1. Introduction

Currently, the central banks of European nations with market economies have the primary statutory objective of achieving and maintaining price stability. The Czech, Hungarian and Polish national banks have already introduced inflation targeting, because these countries are European Union membership candidates, but they did not introduce the euro after their EU accession in 2004, despite it being a future obligation for them. These Central-East European countries have a unique style of capitalism, characterised by underdeveloped capital markets, poor savings accumulation and over-concentrated banking systems (Farkas 2011), resulting in substantial capital imports that accelerated the domestic credit booms in the pre-crisis era (Kovács 2009, Árvai et al. 2009).

This paper aims to analyse the liquidity sensible environment that has defined the range of monetary policy decisions in the selected Central-East European member states over the last decade, using bond and currency markets as indicators and stock markets as control variables. First, it is necessary to define the monetary policy frameworks of these states and describe the expected potential impacts of these policies on, and assumptions regarding, capital markets. Second, it is necessary to analyse how these expectations measured against the experiences of the countries over the last decade. This study applies a method for examining the efficiency of capital markets and identifies different forms of collective behaviours, such as contagion, divergence or interdependence; these phenomena influence the range of available monetary policy decisions.

Following these results, it is necessary to evaluate how inflation targeting supports future euro adoption by answering these questions:

1. Is there any convergence between the capital markets of the euro zone and the selected countries, as required by the Maastricht criteria[1]?
2. Are the national banks in the selected countries able to address financial market crises alone?

2. Theoretical background

This chapter summarises the frameworks, expectations and assumptions regarding capital markets and their interactions with inflation-targeting monetary policies, before defining the different forms of collective behaviours in capital markets.

2.1. Capital markets and inflation-targeting frameworks

Inflation-targeting monetary policy could be defined as a monetary framework that comprises the following four properties: (1) the goal of price stability, (2) an announced numerical or sequential inflation target within a given time period, (3) inflation-forecast targeting (Svenson 1997), and (4) high levels of transparency and accountability (Hamori and Hamori 2010). O'Sullivan and Tomljankovich (2012) summarise the primary benefits attributed to this approach in the literature as follows: substantial declines in inflation and output growth volatility in emerging economies reduces the probability of banking crises and noise in bond markets. The expected noise reduction became significant in light of an article by Bean et al. (2010), which summarises the presumptions of the pre-crisis monetary policy for both the US Federal Reserve System (FED) and the European Central Bank (ECB) – where the assumption of market efficiency as a working approximation for equity and credit markets and where price and financial stability are assumed to be mutually dependent.

The assumption of market efficiency and the expected reduction of noise in bond markets are connected to the first question of this study. The

[1] Focusing on the 4th and 5th criteria, which call for long-term interest rates of no more than two percentage points above the rate in the three EU countries with the lowest inflation over the previous year, and that a national currency's exchange rate remain within certain pre-set margins for two years.

Maastricht-type convergence of capital markets could be temporary or at least biased when they can be described by a complex capital market model, involving the phenomenon of collective behaviour on extreme days. To test these phenomena, this study focuses on the 3-month and 10-year maturities of bond and currency market developments and on the stock market as a control variable between January 1 2002 and August 31 2011 using daily closing values. Our objective is to explore the spill-over effects generated by the FED and ECB on the new EU member states that aspire to adopt the euro.

Bonanno et al. (2001) defined three statistical consequences of complexity in financial markets: first, time series have short and long range memories and only asymptotic stationarity; second, their sectoral intraday cross-correlations are high; and third, they demonstrate collective market behaviours during extreme market events. The contagion, divergence and interdependence terms are consistent with the latter two consequences, with interdependence ruling out any significant changes in the common movement between markets, contagion being important under a significant increase in cross market correlation and divergence being important under a decrease in cross market correlation.

Contagions can be broadly defined as the cross-country transmission of shocks or general cross-country spill-over effects, which do not need to be related to crises. This paper uses the World Bank's very restrictive definition[2] of contagions, as cross-country correlations that increase during "crisis periods" relative to correlations during "tranquil periods". Interdependence can be described as a situation where the difference between correlations under extreme and normal conditions is insignificant.

Definition: *Contagion* (1) occurs between $m_k m_j$ markets when the $\rho^{m_k m_j}$ cross-market correlation becomes significantly higher due to a shock derived from one market ($r^{m}_{n/x}$) spreading to others or as a result of other external factors (Forbes and Rigobon 2002; Campbell et al. 2002; Bekaert et al. 2005):

$$r^{m_i}_{n/x} \neq 0 \rightarrow \rho_n^{m_k m_j} < \rho_x^{m_k m_j}, \quad (1)$$

[2] Forbes and Rigobon (2002) used the World Bank's (2012) definition as well.

Definition: *Interdependence* (2) occurs between $m_k m_j$ markets when the $\rho^{m_k m_j}$ cross-market correlation is not significantly different, but the level of correlation is consistently high (Forbes and Rigobon 2002):

$$r_{n/x}^{m_i} \neq 0 \rightarrow \rho_n^{m_k m_j} \approx \rho_x^{m_k m_j} \tag{2}$$

Definition: *Divergence* (3) occurs between $m_k m_j$ markets when the $\rho^{m_k m_j}$ cross-market correlation becomes significantly lower due to a shock derived from one market ($r_{n/x}^{m}$) spreading to others or as a result of other external factors (Bearce 2002):

$$r_{n/x}^{m_i} \neq 0 \rightarrow \rho_n^{m_k m_j} > \rho_x^{m_k m_j} \tag{3}$$

There could be a number of reasons behind the collective behaviour phenomenon, for example changes in market mood, herding, trade relations[3], credit channels or political connections. However, according to Jentsch et al. (2006), there is a more general reason for collective behaviour that derives from the dynamic properties of extreme events, as extreme events are nested functions of scale-free complex networks. The efficient market hypothesis is consistent with an Erdős and Rényi (1960) random graph or a competitive market model, but there is a more oligopolistic model of a scale-free network that has been developed by Barabási and Albert (1999). Networks among economic actors and financial markets or ordinary enterprises follow this model, according to Berlinger et al. (2011), Benedek et al. (2007), Lublóy (2005) and Vitali et al. (2011). Financial systems are primarily interconnected through the interbank lending market, as the results of Kovács (2009) and Bank for International Settlements (BIS 2011) suggest. Therefore, the vulnerability of a country will not depend on macroeconomic fundamentals or the general soundness of the individual banking systems alone, but will be affected by the maturity structure of foreign claims and the financial relationships between home and host institutions, as Árvai et al. (2009) suggests.

---

[3] The euro zone accounted for 52% of Hungarian exports and 55% of its imports in 2011 (KSH 2012); the euro zone accounted for 47% and 60% of Polish imports and exports in 2010 (GUS 2011, 112), while the corresponding figures for the Czech Republic were 53% and 67% (CZSO 2011).

2.2 The difference between the autonomy and independence of monetary policy

The possibility of barriers between capital markets raises a second question and obviously suggests a more intensive collaboration between the ECB and non-euro-area member states to support official liquidity and maintain the transmission mechanism. In optimal circumstances, a credible and independent central bank would be able to establish a path for short-term interest rates to anchor expectations about future policy rates to influence longer term interest rates (BoE 2000). For example, between September 2008 and February 2010, the reduction in the ECB's short term interest rates generally affected the three month Euro Interbank Offered Rate (EURIBOR) and, in parallel, most bank interest rates on loans for housing and consumption also declined (ECB 2010). Based on the deep economic relationships between the countries in this analysis and the euro zone, the monetary policy environments are already interconnected, with the potential consequence of narrowing the range of decisions available. The autonomy of monetary policy was defined by Plümper and Troeger (2008) and Obstfeld et al. (2005) as the ability of central banks to set prime rates according to macroeconomic conditions, or as the independence from the monetary policies in the key currency areas. This ability is reduced by the degree of monetary interdependence, which is based on trade relationships and cross-border production chains. Therefore, a floating exchange rate regime and free movement of capital does not necessary imply full monetary autonomy as the classic notion of the impossible trilemma would suggest. Global liquidity is able to limit this autonomy by increasing the vulnerabilities of a financial system through substantial mismatches across currencies, maturities and countries, while the supply of global liquidity stems from one or more "core countries" (BIS 2011). Therefore, the BIS recommends wider and more targeted interventions on the national (monetary liquidity) and international (IMF and other regional stabilisation funds) levels (referred to as "official liquidity") in domestic and foreign currencies when private funding or market liquidity contracts suddenly.

Uneven monetary autonomy and central bank independence are not contradictory because this "independence" only refers to its domestic institutional meaning under current law[4], where only the frameworks for

[4] ECB: article 130 of the Treaty on European Union; Act No. 6/1993 Coll. on the Czech National Bank, Article 1 and 6; Act CCVIII of 2011 on the Magyar Nemzeti Bank – Hungarian National Bank, Article 1; The Act on the National Bank of Poland of 29 August 1997, Article 56

central bank activities are defined by the law, instead of its operations. The turbulence in private liquidity and the cross-border lending and ownership in the banking sector suggest more intensive collaborations between EU-27 central banks and financial authorities[5] within and outside the euro zone. The next chapter briefly summarises the primary interactions among the ECB, the FED and the selected central banks with a focus on the patterns of pre-crisis and crisis collaborations.

3. Monetary policy decisions by the ECB and the FED

This paper defines two periods according to the ECB's and FED's interest rate decisions: "period A" covers the era of increasing and consistently high interest rates, while "period B" is a period of expansionary monetary policy with decreased interest rates on the short end of the yield curve and increasing yields on the long end. This chapter briefly summarises the main events of these periods, focusing mainly on the relationships between the ECB and the central banks (Czech National Bank – CNB, Hungarian National Bank – MNB, Polish National Bank – NPB) of the selected countries, especially in the year 2008.

3.1 Period "A"

A cautious monetary tightening characterised both ECB and FED monetary policy during the reconstruction phase after the dot-com bubble – the FED began to cautiously increase its primary credit interest rate from 2% to 6.25% between June 30, 2004 and August 17, 2007. This 42 month period was longer than the corresponding 18 month period when the ECB increased its main refinancing rate from 2% to 4% between December 6 2005 and June 13 2007. This tightening was triggered by the general increase of raw material, food and energy prices (MNB 2008), despite the emerging concerns regarding the sustainability of the housing sector. The FED kept interest rates high until August 17 2007, while the ECB waited until July 9 2008 and increased its interest rates to 4.25% until October 14 2008. This stable period was characterised by emerging risk management and securitisation issues.

[5] Despite the different institutional environments, for example there have been supreme financial supervision authorities in Hungary and Poland since 1999 and 2006, while in the Czech Republic it has been part of the central bank since 1993. (Act No. 6/1993 Coll., on the Czech National Bank; Hungary: law 124 in 1999; Poland: Act on Financial Market Supervision of 2006, No. 157, item 1119).

The ECB's measures to manage money market turbulence during the period from January to September 2008 can be grouped under three headings (ECB 2009):

1. The liquidity provision used earlier in the maintenance period to fulfil counterparties' reserve requirements.
2. Supplementary longer-term (3 and 6 month) refinancing operations occurring since July 2007.
3. Operations in conjunction with the US dollar Term Auction Facility: in 2007, the ECB established a reciprocal currency arrangement (swap line) with the Federal Reserve System – the Eurosystem provided funding in US dollars received via this 28-day and, later, 3-month swap line to its counterparts against collateral eligible for Eurosystem credit operations.

The intensification of the global financial crisis brought challenges for monetary policy in the selected countries, which experienced liquidity constraints in their interbank markets and tensions in their foreign exchange markets. Central bank responses varied depending on the economic conditions and monetary policy framework in place, for example ERM II participants adopted monetary policy measures that frequently mirrored moves by the ECB. However, central banks with inflation targets that did not participate in ERM II tightened their monetary policy stances at the beginning of 2008, with the aim of containing inflationary pressures stemming in large part from food and energy price increases and wage growth. In the first three quarters of 2008, the MNB and PNB each increased their main policy rates by a total of 100 basis points in several steps, while the CNB increased its main policy rate only once, by 25 basis points in February, a move that was reversed in August. The selected non-euro-area member states did not participate in ERM II in 2008, and their currencies appreciated and reached record levels against the euro in the first half of the year. In February 2008, Hungary replaced its exchange rate band for the euro with a free-floating exchange ratio reach its inflation target, thereby fulfilling the nominal Maastricht criteria (MNB 2008). However, after the deepening of the financial crisis in September, global deleveraging and severe problems in the functioning of interbank markets worldwide resulted in a rapid and pronounced depreciation of the Polish zloty and the Hungarian forint (ECB 2009).

As a result of the increasingly deepening crisis, a direct disinflationary effect emerged that affected demand and household consumption; this trend was supported by the expansion of household foreign currency loans and redundancies in the labour market (MNB 2008).

3.2 Period "B"

Central banks had to operate under disrupted monetary policy transmission mechanisms: money market interest rates were largely affected by liquidity disturbances, caused by the lack of trust among market participants and significant declines in markets' balances, due to price decreases and problems with asset valuation (NBP 2009).

Period "B" is characterised by monetary easing; however, period "B" did not occur simultaneously at the ECB and FED (as shown by their policy rates): the FED reduced the prime rate between August 17 2007 and December 17 2008 until it reached 0.5%, while the ECB only reacted after the collapse of Lehman Brothers. The late reaction on the part of the ECB seems reasonable due to its previous liquidity enhancement measures and the significant increase in inflation, resulting from a price surge in the global agricultural and energy commodity markets in 2007 and the first half of 2008. Global inflationary pressures only eased in the second half of 2008; however, at the same time, the previously visible appreciation trend of the Central-East European (CEE) currencies was inverted due to growing risk aversion and the ensuing capital outflows from emerging markets (NBP 2009).

In the second half of 2008, the ECB's main refinancing rate declined from 4.25% to 1% until May 2009, and it tightened the interest rate channels from 200 basis points to 100 bps to reduce interbank market volatility. The financial system recovered quickly, but the crisis spread to the European bond market, causing heterogeneous risk premiums between euro-area member states.

The ECB took the following steps to enhance liquidity management from October to December 2008, as the Annual Report of the ECB (2009) describes:

1. Fixed rate tenders with full allotment (all bids were satisfied), signing to market participants that the ECB was willing to supply as much liquidity as needed to avoid a liquidity crisis.
2. A reduction of the corridor formed by the standing facility rates, i.e., the marginal lending facility and the deposit facility, from 200 to 100 basis points, aiming to further ease banks' liquidity management by offering less expensive central bank intermediation.

3. Supplementary longer-term refinancing operations: one for the length of the maintenance period, two with a maturity of three months, and one with a maturity of six months.
4. Additional US dollar and Swiss franc-providing operations. Market liquidity in the foreign exchange swap market was unusually low due to increased stress and market segmentation, causing US dollar financing to become extremely difficult for institutions outside the United States. The Eurosystem further reinforced its provision of US dollar liquidity to Eurosystem counterparts by adding collateralised repo operations, fulfilling all bids at a fixed rate with overnight, 7-day, 28-day and 3-month maturities, in parallel with EUR/USD foreign exchange swaps.

   On 15 October, the Swiss National Bank and the ECB jointly announced measures to improve liquidity in short-term Swiss franc money markets, whereby the Eurosystem would provide its counterparts with Swiss franc financing via a swap line at a fixed price and with a maximum allotment amount and a 7-day or 3-month maturity.

   The ECB did not undertake any foreign exchange operations in the currencies that participate in ERM II.
5. Expansion of the collateral list.

In response to the tensions that developed in financial markets in late October and November 2008, there was a joint international financial support programme for Hungary to ease the downward pressure on the forint and other currencies in the region. However, the deteriorating economic outlook and external vulnerabilities, combined with credit rating downgrades for Hungary in October and November, resulted in a further sharp depreciation of the zloty, the forint and the koruna (ECB 2009). On 21–22 October, the exchange rate of the forint was subject to significant devaluation pressure in excess of that justified by macroeconomic fundamentals, causing an increase in the base rate of 300 basis points to maintain the stability of the financial intermediary system, contain a further strengthening of capital outflows and devaluation expectations and make speculation against the forint more expensive (MNB 2008). In October and November 2008, the ECB signed agreements to provide euro liquidity to the Hungarian and Polish national banks to improve euro liquidity in their respective domestic financial markets via repurchase agreements worth up to 5 and 10 billion euro (ECB 2009).

Hungary was able to meet its external obligations (97% of GDP at the end of 2007) under these extreme market circumstances due to the

17-month Stand-By Arrangement provided by the IMF (€12.3 billion), ECB (€6.5 billion) and World Bank (€1 billion) under the Fund's fast-track Emergency Financing Mechanism procedures (IMF 2008). This programme had two key objectives: to reduce the government's debt-financing needs and maintain the liquidity and capital adequacy in the banking system. This joint credit line caused a 57% increase in the balance sheet of the Hungarian National Bank (MNB). The MNB took several steps to improve the distribution of interbank forint and FX liquidity and maintain the functionality of domestic financial markets; FX liquidity was improved through two-way O/N FX swap quick tenders and an overnight FX swap standing facility from the €5 billion credit line provided by the ECB. Forint liquidity was enhanced through a reduced reserve ratio, two-week, fixed-rate, and weekly collateralised loan tenders, six-month, variable-rate collateralised loan tenders, as well as secondary market government securities purchases (MNB 2008). The range of eligible collateral was also expanded and made more similar to the set of instruments applied by the ECB.

Polish commercial banks also suffered from limited access to financing currency positions due to the turmoil in international financial markets. Therefore, the Polish National Bank introduced the so-called Confidence Pact in October 2008 to (1) enable banks to obtain financing in the zloty with 7-day and 3-month maturity repo transactions, (2) enable banks to obtain foreign currency financing through FX swaps (USD/PLN, EUR/PLN and CHF/PLN after November) with 7-day and 3-month maturities, and (3) extend the list of securities that were acceptable in transactions with the NBP (NBP 2009). A $20.6 billion IMF Flexible Credit Line was provided for Poland in May 2009 for a one year period, but it was not used (IMF 2009, NBP 2010).

The Czech National Bank also applied reverse 2-week repos and foreign exchange swaps (3-month CZK/EUR) as extraordinary operations to increase liquidity in the secondary government bond market and other channels for banks. However, Czech domestic short-term interest rates were lower than the corresponding rates in the euro-area for most of 2008, as was the case in the previous three years, until euro interest rates fell sharply below Czech rates in the second half of the year. The Czech Republic adopted the role of a “safe haven” in the first half of 2008, but a rapid outflow of short-term investments followed (CNB 2009).

Inflationary pressure eased due to declines in commodity prices; therefore, most central banks with inflation targets (the Bank of England and The Swedish National Bank) decreased their policy interest rates in the fourth quarter of 2008 in response to the weakening economic outlook and the intensification of the global financial crisis. However, the Czech, Hungarian and Polish national banks were only able to decrease their policy rates in November and December, after gaining liquidity through official channels in October.

The experiences of the liquidity disruptions in 2008 are reflected in both the concepts of the new capital and liquidity adequacy regulations in Basel III (Ács 2011) and the *Global liquidity – concept, measurement and policy implications report* of the BIS (2011). The latter clearly states that the role of official liquidity is inevitable when private (market and funding) liquidity declines to an extreme level: central banks are able to provide liquidity in domestic currency, however foreign currency can only be provided through foreign exchange reserves, swap lines between central banks, or dedicated facilities such as IMF programmes.

In summary, this section indicates that foreign exchange markets and foreign currency liquidity play fundamental roles in the selected countries and indirectly and directly affect the government bond market. A Maastricht-type convergence seems to have disappeared between capital markets during the extreme days of 2008, underscoring the relevance of the first research question. The swap lines and collaboration between central banks proved to be essential (including on the level of FED-ECB relations, not only between ECB and CNB-MNB-PNB), but it is necessary to study the differences between ordinary and extraordinary periods in capital markets – focusing on the remarkable forms of collective behaviour.

4. Methodology

To demonstrate the existence of collective behaviours between markets on extreme trading days, it is first necessary to reject the efficiency of the selected markets. To meet the efficiency requirements put forth by Fama (1970), markets have to behave as a random walk describes them – returns should be normally distributed (Jarque-Berra test), without autocorrelation (Ljung-Box test) or heteroscedasticity (ARCH LM test), and should be stationery (ADF test) (Wong and Li 2010, Tsay 2005, Lütkepohl 2004). The rejection of market efficiency allows us to estimate contagions through the use of dynamic conditional correlation after ruling out heteroscedasticity with GARCH-models, following Cappiello et al. (2006).

Time series are generally biased by autocorrelation and heteroscedasticity because of the fat tails of the return distributions and volatility clustering. The different versions of Bollerslev's (1986) Generalised Autoregression and Heteroscedasticity (GARCH) models are widely used methods to provide homoscedastic, standardised residuals. The Asymmetric Power GARCH (APARCH)[6] model (4) developed by Ding et al. (1993) may be the most powerful tool to address the heteroscedasticity bias that results from the asymmetric, fat-tailed assumptions of the distribution:

$$\sigma_t^\delta = \omega + \sum_{i=1}^{p} a_i \left(\left|\varepsilon_{t-1}\right| - \gamma_i \varepsilon_{t-1}\right)^\delta + \sum_{j=1}^{q} \beta_j \sigma_{t-j}^\delta , \tag{4}$$

where ω is a constant term, α denotes the impact of news, $-1 < \gamma_i < 1$ is responsible for the asymmetry function, β is the level of volatility persistence, and $\delta > 0$ provides nonlinearity. The parameters of APARCH have to be defined: "p" and "q" determine the lag numbers of the residuals and volatility, while "o" is a non-negative scalar integer representing the number of asymmetric innovations. A further advantage of the APARCH model is its flexibility – it is simple to convert it to the GJR GARCH and TARCH models and the basic GARCH form. The lag length was optimised on a 1-to-4 scale and selected according to the estimation's Akaike Information Criteria (AIC).

As Forbes and Rigobon (2002) suggest, ordinary cross-correlation is not a suitable tool for specifying the common movement of markets because of heteroscedasticity. Cointegration is also ruled out because it is better to analyse long-term processes; hence, BEKK-GARCH or DCC-GARCH could be adequate solutions following the APARCH step.

This study applies DCC-GARCH[7], following Engle (2002), to analyse the daily common movements of the selected markets. Cross-market correlation is compared using the Ansari-Bradley test because this variance test is not based on the assumption of a normal distribution – as is the case for the widely used t-test. After the identification of common market movements, it is necessary to separate them on the basis of the hub return's extremity or normality.

How can we separate the "extreme" and "ordinary"? Jentsch et al. (2006) defined extreme events[8] by their impact and probability – hence,

---

[6] The estimation based on the UCSD toolbox, developed by Kevin Sheppard: http://www.kevinsheppard.com/wiki/UCSD_GARCH

[7] The estimation based on the Oxford MFE toolbox, developed by Kevin Sheppard: http://www.kevinsheppard.com/wiki/MFE_Toolbox

[8] Definition: *Extreme event* (4) is a $w_x \in W$ event for a W stochastic variable with a $w_x >> w_n$ or $w_x << w_n$ significantly higher impact than the expected in

we have to find a suitable threshold or milestone to form both groups. There are multiple solutions (see Campbell et al., 2002), but this study focus on the fatness of the tails; therefore, it is necessary to separate the empirical distribution by fitting a theoretical normal distribution to it. Therefore, it is reasonable to define extreme returns on the basis of the extreme event definition – that is, "shocks" were the product of the transition from the normal to the extreme return subset.

Definition: *Extreme return* (5) is the extreme change of the m_j market on the fat tails of the r^{m_j} return's probability distribution. This event is related to the skewness of the distribution, while their probability and value differ starkly from the $E(r)$ expected.

$$r_x >> E(r) \text{ or } E(r) >> r_x \text{ where } p_{r_x} << p_{E(r)} \tag{5}$$

Definition: *Normal returns* (6) fit well on the projected theoretical normal distribution – therefore, they are denoted in the study variable r_n.

Definition: *Capital market shock* (7) means the $r_{n/x}$ transition of the return from the r_n normal subset to the r_x extreme subset. The $r_{n/x} \neq 0$ existence of this transition defines both subsets (6), while the totally normal distributed return indicates an $r_{n/x} = 0$ efficient market (7):

$$r_{n/x}^{m_i} \neq 0 \rightarrow r^{m_i} = \begin{cases} r_n^{m_i} \\ r_x^{m_i} \end{cases} \tag{6}$$

$$r_{n/x}^{m_i} = 0 \rightarrow r^{m_i} = r_n^{m_i}. \tag{7}$$

The entire time series can be divided (8) into extreme and normal subsets according to the above definitions:

---

a limited time and space with a $p(w_x) << p(w_n)$ significantly lower probability than the expected, providing a uniqueness (Jentsch et al. 2006).

$$r\begin{cases} r_x \begin{cases} r_x^+ : r_{empirical,l} > r_{theoretical_{normal},l} \\ r_x^- : r_{empirical,i} < r_{theoretical_{normal},i} \end{cases} \\ r_n : r_{theoretical_{normal},i} < r_{empirical,k} < r_{theoretical_{normal},l} \end{cases} \tag{8}$$

where $r_{empirical,i}$ is the i th element of the empirical distribution and the $r_{theoretical_{normal},i}$ denotes the projected normal distribution, $i < k < l$.

Relying on the definition of QQ plots by Deutsch (2002, 690–691), the above separation can be expressed in the following way (9):

$$\begin{aligned} & X_i = \phi_1^{-1}(P_i) = \phi_1^{-1}\left(\frac{1}{T}\right) \text{ for all } i < T \text{, therefore,} \\ & r_n \approx \mu_2 + \sigma_2 X_i, \\ & r_x^+ > \mu_2 + \sigma_2 X_i, \\ & r_x^- < \mu_2 + \sigma_2 X_i, \end{aligned} \tag{9}$$

where X_i denotes the theoretical empirical standard normal distribution, which is represented in the QQ plot by a line with $\mu_2 + \sigma_2 X_i$ slope.

Contagions, divergences and interdependences initiated by one market's extreme days have to be detected for 10 inter-market correlations (6 for currencies). First, it is necessary to decide between interdependence (nonsignificant changes in correlations) and significant correlation changes (such as divergence and contagion) – this could be expressed by the overall weight of significantly different correlations (10):

$$\frac{\sum\left(S_{m_1m_2}, S_{m_3m_4}, \ldots, S_{m_jm_k}, \ldots, S_{m_{n-1}m_{n-2}}\right)}{N}\begin{cases} >50\%, \text{ where is contagion or divergence} \\ \leq 50\%, \text{ where is interdependence} \end{cases} \tag{10}$$

where $s = \begin{cases} \text{1, when correlations are significant different} \\ \text{0, when correlations are nonsignificant different} \end{cases}$, N denotes the number of involved market pairs. Contagions are characterised by significantly higher correlations and divergences are characterised by significantly lower correlations according to the definitions (11). To select between these two forms, the following algorithm was used:

$$g=\begin{cases}1, if\left(\rho_{na}=\begin{cases}0, if\ s=0\\ \rho_n, if\ s=1\end{cases}<\rho_{xa}=\begin{cases}0, if\ s=0\\ \rho_x, if\ s=1\end{cases}\right)\\ 0, if\left(\rho_{na}=\begin{cases}0, if\ s=0\\ \rho_n, if\ s=1\end{cases}\geq\rho_{xa}=\begin{cases}0, if\ s=0\\ \rho_x, if\ s=1\end{cases}\right)\end{cases},$$

Than

$$\frac{\sum\left(g_{m_1m_2}, g_{m_1m_3},\ldots,g_{m_jm_k},\ldots,g_{m_{n-1}m_n}\right)}{N}\begin{cases}>50\%, \text{ where is contagion}\\ \leq 50\%, \text{ where is divergence}\end{cases} \tag{11}$$

Thus the contagion was expressed by weighting against the entire set of correlations, which is a strict rule.

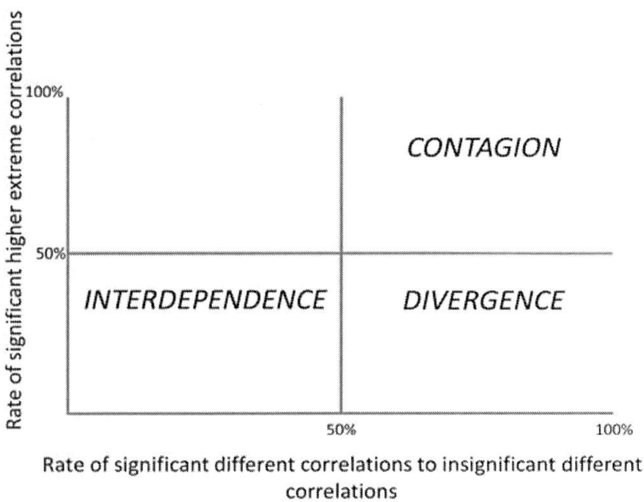

Fig. 9-1 Mapping the difference between contagion and interdependence
Source: Author's calculations

This approach (Figure 9-1) regards market developments in terms of whether they would be signs of shock or contagion. Therefore, a contagiousness ranking could be defined between the three CEE, US and euro zone markets, where markets could be scored according to the number of correlations divided into significantly different parts, and the extreme correlation should be higher on average. The results can be easily visualised in the following way: the "x" axis depicts the rate of significantly different and non-different correlations, while the "y" axis depicts the number of observable correlations, where extreme values are higher than normal.

Although the need for monetary collaboration became obvious in light of the events of 2008, it was necessary to define the patterns that require monetary policy to be conducted with caution. The above methodology can be used not only to test for market efficiency (one of the presumptions of pre-crisis monetary policy), but we are also able to separate the days when this efficiency was most biased (e.g., trading days with extreme returns), as well as the dynamics of common market movements and collective behaviour patterns.

5. Results

Our results are structured in the following manner: after the rejection of the classic form of market efficiency, the patterns of extreme price developments and common movements will be analysed. The impacts of the FED and ECB's monetary policies on the sample countries will be analysed using two event windows on the basis of the increasing and decreasing phases of these two important central banks' main refinancing rates.

According to the results in Table 9-1, the lack of a normal distribution and the heteroscedasticity and autocorrelation of the time series ruled out the classical form of market efficiency. These properties suggest volatility clustering and more frequent extreme jumps in the first differentials of bond market yields, currency rates and stock market indices.

High kurtosis (exceeding the level of 3) could be interpreted as a clear sign of fat tailness and extreme changes, which occurs with enormous magnitude in the bond markets – in contrast to the stock and currency markets with their moderate kurtoses. This result is remarkable, considering that changes in the 3-month yield are primarily affected by monetary policy and changes in international liquidity, while the unregulated stock markets and free-floating currencies seemed to be smoother. The observed heteroscedasticity underlines the appropriateness of employing various GARCH models before estimating the correlations.

As the results in Table 9-2 suggest, heteroscedasticity was ruled out in all of the cases – consequently, bond markets required the highest lag number and the application of the developed GARCH model, while the stock and currency markets were less difficult. Volatility persistence seemed to be an important factor as the close-to-one level of the β coefficient suggests. Market participants and central banks were forced to operate in a market where volatility was self-enhancing.

Patterns of the common market movements differ between market types. Figures 9-2 to 9-5 illustrate the dynamic conditional correlation fluctuations.

Table 9-1 Statistics on market efficiency

Analysed markets	Skewness	Kurtosis	Normal distribution (Jarque-Bera)	Stationarity (ADF-test) 1 lag			Heteroscedasticity (ARCH-LM) 2 lag		Autocorrelation (Ljung-Box) 6 lag	
			p	t statistic		critical value	p		p	
US 3M	0.23	70.0669	0.001	-55.462	*	-1.9416	0		0	
EURO 3M	-0.02	42.0711	0.001	-51.2232	*	-1.9416	0		0.2245	***
HU 3M	1.3047	85.5834	0.001	-50.2077	*	-1.9416	0		0.8346	***
CZ 3M	-3.9396	63.4792	0.001	-46.9896	*	-1.9416	0.846	**	0.0033	
PL 3M	-0.7997	37.5076	0.001	-44.1657	*	-1.9416	0.0334		0	
US 10Y	-0.2763	8.4496	0.001	-52.3948	*	-1.9416	0		0.0188	
EURO 10Y	0.0321	4.96	0.001	-46.9331	*	-1.9416	0		0.0016	
HU 10Y	0.3541	14.6869	0.001	-47.6824	*	-1.9416	0		0.0171	
CZ 10Y	-1.6999	63.9912	0.001	-49.1197	*	-1.9416	0		0.3756	***
PL 10Y	0.6234	16.2843	0.001	-42.2279	*	-1.9416	0		0	
DJI	0.1068	12.2829	0.001	-55.5017	*	-1.9416	0		0	
DAX	0.107	8.2694	0.001	-52.2590	*	-1.9416	0		0.0276	
BUX	-0.093	9.9225	0.001	-47.6622	*	-1.9416	0		0.0178	
PX	-0.5618	17.8663	0.001	-46.4961	*	-1.9416	0		0.0003	
WIG	-0.2971	6.2382	0.001	-46.3625	*	-1.9416	0		0.0002	
EUR/USD	-0.1148	5.2043	0.001	-49.7133	*	-1.9416	0		0.8173	***
HUF/USD	-0.476	7.275	0.001	-50.6851	*	-1.9416	0		0.464	***
CZK/USD	-0.2709	5,5867	0.001	-48.0621	*	-1.9416	0		0.0573	***
PLN/USD	-0.1601	8.5734	0.001	-50.0457	*	-1.9416	0		0.9433	***
*: stationary time series; **: homoscedasticity; ***: lack of autocorrelation										

Source: Author's calculations

Table 9-2 Fitting GARCH model

analyzed markets	AIC	GARCH model	parameters																residuals
																			ARCH-LM
US 3M	2.4777	aparch221	0.0105	ω	0.1925	$\alpha(1)$	0.0236	$\alpha(2)$	-0.626	$\gamma(1)$	0.9995	$\gamma(2)$	0.7836	$\beta(1)$	2.0406	δ			0*
EUR 3M	1.6261	aparch112	0.0210	ω	0.1985	$\alpha(1)$	-0.241	$\gamma(1)$	0.2612	$\beta(1)$	0.5401	$\beta(2)$	2.1090	δ					0*
HU 3M	1.3282	aparch222	0.2087	ω	0.2031	$\alpha(1)$	0.2864	$\alpha(2)$	0.3180	$\gamma(1)$	-0.325	$\gamma(2)$	0.0000	$\beta(1)$	0.5103	$\beta(2)$	0.7890	δ	0*
CZ 3M	1.2870	aparch111	0.0547	ω	0.0157	$\alpha(1)$	-0.999	$\gamma(1)$	0.9371	$\beta(1)$	0.4887	δ							0*
PL 3M	0.7049	aparch112	0.1502	ω	0.3115	$\alpha(1)$	-0.291	$\gamma(1)$	0.1940	$\beta(1)$	0.3894	$\beta(2)$	0.6995	δ					0*
US 10Y	1.8623	gjr111	0.0055	ω	0.0173	$\alpha(1)$	0.0360	$\gamma(1)$	0.9639	$\beta(1)$									0*
EUR 10Y	1.5155	gjr111	0.0036	ω	0.0115	$\alpha(1)$	0.0403	$\gamma(1)$	0.9666	$\beta(1)$									0*
HU 10Y	1.5723	aparch112	0.0836	ω	0.2116	$\alpha(1)$	0.2014	$\gamma(1)$	0.2997	$\beta(1)$	0.4807	$\beta(2)$	1.4632	δ					0*
CZ 10Y	1.4797	aparch112	0.5358	ω	0.0056	$\alpha(1)$	0.9994	$\gamma(1)$	0.0502	$\beta(1)$	0.4051	$\beta(2)$	3.9999	δ					0*
PL 10Y	0.9395	garch23	0.0001	ω	0.2796	$\alpha(1)$	0.0000	$\alpha(2)$	0.2645	$\beta(1)$	0.0807	$\beta(2)$	0.3750	$\beta(3)$					0*
DJI	1.3527	aparch111	0.0153	ω	0.0522	$\alpha(1)$	-1.000	$\gamma(1)$	0.9314	$\beta(1)$	1.3619	δ							0*
DAX	1.6331	tarch111	0.0264	ω	0.0000	$\alpha(1)$	0.1346	$\gamma(1)$	0.9293	$\beta(1)$									0*
BUX	1.7794	gjr111	0.0673	ω	0.0551	$\alpha(1)$	0.0681	$\gamma(1)$	0.8845	$\beta(1)$									0*
PX	1.5973	gjr211	0.0663	ω	0.0050	$\alpha(1)$	0.0700	$\alpha(1)$	0.1242	$\gamma(1)$	0.8303	$\beta(1)$							0*
WIG	1.5750	gjr211	0.0243	ω	0.0000	$\alpha(1)$	0.0453	$\alpha(1)$	0.0447	$\gamma(1)$	0.9180	$\beta(1)$							0*
EUR/USD	0.94313129	garch11	0.0023	ω	0.0468	$\alpha(1)$	0.9490	$\beta(1)$											0*
HUF/USD	1.32536592	gjr112	0.0449	ω	0.0548	$\alpha(1)$	0.1098	$\gamma(1)$	0.1467	$\beta(1)$	0.6939	$\beta(2)$							0*
CZK/USD	1.12197521	garch11	0.0036	ω	0.0436	$\alpha(1)$	0.9512	$\beta(1)$											0*
PLN/USD	1.2732017	aparch112	0.0240	ω	0.1140	$\alpha(1)$	-0.308	$\gamma(1)$	0.3790	$\beta(1)$	0.4950	$\beta(2)$	1.4620	δ					0*

*: no heteroscedasticity

Source: Author's calculations

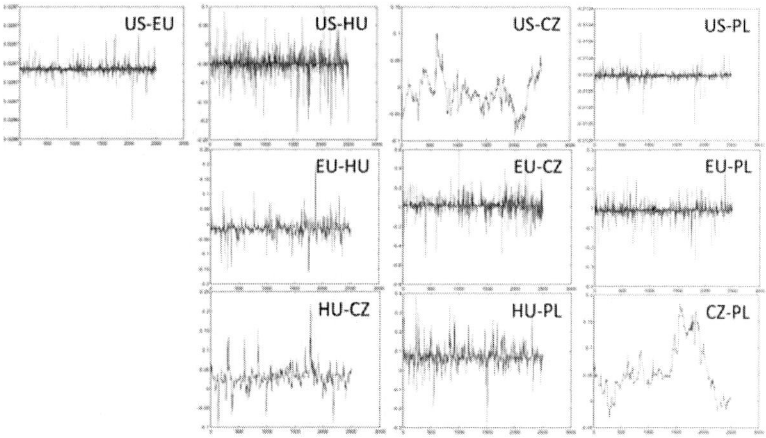

Fig. 9-2 Dynamic conditional correlation between 3-month yields
Source: Author's calculations

Three-month yields exhibit uncorrelated fluctuation, suggesting limited spill-over effects between these maturities in the sample countries. As this is the most liquid maturity and is targeted by monetary policy operations, it is difficult to find any evidence of interdependence or time-variance.

The appearance of the crisis after 2007 had more serious impacts on the 10-year yields, as Figure 9-3 presents. The pre-crisis weak correlation was neutralised by the crisis, which is our first piece of evidence to prove Bearce's (2002) divergence phenomenon. This result is considerable on the basis of the bond market convergence requirements in the Maastricht criteria – Central-East European countries' euro adoption was weakly priced in the pre-crisis era and totally ruled out during the crisis.

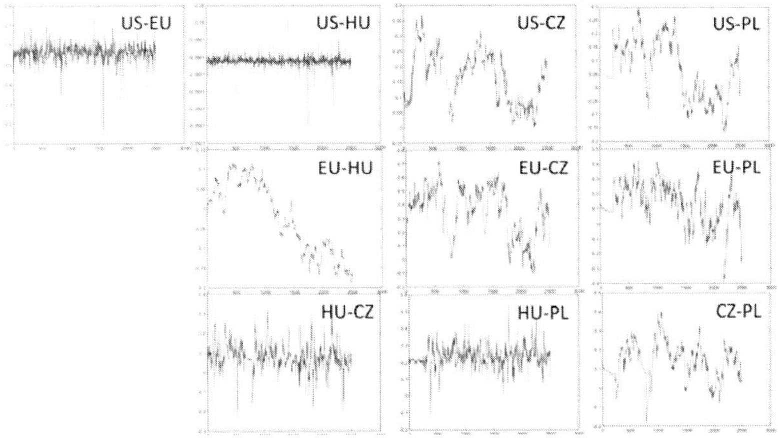

Fig. 9-3 Dynamic conditional correlation between 10-year yields
Source: Author's calculations

There was a correlation between stock markets, as Figure 9-4 suggests. Stronger economic ties between German and emerging European countries implied high correlation compared to the weaker correlation between the US and the other markets in the sample. The strength of the common movement increased dramatically in the second half of the decade – thus, it was already high before the crisis appeared; which is similar to the results obtained by Obstfeld and Taylor (2002) and Goetzman et al. (2005).

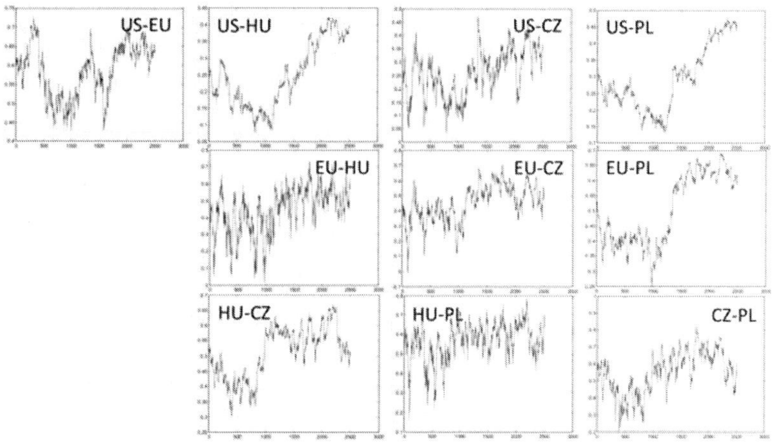

Fig. 9-4 Dynamic conditional correlation between stock markets
Source: Author's calculations

Contrary to the observed weak 10-year bond market convergence, the selected currencies exhibit strong correlation (see Figure 9-5), as shown by Stávárek (2009) and Babetskaia-Kukharchuk et al. (2008). This strong common movement is surrounded by several declines, suggesting there are atypical days when emerging currencies have to follow their own course.

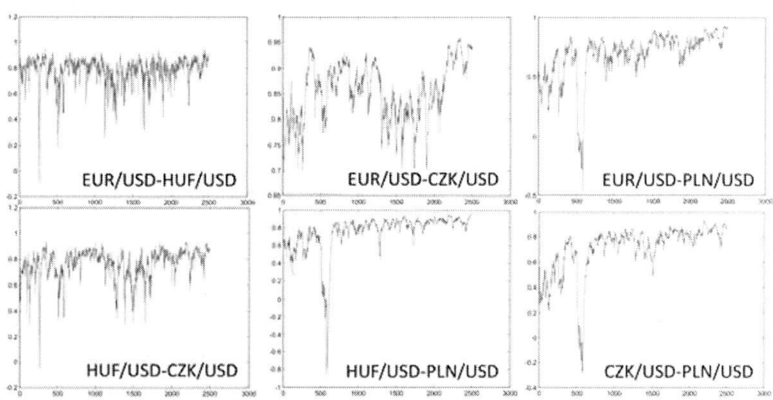

Fig. 9-5 Dynamic conditional correlation between currency pairs
Source: Author's calculations

Table 9-3 Properties of extreme trading days

analyzed markets		US 3M	EUR 3M	HU 3M	CZ 3M	PL 3M	US 10Y	EUR 10Y	HU 10Y	CZ 10Y	PL 10Y
extreme "+"	No	36	60	73	23	60	100	103	91	33	85
	%	*1,44%*	*2,40%*	*2,92%*	*0,92%*	*2,40%*	*4,00%*	*4,12%*	*3,64%*	*1,32%*	*3,40%*
	r	44,79	6,201	3,054	2,278	1,192	3,235	2,144	2,559	2,628	1,57
ordinary		2431	2395	2399	2457	2356	2335	2334	2357	2439	2344
extreme "-"	No	36	48	31	23	87	68	66	55	31	74
	%	*1,44%*	*1,92%*	*1,24%*	*0,92%*	*3,48%*	*2,72%*	*2,64%*	*2,20%*	*1,24%*	*2,96%*
	r	-43,27	-6,694	-3,164	-2,028	-1,143	-3,569	-2,433	-2,895	-2,647	-1,616
kurtosis	e	70,0669	42,0711	85,5834	63,4792	37,5076	8,4496	4,9600	14,6869	63,9912	16,2843
	n	15,2899	7,7186	6,4723	6,1227	4,7224	2,6959	2,6747	3,7812	4,3682	3,4725
analyzed markets		DJI	DAX	BUX	PX	WIG	EUR/USD	HUF/USD	CZK/USD	PLN/USD	
extreme "+"	No	70	47	36	18	67	29	34	29	39	
	%	*2,80%*	*1,88%*	*1,44%*	*0,72%*	*2,68%*	0,0115954	0,0135946	0,0115954	0,0155938	
	r	2,395	3,33	3,724	4,403	2,599	1,555	2,309	1,966	2,227	
ordinary		2355	2351	2409	2420	2332	2395	2353	2367	2359	
extreme "-"	No	78	105	58	65	104	77	114	105	103	
	%	*3,12%*	*4,19%*	*2,32%*	*2,60%*	*4,16%*	0,0307877	0,0455818	0,0419832	0,0411835	
	r	-2,334	-2,742	-3,284	-2,951	-2,212	-1,239	-1,738	-1,401	-1,748	
kurtosis	e	12,2829	8,2694	9,9225	17,8663	6,2382	5,2043	7,2750	5,5867	8,5734	
	n	3,2971	3,0827	3,0188	3,5862	2,8038	2,7427	2,8684	2,7738	2,8646	

Notes: No: numbers of days; %: ratio of extreme days to the entire sample; r: value of the first extreme return; e: endtire sample; n: normal days

Source: Author's calculations

According to these results, we are able make the following statements: 3-month yields and currency rates fluctuated around well-defined correlation levels, while the 10-year yields had a decreasing trend and stock markets had an increasing trend approaching the crisis era.

After the identification of the correlation curves and outliers, it is necessary to define "normal" and "extreme" in the sample markets days.

Trading days with extreme fluctuations were placed in the "extreme subset", as they do not fit the theoretical normal distribution in both of the tails of the empirical distribution (Table 9-3). These extreme days met the definition of extreme events: their mass is insignificant in the entire sample, but they occur in the tails with low probability and high values. The validity of this method was verified by comparing the kurtosis of the entire sample to the subset of “normal” or ordinary days – the observed convergence to 3 was quite impressive.

Extreme jumps were distributed almost symmetrically in the case of the 3M market, while the first extreme return had the highest magnitude. Extreme yield increases characterised the 10Y market; this asymmetry is underlined not only by the number of days but also by the smaller first extreme return. Asymmetry characterised both the stock and currency markets on their negative side – the increased mass of extreme drops is clear in the case of the stock indices, but the currencies were characterised by extreme days primarily after the strength of the currencies had improved substantially.

After the introduction of time-varying correlation patterns and extreme change properties, it is necessary to make a brief comparison between “subsample A” (increases in the main refinance rates of the ECB and FED) and “subsample B” (decreasing interest rate period) for all of the markets.

Considering the shorter period of the ECB refinancing-rate changes – a 34 month increase and 36 month decrease compared to the FED’s 42 and 47 months – there are two common phenomena (Table 9-4). First, the 3-month yields generally declined when the central banks reduced the main refinancing rates – implying some type of implicit spill-over effect between monetary policies. However the decline in 10-year yields was not a broad success, Central-East European national banks had to contend with increasing long term yields in contrast to the general decline in the euro zone and the US. The shapes of the yield curves became steeper in the entire sample, but they were the sharpest in the centre. A maturity transformation in a banking system requires this positive shape of the 10Y-3M spread under constant price level expectations. All of the currencies appreciated against the USD with increased volatility in the interval “B”, while the stock indices were generally devalued according to ECB’s monetary decisions – the FED windows produced a different outcome.

Table 9-4 Market differences under increasing and decreasing interest rates

central bank		ECB					FED				
markets		US	EUR	HU	CZ	PL	US	EUR	HU	CZ	PL
3M	mean "A"	3.809897181	3.5003	7.5218	3.0487	4.8834	3.834701958	2.6703	7.6137	2.3492	4.9094
	variance "A"	*2.061284042*	*0.361*	*0.7361*	*0.5813*	*0.8121*	*1.521848281*	*0.519*	*2.2822*	*0.1307*	*0.9910*
	mean "B"	0.125510778	0.7093	6.9252	1.8194	4.2992	0.761449082	1.6498	7.2524	2.4266	4.7550
	variance "B"	*0.012027703*	*0.2983*	*3.5459*	*0.7010*	*0.5364*	*1.325980386*	*2.3883*	*2.8827*	*1.4100*	*0.9820*
10Y	mean "A"	4.443556107	4.0302	7.2212	4.2229	5.5631	4.533348103	3.7753	7.0318	3.9982	5.5258
	variance "A"	*0.23584287*	*0.0954*	*0.3768*	*0.2221*	*0.1818*	*0.109197037*	*0.1401*	*0.4347*	*0.3113*	*0.4810*
	mean "B"	3.216767531	3.0693	8.0788	4.2510	6.0088	3.434390821	3.3910	7.9372	4.3725	5.9969
	variance "B"	*0.1834048*	*0.1264*	*1.6655*	*0.2821*	*0.0931*	*0.27888403*	*0.3550*	*1.3788*	*0.2493*	*0.0862*
10Y-3M spread	mean "A"	0.633658926	0.5298	-0.3007	1.1743	0.6798	0.698646144	1.1051	-0.5818	1.6490	0.6164
	variance "A"	*1.044591812*	*0.1770*	*0.4704*	*0.1673*	*0.3369*	*1.017479763*	*0.3019*	*1.1300*	*0.1617*	*0.4262*
	mean "B"	3.091256753	2.3600	1.1537	2.4316	1.7095	2.672941739	1.7412	0.6848	1.9459	1.2418
	variance "B"	*0.180085116*	*0.2867*	*0.9540*	*0.5249*	*0.5545*	*0.750074321*	*1.1571*	*1.2308*	*0.9578*	*0.9718*
currency	mean "A"		1.3660	0.0054	0.0506	0.3692		1.2641	0.0050	0.0430	0.3142
	variance "A"		*0.0138*	*0.0000*	*0.0001*	*0.0028*		*0.0030*	*0.0000*	*0.0000*	*0.0007*
	mean "B"		1.3664	0.0050	0.0537	0.3352		1.4013	0.0053	0.0550	0.3609
	variance "B"		*0.0052*	*0.0000*	*0.0000*	*0.0006*		*0.0081*	*0.0000*	*0.0000*	*0.0025*
stock	mean "A"	12164	6632	23516	1588	48793	11264	5473	20459	1366	38962
	mean "B"	10206	5866	19493	1085	38942	10862	6196	20624	1236	41919

Source: Author's calculations

Dividing our samples according to the interest rate decisions of the ECB and FED was useful to separate the pre-crisis and crisis eras and to evaluate possible spill-overs to the emerging European sample, but it is difficult to identify any difference between the two approaches.

The increasing and decreasing periods defined by the FED's main refinancing rate seemed a more appropriate tool to divide the sample markets' common movements into two significantly different components – at least 67% of the market pairs had significantly different correlations in this case (Table 9-5). This result is remarkable because 3M markets seemed to be uncorrelated before the crisis in addition to the consistently high common movements in the currency market. The results concerning the FED's leadership role could be biased by the different length of the two intervals.

Table 9-5 Significant differences in the common movement of the sample

central bank		ECB										
markets		US-EU	US-HU	US-CZ	US-PL	EU-HU	EU-CZ	EU-PL	HU-CZ	HU-PL	CZ-PL	%
3M	Significant difference between "A" and "B" periods	0	0	1	1	0	1	1	1	0	1	60%
10Y	Significant difference between "A" and "B" periods	0	0	0	1	1	1	1	0	0	0	40%
currency	Significant difference between "A" and "B" periods					0	0	0	1	0	0	17%
stock market	Significant difference between "A" and "B" periods	0	0	0	0	1	1	1	1	1	1	60%
central bank		FED										
markets		US-EU	US-HU	US-CZ	US-PL	EU-HU	EU-CZ	EU-PL	HU-CZ	HU-PL	CZ-PL	%
3M	Significant difference between "A" and "B" periods	1	1	1	1	1	1	0	0	0	1	70%
10Y	Significant difference between "A" and "B" periods	1	0	1	1	1	1	1	1	0	1	80%
currency	Significant difference between "A" and "B" periods					0	1	1	1	0	1	67%
stock market	Significant difference between "A" and "B" periods	0	1	1	1	1	1	1	1	1	0	80%

Source: Author's calculations

Therefore, it is necessary to study how the common movements differ under the extreme days defined by US and euro-area benchmarks for the entire sample or the upper subsets. Figure 9-6 demonstrates that it is difficult to define collective behaviours during extreme events. The correlation of sample currencies during the strong appreciation of the euro indicated divergence, meaning a weaker correlation as opposed to the general strong one. However, contagions were identified using the shorter ECB subsets, while the broader FED subsets indicated only interdependence. 3M markets generally exhibit interdependence, as do those of the 10Y, where only the entire sample-based EUR10Y indicated divergence, which means that weak correlations occur when the yield curve decreases substantially, e.g. during monetary expansion, ruling out the possibility of liquidity providing monetary spill-overs between central and emerging countries. During severe decline in the stock markets, only the entire-sample based on the Dow Jones Industrial Average was able to identify contagions – DAX and various subsets indicated only interdependence. The widely accepted hypothesis of trade-relation-based common movements was rejected because of this result and because the stock markets are not consistently interconnected.

Figure 9-7 presents divergences between currencies when the euro depreciated substantially against the USD according to the ECB subsets; sample currencies with weakened correlations are able to depreciate more extensively or remain stable. The 3M markets remained interdependent, but the US10Y market in the entire subset was able to indicate divergence when it increased substantially, meaning loosening common movements under monetary tightening and scarce liquidity. The entire sample based Dow Jones Industrial Average remained able to identify contagions only when the index increased substantially, and "A" periods present a nearly identical picture.

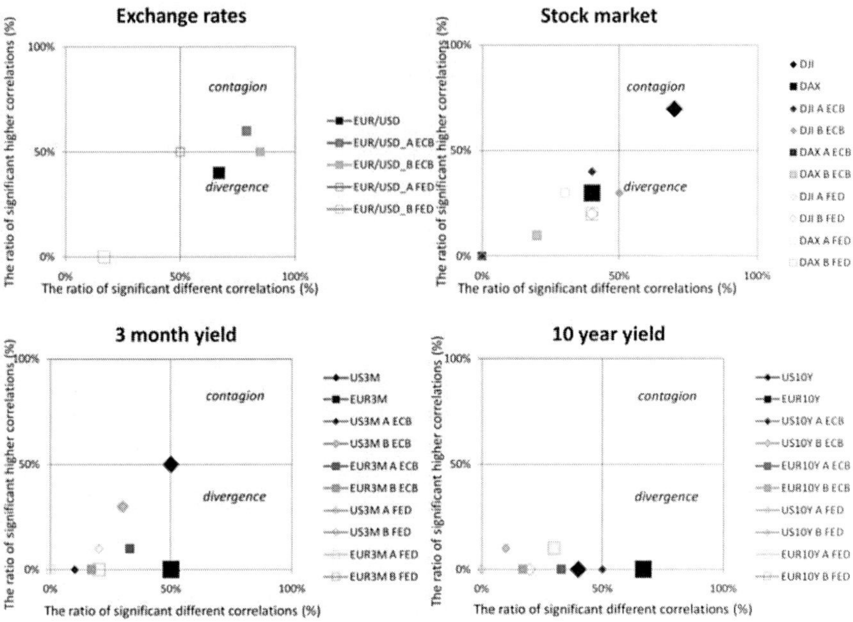

Fig. 9-6 Map of possible contagions, divergence and interdependence, comparing ordinary and negative extreme changes
Source: Author's calculations

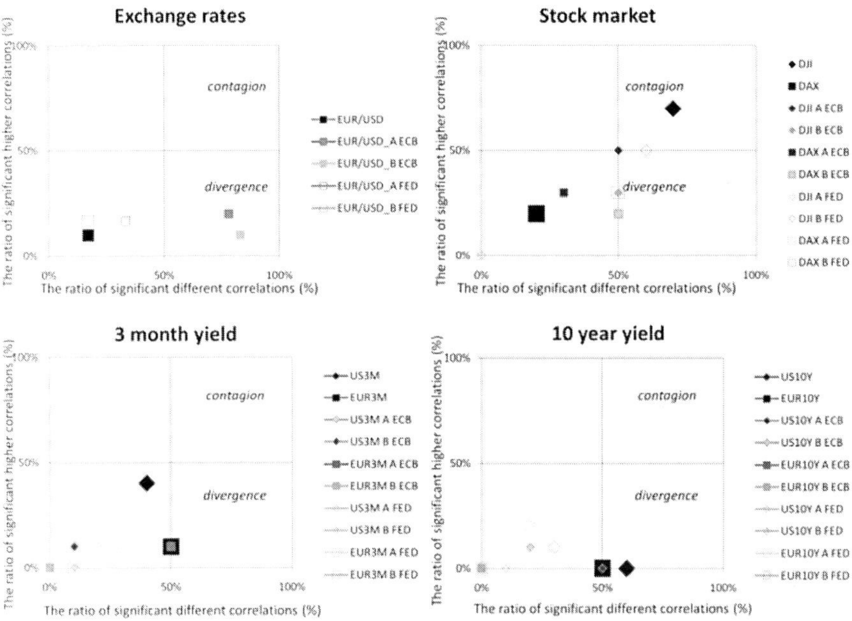

Fig. 9-7 Map of possible contagions, divergence and interdependence, comparing ordinary and positive extreme changes
Source: Author's calculations

These results suggest that thinking of collective behaviour is necessary: cross market-correlation is able to change on the days when one market undergoes extreme changes, but it is difficult to identify such differences in subsets, such as those representing the pre-crisis and crisis periods.

6. Conclusion

The operational autonomy of monetary policy is narrow in the selected Central-East European countries – and the range of decisions is even narrower under turbulent market conditions. The experiences during the crisis in the fall of 2008 underlined that even the former "safe haven" of the Czech Republic required FX liquidity trough swap lines, and the European Central Bank, the Federal Reserve and the Swiss National Bank faced the same problem on a larger scale.

This paper applied a diagnostic model to explore the phenomena that occur in and between markets on extreme trading days. After the rejection of the efficient markets hypothesis, the dynamic, conditional correlations of the markets were analysed under extreme and ordinary trading days to identify the particular forms of collective market behaviours.

Maastricht-type convergence between the selected bond markets was already missing or had disappeared during 2008 due to the crisis, while free-floating currency markets tended to move together without any explicit monetary policy goal. Stock markets, as a control variable, tended to move together in a different way – correlation increased shortly before and during the crisis. The selected markets moved together in a significantly different way than before the FED began to reduce its prime rate, in conjunction with the ECB's decision to ease liquidity conditions without any change in the policy rate. Free-floating exchange rates exhibited that rates were strongly correlated with each other, but these trends were also significantly different under the tight and expansionary monetary policies of the ECB and FED. Contagions and divergence both characterised the currency markets; therefore, investors have to be cautious regarding exchange rate risk. Trade relations characterised stock market correlations well, but contagion between stock markets was only indicated by the Dow Jones Industrial index.

Yield curves' long maturities generally reflected long run risk premiums and inflation expectations. Individual national currencies make it difficult to adapt to downward changes in the principle currencies' yields – even real economies are tied strongly together through trade, corporate ownership and the banking sector, and the primary goal of monetary policy is the same and institutions are harmonised. The Czech, Hungarian and Polish bond and currency markets generally had to contend with loosening connections during difficult times: shocks affected them to a greater extent, while monetary activism was poorly implemented. The monetary autonomy of these countries will not decline after they adopt the euro in the future because this autonomy is also narrow in the present, and its maintenance requires expensive programmes and collaborations. Inflation-targeting monetary policy in the CEE was able to reduce inflation in all of the sample countries, but it was far from effective in reducing the probability of a banking crisis or bond market noise – due to its inability to influence the common lending channels between the euro zone headquarters and CEE subsidiaries of the regional banks. Therefore, we can conclude that inflation-targeting monetary policies have to be maintained in the region, but the free movement of capital and financial innovations requires that central banks increase their institutional capacities both in terms of financial stabilisation and their regional cooperation.

Acknowledgement

The study was created within the framework of project No. TÁMOP-4.2.1/B-09/1/KONV-2010-0005 "Establishment of a Research University Centre of Excellence at the University of Szeged" supported by the European Union and co-financed by the European Social Fund.

References

Ács, A. 2011. "A likviditás dimenziói." [Dimensions of Liquidity] *Hitelintézeti Szemle* 10, 3: 241–261.

Árvai, Zs. and Driessen, K. and Ötker-Robe, I. 2009. "Regional Financial Interlinkages and Financial Contagion Within Europe." IMF Working Paper.

BoE. 2000. "The transmission mechanism of monetary policy." Bank of England, the Monetary Policy Committee.

Babetskaia-Kukharchuk O. and Babetskii I. and Podpiera J. 2008. "Convergence in exchange rates: market's view on CE-4 joining EMU." *Applied Economics Letters* 15: 385–390.

Barabási, A-L. and Albert, R. 1999. "Emergence of Scaling in Random Networks." *Science* 286: 509.

Bean, C. and Paustian, A. and Taylor, T. 2010. "Monetary policy after the Fall." Paper presented at Federal Reserve Bank of Kansas City Annual Conference, Jackson Hole, Wyoming.

Bearce, D. 2002. *Monetary Divergence: Domestic Policy Autonomy in the Post-Breton Woods Era*. Ann Arbor: University of Michigan Press.

Bekaert, G. and Harvey, C. R. and Ng, A. 2005. "Market Integration and Contagion." *Journal of Bussiness* 78, 1: 39–69.

Benedek, G. and Lublóy, Á. and Szenes, M. 2007. "A hálózatelmélet banki alkalmazása" [Application of network theory at commercial banks]. *Közgazdasági Szemle* [Economic Review] 54, 7–8: 682–702.

Berlinger, E. and Michaletzky, M. and Szenes, M. 2011. "A fedezetlen bankközi forintpiac hálózati dinamikájának vizsgálata a likviditási válság előtt és után" [Examination of the network dynamics of the uncovered interbank forint market before the liquidity crisis and after]. *Közgazdasági Szemle* [Economic Review] 58, 3: 229–252.

BIS. 2011. "Global liquidity – concept, measurement and policy implications." *BIS CGFS Publications*, no. 45, November 2011.

Bollerslev, T. 1986. "Generalized autoregressive conditional heteroscedasticity." *Journal of Econometrics* 31, 3: 307–327.

Bonanno, G. and Lillo, F. and Mantegna, R. 2001. "Levels of complexity in financial markets." *Physica A* 299, 1–2: 16–27.

Cappiello, L. and Engle, R. F. and Sheppard, K. 2006. "Asymmetric Dynamics in the Correlations of Global Equity and Bond Returns." *Journal of Financial Econometrics* 4, 4: 537–572.

Campbell, R. and Koedij, K. and Kofman, P. 2002. "Increased Correlation in Bear Markets." *Financial Analysts Journal* 58, 1: 87–94.

CNB. 2009. *Annual Report 2008*. Prague: Czech National Bank.

CZSO. 2011. *Statistical Yearbook of the Czech Republic 2011*. Prague: Czech Statistical Office.

Deutsch H-P. 2002. *Derivatives and Internal Models*. Palgrave.

Ding, Z. and Granger, C. W. J. and Engle, R. F. 1993. "A Long Memory Property of Stock Market Returns and a New Model." *Journal of Empirical Finance* 1, 1: 83–106.

ECB. 2009. *Annual Report 2008*. Frankfurt am Main: European Central Bank.

—. 2010. "Monetary policy transmission in the Euro-area, a decade after the introduction of the Euro." *ECB Monthly Bulletin*, May 2010, 85–98.

Engle, R. F. 2002. "Dynamic Conditional Correlation – A Simple Class of Multivariate GARCH Models." *Journal of Business and Economic Statistics* 20, 3: 377–389.

Erdős, P and Rényi, A. 1960. "On the evolution of random graphs", *Publications of the Mathematical Institute of the Hungarian Academy of Sciences* 5: 17–61.

Fama, E. F. 1970. "Efficient Capital Markets: A Review of Theory and Empirical Work." *Journal of Finance* 25, 5: 383–417.

Farkas, B. 2011. "The Central and Eastern European model of capitalism." *Post-Communist Economies* 23, 1: 15–34.

Forbes, J. K. and Rigobon, R. 2002. "No contagion, only interdependence: measuring stock market comovements." *Journal of Finance* 57, 6: 2223–2261.

Goetzmann, W. N. and Li, L. and Rouwenhorst, K. G. 2005. "Long-Term Global Market Correlations." *Journal of Business* 78, 1: 1–28.

GUS. 2011. *Yearbook of Foreign Trade Statistics of Poland 2011*. Warsaw: Glówny Urzad Statyczny.

Hamori, S. and Hamori N. 2010. *Introduction of the Euro and the Monetary Policy of the European Central Bank*. Singapore: World Scientific.

IMF. 2008. "IMF Executive Board Approves €12.3 Billion Stand-By Arrangement for Hungary." IMF Press Release no. 08/275, November 6, 2008.

—. 2009. "IMF Provides Poland $20.6 Billion Credit Line." IMF Survey online, May 6.

Jentsch, V. and Kantz, H. and Albeverio, S. 2006. "Extereme Events: Magic, Mysteries and Challenges." In *Extreme Events in Nature and Society*, edited by Albeverio, S. and Jentsch, V. and Kantz, H. 1–18. Berlin: Springer Verlag.

Kovács, Gy. 2009: "Financial Stability and the Banking System, or the Imbalance of the Intermediary System." *Public Finances* 54, 1: 49–67.

KSH. 2012. *Catalogue 2012*. Budapest: Központi Statisztikai Hivatal.

Lublóy, Á. 2005. "Dominóhatás a magyar bankközi piacon" [Domino Effect in the Hungarian Interbank Market]. *Közgazdasági Szemle* [Economic Review] 52: 377–401.

Lütkepohl, H. and Kratzig, M. 2004. *Applied Time Series Econometrics*. Cambridge: Cambridge University Press.

MNB. 2008. *Annual Report – Business Report and Financial Statements of the Magyar Nemzeti Bank 2008*. Budapest: Magyar Nemzeti Bank.

NBP. 2009. *Annual Report 2008*. Warsaw: National Bank of Poland.

—. 2010. *Annual Report 2009*. Warsaw: National Bank of Poland.

Obstfeld, M. and Taylor, A. M. 2002. "Globalization and Capital Markets. Massachusetts", National Bureau of Economic Research Working Paper 8846.

Obstfeld, M. and Shambaugh, J. C. and Taylor, A. M. 2005. "The Trilemma in History: Tradeoffs Among Exchange Rates, Monetary Policies, and Capital Mobility." *The Review of Economics and Statistics* 87, 3: 423–438.

O'Sullivanm, R. and Tomljanovich, M. 2012. "Inflation Targeting and Financial Market Volatility." *Applied Financial Economics* 2, 7–9: 749–762.

Plümper T. and Troeger V. E. 2008. "Fear of Floating and the External Effects of Currency Unions." *American Journal of Political Science* 32, 3: 656–676.

Stavárek, D. 2009. "Assessment of the Exchange Rate Convergence in Euro-Candidate Countries." *Amfiteatru Economic Journal* 11, 25: 159–180.

Svenson, LEO. 1997. "Inflation forecast targeting: Implementing and monitoring inflation targets." *European Economic Review* 41, 1111–1146.

Tsay, R. S. 2005. *Analysis of Financial Time Series.* Hoboken, New Jersey: John Wiley & Sons, Inc.

Vitali, S. and Glattfelder, J. B. and Battiston, S. 2011. "The network of global corporate control." http://arxiv.org/abs/1107.5728v2

Wong, D. K. T. and Li, K-W. 2010. "Comparing the Performance of Relative Stock Return Differential and Real Exchange Rate in Two Financial Crises." *Applied Financial Economics* 20, 1: 137–150.

World Bank. 2012. Definitions of Contagion. http://go.worldbank.org /JIBDRK3YC0

ADDRESSING THE CRISIS IN GREECE: THE ROLE OF FISCAL POLICY

ANNA VISVIZI

1. Introduction

The crisis in Greece has defined political and academic debates for more than two years. Following the deadlock-marred Greek Parliamentary elections of May 6, 2012, a new wave of political uncertainty spread over developments in the country, with the possibility of Greece exiting the euro zone becoming an ever more tangible reality that was discussed openly around the world. Although the June 17 elections reduced fears of an imminent "Grexit", Greece remains present in mainstream media coverage worldwide, frequently perceived as a litmus test of the euro zone crisis (Visvizi 2012a). Clearly, the crisis in Greece is by no means a linear and simple process. The events concerning Greece that have shaped popular opinion and imagination since late 2009 form a sequence of different yet interrelated, and to some extent overlapping, crises that have beset Greece since 2008. In other words, it is possible to distinguish between the demand crisis and the liquidity crunch (2008–2009) caused by the global financial crisis, the sovereign debt crisis (2010–present) related to a specific course of action taken by the Greek government in Autumn 2009, and the progressing economic recession (2011–?) that resulted from an inappropriate policy-mix implemented by the socialist government under the aegis of the so-called Troika, i.e., representatives of the International Monetary Fund (IMF), the European Central Bank (ECB), and the European Commission since 2010 (Visvizi 2012c).

Although a rich body of literature has emerged in an attempt to offer insights into the correlated exogenous and endogenous causes of the crisis in Greece, a more focused discussion of the empirical pattern of the phases of the crisis in Greece is still largely absent. Specifically, more insight is required on the question of how particular policy instruments employed by the Greek authorities may have influenced/fuelled the subsequent stages of the crisis. Accordingly, the objective of this paper is to focus on the relatively under-researched issue of the role and efficacy of fiscal policy and fiscal policy measures in addressing the crisis in Greece. The major thesis that this paper advances is that the front-loaded fiscal adjustment measures consistent with the introduction of excessive taxation and marginal expenditure reduction constricted economic activity in the country, leading to an exponential rise in unemployment, a dramatic fall in general government revenue, and increased expenditures on social transfers. Moreover, the paper argues with the very popular – yet inaccurate – view according to which tax evasion was and remains the main reason behind shrinking government revenue in Greece, and thus of the uncertain fate of the two loan facilities generously offered to Greece by its international partners.

The argument is structured as follows: In the first section, the background of the €110 billion financial assistance package that Greece received in May 2010 is discussed briefly, and the major qualitative and quantitative performance criteria attached to the assistance programme are outlined. In the next section, the focus of the discussion is directed towards the scope of fiscal adjustment that was proposed and/or implemented in Greece over the period May 2010–June 2012. In what follows, the efficiency and appropriateness of the fiscal consolidation measures implemented in Greece as a means of addressing the crisis are examined. Subsequently, the thorny issue of tax compliance is raised. Conclusions follow.

2. The background of the €110 billion financial assistance package for Greece

A set of endogenous and exogenous variables led Greece to the brink of losing access to financial markets in early 2010. The state of Greece's public finances was deteriorating, the economic forecasts for the country were alarming, the spreads for Greek treasury bills began rising in an uncontrolled manner, and Greece's credit ratings fell to the "close to junk" category. As the outlook for Greece's public finance was deteriorating (see Table 10-1 for more details), in early 2010 the then IMF managing-director, Dominique Strauss-Kahn, suggested an early debt restructuring for Greece, a proposal rejected by the then Prime Minister of Greece, George Papandreou. As time passed and Greece's inability to service its debt became apparent, in March and April 2010, discussions were held at various levels in the EU regarding the means of addressing Greece's insolvency problem. Although the ECB pushed the limits of its prerogatives by repurchasing Greek bonds, and a bailout was not an option, the European Union (EU) did not have a mechanism to assist Greece. Therefore, two alternative methods to approach the crisis in Greece were discussed in the EU. Some EU leaders suggested a strictly European solution whereby the EU member states would offer bilateral loans to Greece. This approach was stymied by a view promoted by Angela Merkel, who argued that the IMF's involvement was needed. The IMF's engagement with a possible future rescue package for Greece offered the promise that conditions would be attached to the rescue loan granted to Greece. These loan conditions would in turn increase the probability that Greek authorities would comply with the terms of the loan and consequently not only repay it but also improve Greek public finances in line with the provisions of the Stability and Growth Pact (Visvizi 2012b).

In May 2010, a financial assistance programme for Greece was agreed on by the Eurogroup and the IMF Board. This unprecedented loan, with a total value of €110 billion, was to be disbursed in twelve tranches over the period 2010–2013. The loan consisted of a €30 billion Stand-by Agreement (SBA) approved by the IMF and €80 billion in bilateral loans granted to Greece by euro zone member states, centrally pooled and managed by the European Commission. The implementation of the programme was to be overseen by the representatives of the Troika. The major objective of the joint EU-IMF €110 billion assistance package was to aid Greece in overcoming its debt crisis, revive growth, and modernise its economy. It was expected that by 2012, Greece would regain its ability to finance its debt. The major quantitative targets of the economic reform programme that the Greek government suggested, included a reduction in the gross government deficit, a gradual reduction in the debt to GDP ratio, and the restoration of economic growth.

In principle, the economic reform programme approved by the Troika in May 2010 was based on fiscal consolidation and fiscal discipline that – coupled with structural reforms – were expected to yield positive outcomes in the form of growth and increased government revenue. The fiscal consolidation measures included in the Memorandum of Understanding (MoU) of May 2010 included front-loaded revenue enhancing measures, i.e., increases in tax rates and a broadening of the tax base, as well as plans for reducing expenditures, including reductions in public investments, the public sector's operating costs and the wage burden. These measures were to be complemented by structural fiscal reforms focusing on tax administration, the reform of the tax collection mechanism, enhanced auditing, simplifying the general tax framework, and combatting tax evasion. The structural reform measures listed in the programme included public administration reform, labour market and wage-negotiation reform, pension reform, healthcare reform, business environment reform, reforms aimed at promoting foreign direct investment and exports, and reforms increasing the levels of absorption of structural and cohesion funds.

Table 10-1 The Greek economy: major macroeconomic & fiscal indicators 2008–2012

	2008	2009	2010	2011	2012 (target/ forecast)
Total revenue					
% GDP	40.7	38.2	39.7	40.9	42.4
in m. of EUR	94,833.0	88,601.0	90,247.0	88,075.0	86,267.50
Total expenditure					
% GDP	50.6	53.8	50.2	50.1	47.7
in m. of EUR	117,963.0	124,646.0	114,106.0	107,769.0	97,050.9
Primary deficit/balance					
% GDP	-4.8	-10.4	-4.7	-2.2	-1
in m. of EUR	-11,193.0	-24,128.0	-10,666.0	-4,664.0	-2,034.6
Overall balance/deficit					
% GDP	-9.8	-15.6	-10.5	-9.2	-7.3
in m. of EUR	-23,130.0	-36,045.0	-23,859.00	-19,694.00	-14,852.6
Gross government debt					
% GDP	113	129.4	145	165.3	162.1
in m. of EUR	263,284.0	299,685.0	329,535.0	355,617.0	329,810.30
GDP					
growth rate	-0.5	-3.6	-3.7	-6.9	-6.0*
in m. of EUR	232,920.3	231,642.0	227,317.9	215,088.2	202,182.9*
Current account balance					
% GDP	-17.9	-14.3	-12.3	-11.3	-7.8
in m. of EUR	-41,692.7	-33,124.8	-27,959.1	-24,304.9	-15,869.9
Unemployment					
in %	7.7	9.5	12.6	17.7	19.7
Inflation rate (HICP)					
in %	4.2	1.3	4.7	3.1	-0.5

Source: Eurostat; forecasts for 2012 from: European Commission (2012b); * from Alpha Bank (2012)

Overall, the objectives set in the MoU followed the traditional recipe of fiscal consolidation that the IMF tends to offer as a lender of last resort. In this sense, these objectives delineated a routine means of assisting a country in the restoration of its shattered public finance. In the case of Greece, however, as insiders would have argued, the programme suffered from three significant drawbacks from the beginning. On the one hand, the programme was founded on incorrect assumptions regarding the nature of the crisis in Greece. That is, the crisis was initially approached by Greek authorities and Greece's European and international partners as a liquidity problem. Thus, the structural causes of the crisis were downplayed in the MoU. On the other hand, the fiscal consolidation targets and especially the extremely short time-span within which fiscal consolidation was to be implemented, were overly ambitious and thus unfeasible.

Finally, it is important to emphasise that the MoU of May 2010 was largely identical to the provisions of the Updated Hellenic Stability and Growth Programme (SP 2010) approved by the Ecofin in February 2010. In addition, the MoU incorporated an excessively stringent Tax Law in April 2010 (applied retroactively as of January 2010) passed in haste by the PASOK parliamentary majority prior to the arrival of IMF officials in Athens. In this sense, the design of the fiscal consolidation programme of May 2010 created vast opportunities for the Greek socialist government (PASOK) to employ the programme in an instrumental way. Here it is worth considering the fact that the fiscal consolidation programme assumed the possibility of cyclical de facto readjustment of the programme's quantitative objectives. That is, if a progress report produced by the Troika on a three-month basis were to reveal discrepancies in the quantitative performance criteria, to keep the programme on target, new fiscal policy measures would be introduced to guarantee the programme's success. This mechanism allowed the socialist government to shift the burden of fiscal adjustment away from the public sector and thus away from expenditure reducing measures towards the private sector and revenue enhancing measures. Specifically, as presented in Table 10-2, several of the expenditure reducing measures were either not implemented or came into force with a significant delay or in an amended, "soft" version, thus having little impact on the strained state budget.

Table 10-2 Major consolidation measures in the authorities' programme of May 2010: commitments vs. implementation

	Revenue-enhancing measures	Implementation
1	Increase in VAT rates & base	04/2010
2	Increase in excise tax on fuel	01/2010
3	Increase in excise tax on cigarettes	01/2010
4	Increase in excise tax on alcohol	01/2010
5	Luxury goods tax (yachts, cars, pools)*	01/2010
6	Taxation on unauthorised establishments	01/2010
7	Gaming royalties	01/2010
8	Gaming licenses	01/2010
9	Special/emergency levies on profitable firms	01/2010
10	Levies on illegal buildings	01/2010
11	Green tax	01/2010
12	Presumptive taxation ("amnesty")	01/2010
13	Increase in administratively set prices of real estate	01/2010
14	Increase in taxation of real estate	04/2010
15	Privatisation	Practically none until 09/2012
	Expenditure-reducing measures	Implementation
1	Wage bill (13th, 14th wage, allowances)	Late 2011, several exceptions applied
2	Intermediate consumption	11/11 & 07/12
3	Pension cuts & freeze	2010 & 2011 & 2012
4	Elimination of solidarity allowance (introduced 10/09)	No
5	Public investment reduction	2010, 2011, 2012
6	Introduction of unified public sector wages	11/2011, several exceptions applied; the majority of state-owned enterprises (SOEs) did not conform with it;
7	Local administration reform ("Kalikrates") savings	questionable
8	Reduction in operational expenditure	minimal
9	Reduction in public employment	illusory
10	Unidentified measures	

Source: Adapted by the author from: European Commission (2010)

Simultaneously, all of the planned revenue enhancing measures were implemented on time with further policy instruments being added periodically, thus increasing the tax burden on the private sector. Increases in taxation, e.g., personal and corporate income taxes, and the imposition of new taxes, e.g., emergency contributions from vehicles, yachts, motorbikes and pools; levies on credit cards and cheques; and surcharges on mobile telephony, have been complemented by the introduction of the so-called income thresholds. These administratively established thresholds effectively increase the taxable income base, in that taxation – rather than being imposed on real income – is imposed on an estimated (and thus usually exaggerated) annual maintenance cost of a vehicle, a house, an apartment, etc. The thresholds are also imposed on tuition fees, healthcare expenses, etc. A focused study of these thresholds would reveal a direct correlation between their imposition and plummeting consumer demand for goods and services. As the discussion in this paper will depict, as a result of the overemphasis on revenue-enhancing measures, an expenditure drift occurred over the period 2010–2011. The socialist government sought to balance this situation with additional tax increases, a practice that the authorities legitimised by producing the myth of tax evasion in Greece.

3. The scope of fiscal consolidation in Greece 2010–2012

To obtain insights into the scope of the fiscal adjustment in Greece, in the following paragraphs, the milestones of the (planned) fiscal adjustment effort over the period 2010–2012 are described. By contrast, Table 10-3 offers a summary picture of the scope of the fiscal consolidation process in Greece as recorded by IMF authorities. Six milestones in the fiscal adjustment effort in Greece can be distinguished. These include: 1) provisions of the MoU of May 2010 for the period 2010–2012; 2) the Medium-Term Fiscal Adjustment Strategy (MTFS) of June 2011 for the period 2012–2015; 3) additional, very specific tax laws introduced in September 2011 following a rather difficult negotiation round with the Troika; 4) the "voluntary bond exchange programme" of November 2011; 5) the 2nd MoU of March 2012; and 6) measures discussed by the coalition government in summer 2012 to be implemented as of 2013.

Table 10-3 The scope of fiscal adjustment: measures executed including carry-over impacts

	Deficit (outcome or projection)			Measures (implemented in or identified for a given year)	
	in m. of EUR	% GDP		in m. of EUR	% GDP
2009	36,624.0	15.8	in 2010	19,074.0	8.4
2010	24,125.0	10.6	in 2011	16,680.0	7.7
2011	20,002.0	9.3	in 2012	13,0191.0	6.5
2012	14,779.0	7.3	for 2013	1,584.0	0.8
			in 2013	7,639.0	3.8
2013	9,359.0	4.6	for 2014	3,065.0	1.5
			in 2014	4,016.0	1.9
2014	4,404.0	2.1			
			Cumulative	51,969.0	30.6

Source: Adapted by the author from European Commission (2012a)

(1) The fiscal consolidation measures included in the MoU of May 2010 aimed to increase tax revenue and cut expenditures. The measures designed to increase tax revenue were largely based on the provisions of the Tax Law adopted on April 23, 2010 (Law 3842/2010). This law provided for increases in VAT rates; increases in the excise taxes on fuel, cigarettes and alcohol; the introduction of a luxury goods tax (yachts, pools, and cars); special emergency levies on profitable firms; presumptive taxation (frequently inaccurately referred to as a "tax amnesty"); and steep increases in tax rates on property, followed by the introduction of new tax measures on property (European Commission 2010, 17). According to the government plans, revenues would be increased by the equivalent of approximately 4% of GDP through 2013 (MoU 2010, 8). The cuts in spending were to be achieved through nominal wage cuts in the public sector of approximately 7% of the basic salary (thus leaving other forms of compensation and benefits – notably constituting a lion's share of remuneration in the public sector – intact); reductions in Easter, summer and Christmas bonuses and allowances; nominal pension cuts of 9% through a reduction in Easter, summer and Christmas bonuses; and a reduction in the largest pensions. Other measures included intermediate consumption cuts (e.g. managing ministry expenses) and a reduction in public investments (MoF 2010a). Overall, the government presented a rather ambitious programme of fiscal consolidation of a rare scale, i.e., 7.8% of GDP in the first year of the process (MoF 2011a, 8). In line with the government's plans, the reduction in the general government deficit of

5.0 percentage points (p.p.) in 2010 was to be followed by a 3 p.p. reduction in 2011, thus bringing the deficit from 15.4% of GDP in 2009 to 7.4% in 2011. The government declared that "fiscal measures will amount to more than 8 p.p. of GDP, but the nominal deficit drift in 2011 (the increase in interest payments, pension expenditures and other structural expenditures that would take place without the measures) is expected to reach 5 p. p. of GDP" (MoF 2011a, 8).

(2) The Medium-Term Fiscal Strategy 2012–2015 (MTFS) approved by the Greek Parliament in June 2011 provided for additional fiscal consolidation measures valued at €28.3 billion (12% of GDP) for the period 2011–15. The MTFS' objective was to reduce the general government deficit from 7.5% of GDP in 2011 to 2.6% of GDP in 2014. The MTFS included additional fiscal consolidation measures worth €6.5 billion or 2.9% of GDP in 2011 (23.1% of the total fiscal effort), €6.8 billion or 3.0% of GDP in 2012 (24.0% of the total), €5.2 billion or 2.2% of GDP in 2013 (18.5% of the total), and €5.4 billion or 2.2% of GDP in 2014 (19.3% of the total fiscal effort). The government's plan was to further reduce the general government deficit to approximately 1% of GDP in 2015, with measures worth €4.3 billion or 1.7% of GDP. Regarding reductions in public expenditures, the MTFS aimed to decrease such expenditures from 51.4% of GDP in 2011 to approximately 44.4% of GDP in 2015 after the implementation of the measures. These reductions would include cuts in social transfers from 24% of GDP in 2011 to 20.0% in 2015; a reduction in the public sector wage bill from 9.6% of GDP in 2011 to 6.6% in 2015; and a reduction in intermediate consumption from 5.2% of GDP in 2011 to 3.0% in 2015 (MoF 2011b, 2–3). Regarding revenue measures, the MTFS foresaw a decrease in public revenues from 40.9% of GDP in 2011 to 37.6% of GDP in 2015 following the lapse of certain one-off measures taken in 2010 and 2011. However, public revenues were also expected to increase to 43.2% of GDP by 2015. "This rise in general government revenues [would] be driven mainly by increases in direct tax revenue (from 7.0% of GDP in 2011 to 8.2% in 2015); in indirect tax revenue (from 12.2% of GDP in 2011 to 13.2% in 2015); and a rise in social contributions from 9.5% of GDP in 2011 to 10.5% in 2015" (MoF 2011b, 3).

(3) In September 2011, on the occasion of a periodic review mission to Greece and in the face of a significant fiscal drift, dramatic negotiations took place in Athens with the Troika's representatives leaving the negotiating room. As news reports suggested, the subject of the disagreement was the larger than expected budget deficit projected for 2011. According to the Troika, the projected deficit was approximately

8.6%–8.7% of GDP due to omissions and gaps in the government's policy. The government maintained that the deficit would be more than 1.1 p.p. smaller than the IMF's estimates. On this basis, the government did not want to introduce any additional measures to balance out the expenditure drift. There was also a significant disagreement on the issue of privatisation, which in any case was delayed by the socialist government. As a result of the September talks with the Troika, the disbursement of the 6th tranche of the financial assistance to Greece was halted. In addition, the Troika called for additional measures valued at €1.7 billion on the grounds of a revenue-lag of ca. €1.1 billion and increased spending of €600 million related to pension funds. To raise the required €1.7 billion and thus release the disbursement of the 6th tranche of the loan, the PASOK government introduced a new tax on property. This highly controversial tax will be discussed in the next section.

(4) In February 2012, a "voluntary bond exchange programme" brokered by the Institute of International Finance (IIF) was enacted. The value of the bond exchange programme was set at a level of 53.5% (compared to the initially planned 50%). In other words, in line with the agreement, bonds in the hands of private creditors will be exchanged for new ones with nominal values corresponding to 46.5% of the "old" bonds. The actual loss that the creditors will incur amounts to, on average, 74%, largely due to the loss of future interest payments. The new bonds are issued by the Greek government (31% of the total) and the European Financial Stability Fund (EFSF) (15%) under English law (previously, the bulk of Greek bonds had a Greek law clause attached to them). As for the interest rates, depending on the maturity of the bonds, their holders will garner a 2% profit (for bonds maturing over the period February 2012 – February 2015), a 3% profit (for bonds maturing over the period February 2015 – February 2020), and a 4.3% profit for bonds maturing over the period February 2020 – February 2042. Moreover, as of 2015, the creditors participating in the bond exchange scheme will be entitled to a minor increase in interest rates should economic growth in Greece exceed the targets established in the agreement with the EU and the IMF. As a result of the programme, the share of Greek public debt that is held by private creditors will be reduced by 53.5%, which constitutes approximately 2/3 of Greek debt. Since in 2011 the value of Greek debt amounted to ca. €356 billion (ca. 165% of GDP), the bond exchange programme is expected to result in an effective debt reduction of ca. €109 billion. This reduction will allow Greece's debt burden to be reduced by €3.2 billion annually, which – under specific circumstances – could allow the debt level to reach 120.5% of GDP by 2020 (Visvizi 2012d).

(5) On March 15, 2012, the IMF Executive Board approved a four-year €28 billion arrangement under the Extended Fund Facility (EFF) for Greece in support of the authorities' economic adjustment programme. The details of the programme were laid out in the Second Memorandum of Understanding (MoU II) supported by a financial assistance package of a total value of €130 billion co-financed by the IMF and the EU. The IMF's decision to participate in the EU-IMF €130 billion four-year financial assistance programme for Greece completed the chain of events that was set in motion on October 26, 2011. In line with the agreement reached at that time, following a debt-restructuring arrangement, a new rescue package would be offered to Greece. The purpose of this package was to assist the country with meeting its payment obligations and to recapitalize Greek banks that would incur huge losses as a result of the bond exchange scheme. The support from the EU and IMF was conditional on Greece securing private creditors' participation in the "voluntary bond exchange programme" and adopting a series of additional reform and fiscal consolidation measures. The MoU II primarily concerned structural spending reforms, which required additional measures beyond those already approved in the context of the 2011 MTFS and the 2012 budget. The programme required 1.5% of GDP worth of measures in 2012, 1.5% of GDP in tax administration improvements, and a further 5.5% of GDP worth of spending measures in 2013–14 to achieve the primary surplus target of 4.5% of GDP by 2014. As stated in MoU II, "[t]he bulk of adjustment will be achieved through expenditure cuts that aim at permanently reducing the size of the state and improving government efficiency, including by closing entities that no longer provide a cost-effective public service and by targeted reductions in public employment. Many of these cuts will need to fall on social transfers, the category of spending which increased most explosively in the post euro accession period" (IMF 2012, 7). The first tranche (€1.65 billion) of the financial aid was disbursed on Friday, March 16, 2012.

(6) Shortly after the Parliamentary Elections of June 17, 2012, which resulted in the formation of a coalition government (Visvizi 2012a), additional fiscal consolidation measures were discussed. To ensure that the 2012 budget deficit remained manageable, the governing coalition agreed on additional measures generating €3 billion in expenditure savings. These measures would involve reductions in ministry operating costs, the cancellation of some benefits received by the cabinet, as well as further reductions in pension levels and social transfers, among other measures. Moreover, throughout the summer of 2012, discussions were held regarding additional measures worth a total of €11.5 billion to be

introduced over the period 2013–14. These measures (to be approved in September 2012) foresee a significant decrease in the general government expenditures to be achieved, among others, via reduction of employment in the public sector.

4. Expenditure-reducing measures in Greece: their efficiency and appropriateness

In discussing the efficiency and appropriateness of the fiscal consolidation measures implemented in Greece over the period 2010–2012, it is necessary to emphasise that contrary to the initial provisions of the MoU, the burden of fiscal adjustment was shifted towards the private sector. Table 10-2 attests to this shift. Moreover, although – as seen from the perspective of the last two years – Greece's consolidation efforts have been considerable, neither the revenue enhancing measures nor the expenditure reducing efforts were as successful as the government and the Troika had expected. This raises some questions about the appropriateness of the design and of the assumptions underlying the fiscal consolidation programme agreed for Greece. For instance, one of the questions is, why regardless of the obvious signs of a deepening recession in the Greek economy, additional strain was imposed on the private sector via multiple increases in taxation. This issue is particularly relevant given the fact that one of the major weaknesses of the Greek economy is related to the excessive size of the public sector and the abusive role of the state in the economy. It is the private sector that – irrespective of the squeezed liberal space in Greece – used to keep the economy going and provided the means to finance the public sector. Paradoxically however, the fiscal consolidation programme implemented over the period 2009–2012, rather than supporting the "healthier lung" of the Greek economy, in a systematic way led to the exhaustion of the private sector. Clearly, several other questions regarding the empirical pattern of fiscal adjustment in Greece still need to be answered in future research. In the following paragraphs, the largely failed attempts at reducing expenditures will be discussed. In the next section some details explaining the revenue drift will be outlined.

One of the flagship reforms advertised by the PASOK government throughout 2010 concerned the pension system. The objective of the reform was to simplify the fragmented pension system, enhance transparency and fairness, increase and equalise the retirement ages[1] and

[1] For instance, the statutory retirement age for women was to be extended by 5 years to age 65 to match the retirement age for men. Successively, the statutory

decrease the unfounded generosity of retirement benefits available to the public sector employees,[2] while preserving adequate pension levels for the low- and middle-income earners (MoU II, 8). Moreover, to generate further savings, state contributions (in the form of grants) to the supplementary (public) pension funds that exist in Greece were to be decreased by reducing the number of the funds (from 13 to 3 by the end of 2018) and by diminishing the value of transfers to eligible pensioners.[3] None of the above plans was implemented until 2012. Instead, the socialist government introduced three successive cuts to pension levels over the period 2010 – May 2012. However, irrespective of the dramatic cuts in pension levels, the general government expenditures on pensions and grants to social security funds increased substantially over the period 2010–2012 (see Table 10-4 for details). One of the reasons behind this "overshooting" is related to the government deliberately avoiding restructuring the public sector.

---

retirement age was to be extended to age 67 for both men and women. In addition, early retirement below the age of 60 was to be curtailed. In line with the provisions of the existing regulations, employees can draw a pension below that age if they have paid contributions for a certain number of years or had children under 18.

[2] In line with the existing regulations, upon their retirement the public sector employees would receive a generous one-off payment/bonus ranging from €30,000 for the lowest-rank employees to ca. €160,000 for the medium-rank civil servants. The retirement bonuses granted to employees of the Bank of Greece would reach the value of €400,000. As the data revealed by the coalition government in August 2012 suggest, these values are disproportionate to the total value of individual contributions and beyond what the retirement funds can afford. In August 2012, Antonis Samaras, head of the coalition government, ordered the bonuses disbursed in 2011 and 2012 to be paid back.

[3] It should be noted that several of the funds had very good financial positions, which was a reflection of prudent financial management by the individuals who established them. Consequently, the complementary pension transfers to fund members that these funds could afford did not constitute any burden whatsoever on the state budget. Of course, contrasting examples exist. The thrust of the reform was to treat all funds – unfairly so – as if all of them were in financial difficulty.

Table 10-4 Expenditures on pensions & contributions to social security funds in millions of EUR

	2010	2011	2012
Pensions	6.25	6.572	6.511
Funds	10.376	11.78	13.119
Sum	16.626	18.352	19.63
% GDP	7.31	8.53	9.71*
*indicates GDP size with a recession estimated at 6%			

Source: MoF (2010b, 2011c, 2012)

The question of the size and efficiency of Greece's public sector has been a recurrent topic in the official discourse on the crisis in Greece. Low productivity, a lack of transparency, a high degree of unionisation, corruption, and causing a burden on the state budget are the most accurate descriptors of the public sector in Greece. "Low and middle-rank civil servants have higher wages than similar private sector employees, although they work on average fewer hours and have greater job security" (OECD 2011a, 11). The public sector in Greece nourishes clientele's connections and generates countless functional spill-overs for the entire economy. In this sense, the Greek public sector resembles bureaucratic communist public sectors. Regarding the size of the Greek public sector, it is not easy to reconcile the official data produced by relevant ministries or published by international institutions such as the OECD or IMF. Specifically, data provided by the Greek Ministry of Administrative Reform indicate that the general government employment was 715,882 in 2009, 683,627 in 2010 and 664,223 in 2011 (European Commission 2012a, 24). These numbers would suggest a rather small public sector, an observation also made by the OECD (2011b, 2). It is important to stress, however, that the official records do not include all of the employees of state-owned enterprises (SOEs); the data do not include countless experts and committee members employed (and remunerated generously) by all of the ministries and other government bodies; the data do not include employees without tenure, referred to in Greece as "*stagiaires.*" Accordingly, the above numbers concerning the size of the Greek public sector should be increased by another 250,000, with the cost of its maintenance "hidden" in extra-budgetary accounts. To obtain a complete picture of the scale of the problem that the public sector generates in Greece, it is worth noting that in late 2009, ca. 100,000 public sector employees opted for early retirement, fearing the consequences of the planned pension reform and taking advantage of the generous compensation and benefit schemes that the public sector pension regime used to offer.

Overall, the question of the size of the public sector in Greece and the cost that it generates for the state budget has been beset by confusion and conflicting arguments during the last two years, with the socialist government being unwilling to downsize it and the Troika exerting no particular pressure on the government to change the status quo. In 2011, the plan was to place some 30,000 employees on reserve; an alternative solution was to move employees across the public sector according to demand. While the successes of the first measure were insignificant, the alternative solution produced anecdotal outcomes in the form of, for example, public railway company employees being moved to state museums and crowding the museum cafeterias rather than offering assistance to tourists.

Considering the problem of the public sector from the fiscal consolidation perspective, as Table 10-5 demonstrates, the nominal value of expenditures on wages and salaries (however, including only the central government, hospitals and other government bodies and excluding the SOEs[4]) decreased slightly over the period 2010–2012. However, given the economic recession, the percentage change in expenditures relative to GDP has been negligible, thus indicating a sustained need of serious consolidation efforts in the public sector. Until now, as a means of avoiding the political cost related to possible public sector restructuring, the PASOK government deliberately channelled the burden of fiscal adjustment in Greece to the already squeezed private sector. In this way, the public sector, including the civil servants, SOEs and the powerful trade unions, were spared from the dramatic experience of fiscal adjustment that the rest of the Greek society endured over the period 2010–2012.[5] One could argue that as a result of this politically driven selective approach to how to split the burden of fiscal consolidation, the PASOK government aggravated the cleavage that exists between the public and the private sectors in Greece and thus between the relevant groups of the population. It is worth noting that any media discussion of downsizing the public sector stumbles on the argument that public sector employees will be fired.

[4] In August 2012 it was revealed that the majority of SOEs did not conform to the 2011 law providing for the introduction of a uniform salary scheme for the civil servants and the SOEs, i.e., they maintained the excessively high levels of salaries, compensation and benefits intact.

[5] Note, that wages in the private sector have been substantially reduced in 2011 and 2012, while the minimum salary level for employees under the age of 25 has been set at the level of €571.

In this context, the negative socio-economic consequences thereof are pointed to. At the same time, however, people seem to have reconciled with the 1 million-plus unemployed individuals who lost their jobs in the private sector.[6] The paradox is that these individuals would not have lost their jobs had the socialist government restructured the public sector, hence had it reduced the general government expenditure, and – through liberalization and deregulation – limited the role of the state in the economy. In this way, there would be no need to move to excessive taxation aimed at balancing the expenditure drift.

Table 10-5 Expenditures on wages & salaries 2010–2012, in millions of EUR

		2010	2011	2012
Central government	wages & salaries	12,180	11,340	10,439
	other allowances	312	7	283
	productivity bonus	597	517	36
	ΕΟΠΥΥ	0	0	444
Salaries for hospital personnel and other government bodies		3,318	3,102	2,765
Sum		16,407	14,970	13,967
% GDP		7.22	6.95	6.91*
*based on the assumption of a recession of the size of 6% of GDP; ΕΟΠΥΥ: National Organisation for Healthcare Provision;				

Source: MoF (2010b, 2011c, 2012)

Overall, as depicted in Table 10-6, some progress has been achieved with regard to controlling expenditures in Greece during 2010–2012. However, the failed pension system reform did not yield any outcomes in the form of reduced expenditures. Rather, the three consecutive cuts in pension levels forced many elderly citizens into poverty. Moreover, the local administration reform known as "*Kalikrates*", which the PASOK government argued was a major achievement in terms of savings, led to organisational chaos in municipalities rather than decreasing public expenditures. Notably, although presented as a novelty, the local administration reform was scheduled and planned for years by the socialists, mainly to influence the distribution of political support in the

[6] The tragedy of the situation is that the majority of these unemployed are not eligible for unemployment support/benefits, as is the case with self-employed owners of shops, taverns, small manufacturing entities, etc.

Greek countryside in view of future elections. Finally, the restructuring of the public sector, a reform that would have yielded multiple gains for the Greek economy, has been largely avoided by the PASOK government for reasons of political convenience.

Table 10-6 General government expenditures: major categories of expenditure 2007–2011, excluding extra-budgetary funds

	2007	2008	2009	2010	2011
Compensation of employees, payable					
% GDP	11.4	12	13.4	12.2	12.1
in m. of EUR	25,464.0	27,986.0	31,002.0	27,770.0	26,066.0
Social benefits (other than in kind social transfers)					
% GDP	17.9	19.6	21.1	20.8	21.9
in m. of EUR	39,941.0	45,757.0	48,972.0	47,220.0	47,026.0
Expenditures on local government					
% GDP	2.7	2.9	3.3	2.8	2.9
in m. of EUR	6,013.0	6,675.0	7,651.0	6,465.0	6,306.0
Total general government expenditures					
% GDP	47.6	50.6	53.8	50.2	50.1
in m. of EUR	106,009.0	117,963.0	124,646.0	114,106.0	107,769.0

Source: Eurostat

5. Revenue-enhancing measures in Greece: their efficiency and appropriateness

The government sought to increase revenues by broadening the tax base and introducing new temporary and permanent tax measures. Over the period 2010–2012, several tax increases (affecting both natural and legal persons) were introduced, while tax exemptions and discounts were largely abolished. However, as Table 10-A1 demonstrates, irrespective of increased excise duties, the steep increases in taxation, and regardless of a number of emergency levies imposed on companies, personal income, property, and the so-called luxury goods, a significant revenue-drift has occurred over the period 2010–2012. Rather than being offset by expenditure reducing measures, the revenue-drift was addressed with further increases in taxation. As the tax measures introduced over the period January 2010 – March 2012 have been incommensurate with the companies' and individuals' ability to pay, the private economy contracted and unemployment exploded to 23.1% in May 2012, compared to 16.8% in May 2011 (ELSTAT 2012b).

According to the results of a study conducted on a sample of 1,200 small and medium-sized enterprises in Greece, 64.7% anticipate that the situation of their businesses will deteriorate in the second half of 2012. The commercial and services sectors will be the most affected by the worsening economic situation in the country. The same study reveals that almost 190,000 enterprises face a high risk of closing. The net loss of businesses during the next 12 months is estimated to be 67,000, which implies a risk of further job losses amounting to 260,000, including employers, the self-employed and employees (IME GSEVEE 2012). Currently, several of the companies that continue to exist either do not remunerate their employees in full or do not do so regularly and on time. Finally, it should be noted that the general government revenues from taxation decreased by ca. 8% in 2010 and by a further ca. 4% in 2011. Further decrease in revenue collection on account of taxation is expected to take place in 2012. In addition, companies' contributions to the public insurance funds decreased dramatically over the period 2010–2012, thus creating an additional strain on the state budget. Specifically, data indicate that by July 2012 these funds consumed 74.2% of resources assigned to them in the 2012 state budget. Taking into account the estimates of an economic recession of at least 6% in 2012, the prospects for the execution of the state budget are grim. It is for this reason that the Troika demanded that the new coalition government imposed an additional €3 billion in expenditure-reducing measures for 2012 alone. As noted earlier, a package of additional measures of the value of €11.5 billion for the years 2013–2014 was scheduled to be approved by the Greek Parliament in September 2012.

With regard to indirect taxation, over the period 2010–2011, VAT rates were raised three times, i.e., in March 2010 (from 4.5% to 5.0%, 9.0% to 10.0%, and 19.0% to 21%), in July 2010 (from 5.0 to 5.5%, 10.0% to 11.0%, and 21% to 23%), and in January 2011 (from 5.5% to 6.5% and 11% to 13%). It should be noted that the range of goods and services covered by the highest VAT rates increased significantly, and the lowest rate is rarely applied. Faced with a demand crisis and negative consumer sentiments, Greek businesses were forced to absorb the successive increases in VAT rates, thus decreasing their already marginal gains, to maintain price levels. In this context, it is important to highlight one of the most contested changes in VAT policy, which concerns the gastronomy sector, retail food and beverages. As of September 2011, VAT rates increased from 13% to 23%, thus causing an additional pressure on the owners of restaurants, bars, taverns, etc. Clearly, the majority of prices increased in such establishments, thus affecting the already damaged competitiveness of these sectors that are so important for the Greek tourism industry.

Regarding excise duties and other taxes imposed on the petroleum products sector, over the period June 2010–June 2012, the cost of petroleum products increased, mainly due to taxes, by 80%, with the average price for 1 litre of unleaded petrol reaching €1,743 by the end of July 2012.[7] Further increases in price levels are expected due to a rise in distillation costs (POPEK 2012). Considering the declining purchasing power of Greek consumers, in the first half of 2011, consumption levels plummeted to 35% compared to a comparable period in 2008. A 13% decrease in gasoline consumption was recorded in the first quarter of 2011 (compared to the first quarter of 2010) in addition to a 19% decrease in diesel consumption. Accordingly, since 2010, more than 1,200 gasoline stations have been closed, and 1,000 more will close by the end of 2012, thus causing job losses of ca. 5,000.

Another highly contested set of tax measures concerns property taxes. To understand these measures, it is necessary to outline some basic features of the Greek property market. That is, 8 out of 10 Greeks own some form of property, such as an apartment, a house, a plot of land, or a property designed for professional use. In Greece, it is common to inherit property. Thus, owning property is not the same as having income. Nevertheless, confusion and several myths beset the issue of property (taxation) in Greece, with the most common misconception being that property owners should be paying extra taxes simply because they own it. This incorrect view, expressed frequently in the public discourse in Greece, links – wrongly so – ownership of property to the ability to pay increased taxation. Clearly, and it should be emphasized, as long as property is not rented or subject to a sales contract, it generates no profits. Thus, the owners' ability to pay taxes on account of owning either a plot of land, a house/apartment used for living, or an unrented apartment is nil, because no correlation between owning a property and the income level exists.

---

[7] According to the 2012 Bloomberg Gas Price Ranking that sorts 60 countries by average price at the pump and by "pain at the pump", locates Greece at the 9th position as regards the "most-expensive-gas", and at the 26th position as regards the "pain at the pump", i.e. well ahead of the UK, France or Germany.

The steep increases in property taxation in Greece have had severe ramifications, e.g., on the rental market, the construction sector and 130 related industries and on general government revenue (see Table 10-A1 for details). With respect to the rental market, as the economy contracts, demand falls, and the tax burden increases, a 50% decrease in rents (for offices, stores, and apartments) has taken place across Greece, with countless stores and offices available for rent even in central locations of Athens. Despite the fact that a 20–30% decrease was observed in rental prices over the period 2010–2012, demand still does not match supply. Accordingly, the number of transactions in the real estate sector decreased from nearly 40,000 in the fourth quarter of 2007 to less than 10,000 in the fourth quarter of 2011, while the value of the transactions plummeted. Regarding the construction sector, it should be noted that following the liquidity crunch in 2009 and 2010, augmented by increases in taxation, the number of building permits decreased from 42,891 (over the period May-April 2010–211) to 35,393 (over the period May-April 2011–2012), constituting a 17.5% decline. However, the decline in building area was even more spectacular, reaching a value of 30.5% over the same time-frame (ELSTAT 2012a, 3).

As a footnote in the discussion of property taxation in Greece, one should mention yet another direct tax levied on it. Imposed temporarily for a period of two years, i.e., 2011 and 2012, this special property tax imposes payments on real estate (€0.50 – €20.00 per square metre) to be collected via electricity bills. The planned revenue increase from this measure was estimated to be €1.7 billion annually. The enforcement of this measure was to be improved by eliminating access to electricity in cases of non-payment. Several problems, contingencies and controversies plague this tax measure. On the one hand, a very important constitutionality question was raised in that it is illegal for the Public Power Corporation (ΔΕΗ) to arbitrarily decide to shut off power for reasons other than electricity consumption. In fact, in March 2012, the Council of the State ruled against power being shut off if the property tax is not paid. On the other hand, several unintended exceptions in the imposition of this tax measure were revealed; similarly, several accounting mistakes were detected. Finally, the primary problem related to this tax measure is that it is detached from the income of the tax payer. Although in March 5, 2012, the Council of Ministers decided to replace the special property tax with a new tax as of 2013, to generate revenues €2.3 billion per year, the fate of this tax measure remains uncertain. The most probable scenario is that it will be incorporated in the ordinary property taxation.

In any discussion on fiscal consolidation and structural reform, the question of privatisation cannot be omitted. In the case of Greece, the privatisation process is particularly important in that rather than producing imminent privatisation receipts,[8] it may trigger a path-dependent restoration of the Greek economic system and thus push Greece onto a growth path. In other words, it has to be noted that privatisation in Greece should not be conceived of as a fire-sale to generate one-off revenues. Rather, privatisation should be regarded as a process that will allow for the deregulation, liberalization and restructuring of the Greek economy, downsizing the public sector, and limiting general government expenditures (Visvizi 2012b). In addition, an added bonus of privatising the SOEs is that it may contribute to breaking the monopoly and the influence that the trade unions exert in Greece. Nevertheless, although privatisation holds a great deal of promise, it seems that Greece's socialist government and the Troika itself adopted a misconceived approach to this process. Although over the period 2004–2009, the then centre-right government of Nea Democratia successfully accomplished privatisations valued at €11 billion, thus suggesting that privatisation in Greece is feasible, the MoU of 2010 contains only the following laconic statement on the matter: "Prepare a privatisation plan for the divestment of state assets and enterprises with the aim to raise at least €1 billion a year during the period 2011–2013" (MoU 2010, 45).

In 2011, the Troika exerted significant pressure on the government to draft a privatisation plan valued at €50 billion; however, without any tangible results. In contrast, the MoU II includes several provisions on privatisation, the most specific of which is that "the government anticipates €50bn in proceeds over the lifetime of the asset sale program, including at least €19bn through 2015" (European Commission 2012a, 108). Although in August 2012 the coalition government opened several tender procedures for the exploitation of property and for the acquisition of shares or licences, the fate of privatizations in Greece remains uncertain. Undeniably, the most difficult of all will be privatization of the SOEs. At this point several unresolved questions remain, for instance: which model of privatisation should be followed? Here, it seems that the experience of the successful privatisation process in Poland in the early 1990s has been neglected by the Greek authorities and the Troika.

[8] The interesting point here is that receipts from any potential future successful privatizations in Greece will not be directed to the state-budget, but to the treasury established especially for this purpose, the Hellenic Republic Asset Development Fund S.A. Accordingly, any proceeds from privatizations will be reserved for servicing Greece's debt.

Moreover, the legal framework for the privatisation process remains a sensitive issue. Therefore another question is whether those responsible for the process will be granted immunity, thereby shielding them from possible unfounded future accusations of political adversaries. As long as the above questions remain open, the odds for privatisation in Greece seem low.

6. The (thorny issue of tax compliance and the) myth of tax evasion

The notions of tax evasion, tax compliance and corruption have been making the headlines since late 2009, depicting Greece – at least at the popular level and undeservedly so – as a nation of corrupt, notorious tax dodgers. As will be argued in this section, to avoid politically costly restructuring of the public sector, the tax evasion argument was employed instrumentally by the Greek socialist government over the last couple of years to manipulate public opinion (at home and abroad) into believing that tax evasion and corruption were the causes of Greece's downturn. Furthermore, as fiscal consolidation in Greece over the period May 2010 – June 2012 did not yield the expected results and an expenditure drift occurred, the same argument of tax evasion was employed by the PASOK government to legitimize additional tax increases. In other words, since late 2009, the socialist government embarked on a strategy of a ceaseless talk of tax evasion, of the necessity to enhance fiscal audit and to "catch" the tax dodgers. Unsurprisingly, in the public discourse tax dodgers were associated mostly with the rich and with the successful members of the society. It can be argued therefore that tax evasion and corruption were employed instrumentally by the socialist government for two correlated reasons. On the one hand, they served the purpose of diverting the society's attention from the real causes of the crisis, i.e. the huge public sector and the abusive role of the state in the economy, in order to create an opportunity structure enabling the government to avoid the politically costly structural reforms. On the other hand, the same arguments were employed to create an image of a committed socialist government engaged with issues of social justice. This in turn was to improve the popularity of the government and the social support for it. Sadly so, the myth of tax evasion and corruption in Greece fell on a fertile ground of naivety, misconceptions and stereotypes about Greece and about the causes of the crisis. Accordingly, to a considerable extent the myth of tax evasion dwarfed the talk of reforms and economic growth in Greece. As the argument of tax evasion and corruption seems to be returning to the public discourse regarding the crisis in Greece, it is necessary to make some points on it by means of clarification.

According to the Transparency International Corruption Perceptions Index 2011, Greece occupies the daunting 80th position with a score of 3.4 (on a scale up to 10.0) and is comparable to El Salvador, Colombia, Morocco, Peru and Thailand. Amongst its European peers, Greece is followed only by Bulgaria, which receives a score of 3.3. It would seem that the results of the Eurobarometer (2012) survey released in February 2012 confirm these results, in that 98% of Greek respondents perceive corruption to be a major problem in Greece, and 80% of Greek respondents believe that corruption within their country is more widespread than in other EU countries. As revealing as these findings may be, they are based on perceptions aggregated through opinion polls and surveys. Even if Transparency International seeks to have its surveys peer reviewed, the initial dataset remains subjective. It has long been demonstrated that scandals, crises, and allegations of corruption (frequently fuelled by the media and employed instrumentally for domestic politicking) affect people's perceptions of the degree of corruption.

The notions of tax evasion and corruption are frequently (and wrongly) blended into a single concept in the public discourse on Greece and seem to preoccupy some politicians and opinion-makers at home and abroad. Therefore, it is pertinent to elucidate some numbers that are readily available on the OECD portal. The provisional data for 2010 indicate that total tax revenue as a percentage of GDP was 30.9% in Greece, compared to 36.3% in Germany, 28% in Ireland and 48.2% in Denmark. The value of taxes on goods and services in 2009 as a percentage of GDP reached 10.8% in Greece, 11.1% in Germany, 10.1% in Ireland, 11.7% in Poland and 15.4% in Denmark. The major difference in the shares of tax contributions to total GDP is identifiable for taxes on income and profits. In 2009, their share as a percentage of GDP reached a value of 7.6% in Greece, compared to 10.8% in Germany, 10.1% in Ireland and 29.4% in Denmark.

In this context, an OECD report (OECD 2011a, 10) notes that "personal income tax revenues are more than 5% of GDP below the euro-area average, although statutory rates are not especially low." The OECD further suggests – rightly so – that the so-called self-employed, including plumbers, electricians, nurses etc., might be the culprits in this regard. The August 2011 OECD Economic Survey on Greece stated that "[i]f Greece collected its VAT, social security contributions and corporate income tax with the average efficiency of OECD countries, tax revenues could rise by nearly 5% of GDP." Notably, the value of the VAT Revenue Ratio (VRR) for Greece is 0.41 (OECD 2011c). This finding implies that 59% of potential revenues from VAT are not collected. This number would seem to confirm the argument of tax evasion in Greece, were it not for the observation that the VRR levels for the UK and Spain are the same as that of Greece. Moreover, the VRR value for Germany, 0.55, falls below the 2008 OECD average (unweighted) of 0.58.

Overall, the numbers presented here clearly suggest that, although tax evasion exists in Greece, it is not as severe a problem as the media and some politicians portray it to be. Until 2010, in some cases, Greece fared better than other countries, and in some cases the performance of Greece was comparable to countries that no-one would dare to call countries of tax dodgers. The paradox is that, like in a self-fulfilling prophecy, as a result of excessive taxation that caused an exponential contraction of the private economy, data for 2011 and 2012 may reveal heightened levels of tax evasion as well as growth of the grey sphere of the economy. Whereas neither of these two is a welcome development, both of these phenomena serve as a depiction of how the state has crowded out private agents from the economy to a clear detriment of fiscal consolidation and the reform process. Consequently, the insistence by some politicians in the West, including the Troika, regarding the argument of tax evasion in Greece is worrying in that it overshadows the necessary debate on transforming the Greek economic system. The danger here is that an overemphasis on tax evasion, and the resulting overemphasis on increasing taxation (a new tax law is to be submitted to the Greek Parliament in September 2012), rather than a focus on creating conditions for growth (via a sustained effort at restructuring the public sector, liberalisation, deregulation and privatisation), is counterproductive and thus is likely to capsize genuine efforts at rescuing Greece (Visvizi 2012e).

7. Conclusions

The objective of this paper was to discuss the background and the scope of the fiscal consolidation process implemented in Greece over the period May 2010 – June 2012. A particular focus of the discussion was placed on the efficiency and appropriateness of the fiscal policy measures introduced by the socialist PASOK government as a means of addressing the sovereign debt crisis in Greece. It was argued that contrary to the government's assertions and provisions included in the MoU of May 2010, the government deliberately channelled the burden of fiscal adjustment towards the private sector of the economy to avoid the politically costly necessities of reducing expenditures and restructuring the public sector.

Consequently, as a result of tax-based fiscal adjustment, significant contractionary effects have occurred in the Greek economy, and general government revenues plummeted. Neither exports nor domestic demand could offset these contractionary effects. Therefore, in mid-2012, i.e., more than two years after the launch of the generous EU-IMF €110 billion financial assistance programme for Greece, despite the "voluntary bond exchange programme" followed by a second financial package worth €130 billion, the outcomes of fiscal adjustment in Greece remain at least uncertain. Clearly, the coalition government formed in Greece after the June 17 elections seems committed and able to navigate the stormy waters of fiscal consolidation. Nevertheless, the domestic and external challenges that the coalition government faces are not conducive to success (Visvizi 2012a). Having said that, several practical and theoretical questions emerge that will be addressed in future research. Specifically, on the one hand, it is necessary to investigate the empirical pattern of the IMF intervention in Greece and its variability. On the other hand, it seems that a closer examination of the theoretical aspects of fiscal consolidation in Greece would be needed.

In the rich body of literature on the variability of fiscal consolidation, a number of assumptions and hypotheses regarding the efficiency of fiscal consolidation have been tested. In this strand of research, the major question is which of the two alternative means of fiscal consolidation, i.e., expenditure reduction or revenue enhancement, produces better results. Moreover, additional questions include what can serve as a driver of growth in periods of fiscal consolidation, i.e., domestic demand or exports, and what the role of monetary policy vis-à-vis fiscal consolidation can be. Overall, research suggests that "spending-based adjustments are considerably less contractionary than tax-based adjustments" (Guajardo et al. 2011, 26). In this context, Konstantinou and Tagkalakis (2010, 3) conclude that "cuts in direct taxes generate a positive effect on consumer and business confidence (…). [At the same time], higher government wage bills and government investment reduce confidence, possibly because they entail a permanent increase in the size of the public sector, which would have to be financed by higher future taxes." Addressing the question of the efficiency of fiscal adjustment in the face of a considerable debt-to-GDP ratio, Deák and Lenarčič (2011) observe that "a government spending shock has a positive and a tax receipt shock a negative effect on output over time. However, if the debt-to-GDP ratio is above [a certain] threshold, then fiscal policy has no significant effect on output." Each of these contributions offers important insights likely to benefit the study of the theoretical and empirical patterns of fiscal consolidation in Greece over the period 2010–2012. Treating these studies as a point of departure, it would be particularly interesting to examine the fiscal consolidation process in Greece from the perspective of the "expansionary fiscal consolidation" hypothesis (Giavazzi and Pagano 1990) in the absence of monetary policy. It should be noted of course that Perotti (2011) questions the hypothesis of expansionary fiscal consolidation and its applicability in the euro zone. He argues that limited policy options are available to euro-zone members, i.e., "a depreciation is not available to EMU members, except possibly vis-à-vis non-euro members. [And] an expansion based on exports is not available to the world as a whole." Therefore, as Perotti suggests, the odds of expansionary fiscal consolidation in the euro zone are low. Yet, because several euro-zone members are currently undergoing fiscal consolidation, it could still be of benefit to test the Greek case against the expansionary fiscal consolidation hypothesis and to draw relevant lessons from it. The questions to be addressed therefore would include whether an alternative – to monetary policy measures – policy-mix exists to effectively address fiscal imbalances in countries that are members of a monetary union. In the specific case of the EMU, would it be consistent with domestic-level solutions, with euro-zone-wide approaches, or with a combination of both of them? The Greek case bears the promise of providing some insights on these questions.

References

Alpha Bank. 2012. "Εβδομαδιαίο Δελτίο Οικονομικών Εξελίξεων." [Weekly Economic Report]. August 16.

ELSTAT. 2012a. "Building Activity Survey." April, Piraeus: Hellenic Statistical Authority.

—. 2012b. "Labour Force Survey." May, Piraeus: Hellenic Statistical Authority.

Eurobarometer. 2012. "Corruption." Special Eurobarometer 374. Field Work: September 2011. European Commission.

European Commission. 2010. "The Economic Adjustment Programme for Greece." European Economy Occasional Papers 61, May, Brussels: Directorate-General for Economic and Financial Affairs.

—. 2012a. "The Second Economic Adjustment Programme for Greece." European Economy Occasional Papers 94, March. Brussels: Directorate-General for Economic and Financial Affairs.

—. 2012b. "Spring Forecast 2012." European Economy 1/2012, Brussels, May.

Deák, S. and Lenarčič, A. 2011. "The Macroeconomic Effects of Fiscal Policy Shocks in Good Times and Bad." Working Paper 1/1765, Centre for Economic Policy Research, February.

Giavazzi, F. and Pagano, M. 1990. "Can Severe Fiscal Contractions Be Expansionary? Tales of Two Small European Countries." *NBER Macroeconomics Annual* 5, edited by Blanchard, J. and Fischer, S., 75–122.

Guajardo, J. and Leigh, D. and Pescatori, A. 2011. "Expansionary Austerity: New International Evidence." IMF Working Paper WP/11/158, International Monetary Fund, July 2011.

IME GSEVEE. 2012. "Economic Climate Trends July 2012." IME GSEVEE Survey (conducted by Marc A.E.). Athens: Small Enterprises Institute (IME GSEVEE).

IMF. 2012. "Greece: Letter of Intent, Memorandum of Economic and Financial Policies, and Technical Memorandum of Understanding Policies." International Monetary Fund. March 9.

Konstantinou, P. and Tagkalakis, A. 2010. "Boosting confidence: is there a role for fiscal policy?" Working Paper no. 113. Athens: Bank of Greece, April.

MoF. 2010a. "Hellenic Stability and Growth Programme Newsletter." Athens: Hellenic Ministry of Economy and Finance, May 17.

—. 2010b. "Budget Execution Bulletin." Athens.

—. 2011a. "National Reform Programme 2011–2014." Athens, April.

—. 2011b. "Greece: Medium-Term Fiscal Strategy 2012–2015." Athens: Ministry of Finance. June.

—, 2011c. Budget Execution Bulletin. Athens.

—, 2012. Budget Execution Bulletin. Athens.

MoU. 2010. "Greece: Memorandum of Economic and Financial Policies." Athens. May 3.

OECD. 2011a. "Greece." OECD Economic Surveys. August.

—. 2011b. "Country at glance: Greece." Government at a Glance 2011. June 24.

—. 2011c. "OECD's Current Tax Agenda." OECD Report. April, 2011.

Perotti, R. 2011. "The "Austerity Myth": Gain Without Pain?" NBER Working Paper No. *17571*. November.

POPEK. 2012. "ΔΤ για τις τιμές και την ανάγκη μείωσης των φόρων στα καύσιμα" [Press release on the need to reduce taxation on fuel]. Press Release 09.07.2012, No. 681. The Pan-Hellenic Federation of Fuel Station Owners and Oil Traders (POPEK).

SP. 2010. "Report to the implementation of the Hellenic Stability and Growth Programme and Additional Measures in response to COUNCIL DECISION 6147/10, March 8, 2010." Athens: Hellenic Ministry of Economy and Finance. March.

Transparency International. 2011. "Corruption Perceptions Index." Report 2011.

Visvizi, A. 2012a. "The June 17 Elections in Greece: Domestic and European Implications". PISM Policy-Paper no. 31, June 2012, Polish Institute of International Affairs (PISM), Warsaw.

—. 2012b. "The crisis in Greece and the EU-IMF rescue package: determinants and pitfalls." *Acta Oeconomica* 62, 1: 15–39.

—. 2012c. "The crisis in Greece & the EU economic governance: lessons & observations." In *European integration process in the new regional and global settings,* edited by Latoszek, E. et al. Warsaw: University of Warsaw Press, 183–204.

—. 2012d. "Greece: The riddle of perplexity." Euro&Finance / Analysis, Euractiv, March 19, http://www.euractiv.com /euro-finance/greece-riddle-perplexity-analysis-511576

—. 2012e. "Greece: The odds of growth." *Euro&Finance / Analysis*, Euractiv, February 28, http://www.euractiv.com/euro-finance/greece-odds-growth-analysis-511153

Appendix

Table 10-A1 The revenue drift: recurring revenue – direct & indirect taxes: 2009-2012 (in millions of EUR)

			2009	2010	2011			2012		
			executed	executed	drift	target	executed	drift	MTFS	target
I.	Direct taxes		22 192	20 265	-7.3%	21 859	20 157	-1,90%	20 554	23 552
1	Income tax			14 317		15 704	12 782		12 656	15 132
		personal income tax		943		10 760	8,16		8 313	11 200
		corporate income tax		3 167		3 044	2,76		2 660	2 320
		other		172		1 900	1 862		1 863	2
2	Property taxes			487		895	1 172		732	2 907
3	Direct Tax Arrears			289		2 430	1 917		2 724	2 185
4	Other direct taxes			2 571		2 830	4 285		4 442	3 298
II.	Indirect taxes		31 097	31 004	-8.3%	33 815	28 587	-5.4%	30 219	26 881
1	Transaction taxes			18 457		20 205	17 744		18 372	16 537
1.1		VAT		17 375		19 015	16 887		17 361	15 687
		fuel		2 653		2 535	2 847		2 587	2 658
		tobacco		779		930	844		785	750
		other		13 943		15 550	13 197		13,16	12 279
1.2		Other transaction taxes (capital transfers & stamp duty)		1 082		1 190	857		1 011	903

Continued on next page

**Table 10-A1 The revenue drift: recurring revenue – direct & indirect taxes: 2009-2012 (in millions of EUR)
(continued)**

		2009	2010	2011			2012		
		executed	executed	drift	target	executed	drift	MTFS	target
2	Consumption taxes		11 824	-7.8%	12 830	10 131	-6.3%	10 813	9 630
2	on insurance premiums		404		380	379		389	343
2	on vehicles		249		490	100		170	91
2	excise tax on fuels		5 698		5,7	4 653		4 698	4 727
2	other excise taxes (tobacco etc.)		3 382		4 090	3 509		3 629	3 120
3	road duties		1,59		1,4	1 117		1 343	1 011
3	other consumption taxes		501		770	372		584	338
	Indirect tax arrears		339		390	375		608	374
	Other indirect taxes		384		390	337		426	340
	Total tax revenue (I + II)	55 907	51 269	-7.9%	55 674	48 774	-3.9%	50 773	50 403

Source: MoF 2010b, 2011c, 2012: State Budget Execution Bulletin, Ministry of Finance Hellenic Republic, Athens.

THE CAUSES OF SLOW GROWTH IN HUNGARY

PÉTER MIHÁLYI

1. Introduction

In his 1966 Inaugural Lecture at Cambridge titled *On the Causes of the Slow Rate of Economic Growth in the UK*, the Hungarian-born British economist Nicholas Kaldor presented a series of "laws" to account for the growth rate differences between Britain and 12 more successful economies, such as the US, Germany and France. He called his method Circular Cumulative Causation, a multi-causal approach where the interdependencies between the explanatory factors were strong and the variables were interlinked in the determination of the outcome. In Kaldor's interpretation, the UK's main problem at that time was the slow growth of productivity, caused by slow growth in the manufacturing sector. Why did that matter? He found that industrial productivity was positively related to the growth of industry – i.e. the law of increasing returns to scale was strongly manifested. The objective, methodology and central analytical concepts of this paper are similar. We will examine the causes of slow growth in the Hungarian economy. As will be seen, the increasing returns to scale, which Kaldor took from Young's (1928) seminal study, also occupy a central position in this paper.

2. The Facts

2.1 The Red Queen paradox

For average Hungarians, the regime change of 1989/1990 did not produce the expected result: the country was unable to catch up with the Western market economies, even after two decades. While fundamental changes did occur on a broad front, our economic rivals also advanced as fast as Hungary. This is the so-called Red Queen Paradox, an often-used metaphor in everyday life, such as in economics, arms races, and evolutionary biology.

The Red Queen is a fictional character in Lewis Carroll's fantasy novella *Through the Looking-Glass*, the sequel to *Alice's Adventures in Wonderland.* Speaking with Alice, the central heroine of both works, the Red Queen describes her empire as a system in which "it takes all the running you can do to keep in the same place." In narrow, economic terms this is a perfect depiction of *capitalist rivalry*: if your competitors are moving ahead, you must move faster to not lose ground. In broader evolutionary terms (Van Valen 1973), the message is, "For an evolutionary system, continuing development is needed just to maintain its fitness relative to the systems it is co-evolving with."

2.1.1 Competition worldwide

While the Red Queen Paradox is not well known in Hungarian economic parlance,[1] its primary message did become frequently used in policy discussions: Hungary must grow twice as fast as the EU countries to catch up with them.

Is it possible to catch up with the forerunners and leave them behind? The first intuitive answer is yes. Hungary has a mid-sized developed economy with a per capita GDP level 25% higher than the world average. Between certain selected years – such as 1997–2006 – the Hungarian economy did grow faster than the EU-15,[2] and there were four calendar years (2002–2005) when the Hungarian growth rate was at least twice as high as the EU-15 average. Furthermore, if we disaggregate growth by regions, the numbers show that the Central Hungarian Region's per capita GDP surpassed the EU-27 average in 2004. Why should there be any doubt that the performance of the most developed Hungarian region can be emulated by the country as a whole in the next 2 to 3 decades?[3]

Yet there are good reasons to be wary of all this optimism. First, as shown elsewhere (Mihályi 2011a, b, c), during the last 140 years, Hungary had been unable to sustain above-average growth rates except for very short cyclical upswings. Kornai (1972) described this feature as the alteration of rush and harmonic growth periods. As illustrated in Figure 11-1, the exceptionally high and low growth rates should be interpreted in a comparative perspective, as the Red Queen Paradox

[1] L. Carroll's name is known thanks to his first book, which was translated into Hungarian in the 1930s.
[2] EU-15, as defined in EU statistics: Austria, Belgium, Denmark, Finland, France, Germany, Greece, Ireland, Italy, Luxemburg, the Netherlands, Portugal, Spain, Sweden and the UK.
[3] Continued EU assistance can be also taken into account.

suggests. During this long time span, when Hungary was sometimes capable of producing a high average rate – such as the 3.8% in 1950–1973 – the EU-12 countries[4] displayed even higher growth rates. Between 1990 and 2008, Hungary outperformed the EU-12, but its 2.2% growth was not particularly outstanding relative to the world average. In examining the entire period, there were several countries that produced 2 to 3 times higher than average growth rates for a sustained period of time (e.g., Venezuela in 1870–1949; Japan, Taiwan, Hong Kong in 1950–1989; Vietnam, Ireland, and Lebanon in 1990–2008). Hungary was never such a star-performer.

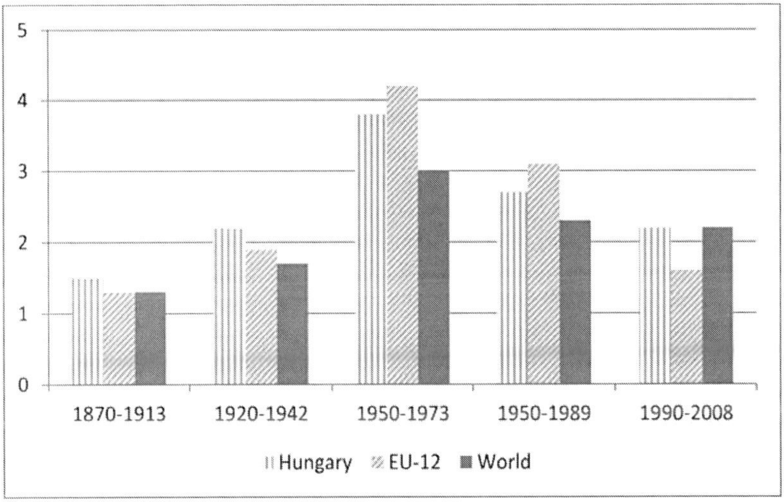

Fig. 11-1 Long term growth rates of GDP/head in Hungary, in EU-12 and the world, 1870–2008 (Annual average changes in percentage)
Source: Mihályi (2011a) based on Maddison (2010)

Second, the example of the former German Democratic Republic is also compelling. In spite of the billions of Euros channelled from West Germany towards the Eastern Länder, the level gap hardly shrank after unification. Using a sophisticated econometric forecasting technique, Aumann and Scheufele (2010) concluded that it may require another 50 years for the Eastern provinces of Germany to eliminate the gap with their

[4] EU-12, as defined in Maddison (2010): Austria, Belgium, Denmark, Finland, France, Germany, Italy, the Netherlands, Norway, Sweden, Switzerland and the UK.

Western peers. Third, there are important examples even among developed countries, where the distances actually grew between competitors. Using the US as a benchmark (= 100), Switzerland once achieved 93% and then fell back to 81%, Italy slid from 70% to 64%. The case of Japan is even more striking. Once widely admired, Japan climbed to 82% by 1996, but then by 2008 fell to 73% of the US income level. The list of failed catching-up stories is even longer if 5 to 6 Latin American countries and 8 to 10 African countries are included, where growth was not simply slower than in the US but actually negative.[5]

2.1.2 Competition among the transition economies

Once Hungary joined the European Union in 2004, a new type of rivalry started; a competition between the former socialist countries in catching up with the core countries of the EU-15. Hungary was first compared with Slovakia, the Czech Republic and Poland – the so-called Visegrád countries – but later the three Baltic countries were included in the standard analysis. During the first post-communist decade, Hungary always fared favourably in this comparison. However, in the next 10 years, this advantage was lost. As Figure 11-2 illustrates, Hungary hardly made any advancement between 1989 and 2010 relative to her new peers. Relative to the EU-15 average, Hungary advanced merely 1 percentage point in 20 years, from 54% to 55%. In the same period, Poland advanced from 38% of the EU-15 average to 55% (a total of 17 percentage points).

While the raw data and the visual presentation suggest that Hungary's performance in this kind of Red Queen Race was just about "normal," this is not the public perception. In regard to comparison, people usually disregard the weaker competitors and envy the stronger ones. There are not many Hungarians who are impressed by a scholar or politician saying that Russia or Ukraine displayed an even worse performance than "we did". Instead, they point to Poland and Slovakia, which were able to significantly reduce the gap separating them from the more advanced EU countries. For the average Hungarian, the case of Slovakia is even more relevant because this country was not only better in relative terms but also surpassed Hungary in absolute terms by 2007.

[5] All figures cited in this paragraph were calculated from Maddison (2010).

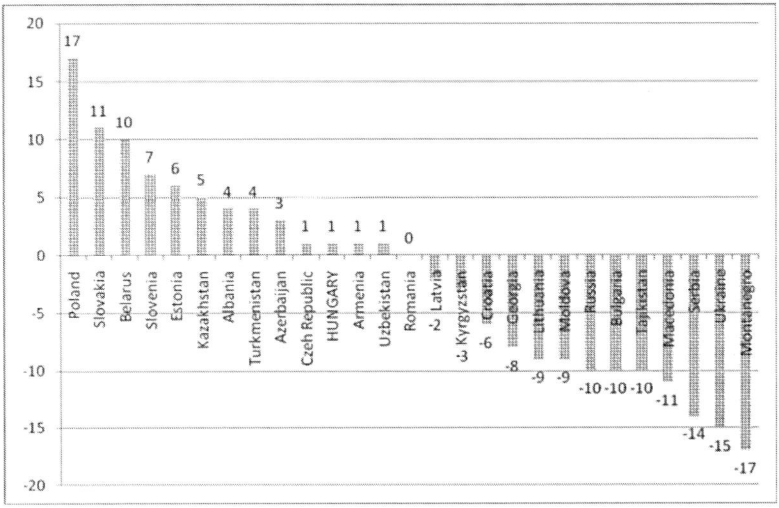

Fig. 11-2 Economic convergence of selected transition economies towards the average of EU-15 between 1989–2010
(Percentage points, GDP/head at purchasing power parity, EU-15 = 100)
Source: Author's calculations based on Darvas (2011) raw data and methodology

2.2 Natural endowments and economic policies matter

Since the previously mentioned Kaldor study (1966), analytical frameworks and tools have been significantly enriched. When countries at comparable levels of development are assessed today, the "laws" that might explain their differences are formulated at least in three separate dimensions: (i) natural endowments; (ii) economic policies; (iii) balance-of-payments; and (iv) supply-side analysis. In the next few paragraphs, "laws" (i) – (iii) will be briefly discussed to leave space for the fourth explanatory dimension, the mechanisms determining the supply-side of the economy, and within this, the changes in productivity.

2.2.1 Unfavourable geography

The success of the Japanese economy during the 1960s was used to belittle the importance of natural endowments in many parts of the world, including Hungary. "Japan has no raw materials, yet she is producing miraculous growth rates" was the resounding verdict at that time. However, after the first oil shock in 1973 and the rapid enrichment of some OPEC countries this alleged "law" went slowly out of fashion. Beyond the oil-rich Arab countries, the examples of Norway, the UK and – more recently – post-communist Russia have convinced everyone that the availability of raw materials is a major economic asset that can greatly contribute to the growth of a country. Similarly, the same holds true for monopoly positions (such as sea ports, maritime transit routes, summer beaches, and winter ski resorts). In this context, it is worth mentioning how in his latest book Jeffrey Sachs (2011) challenges the conventional view regarding European vs. USA comparisons. According to Sachs, America's long-standing advantage in per capita GDP has been due to its geography rather than its economic system. America has vastly more land and natural resources per person than does Western Europe. This has been the source of its enduring advantage, rather than the allegedly better incentive mechanism, the lower taxes, the better institutions or the restrained activity of the state (Sachs 2011, 225–226).[6] Without any further illustration and/or explanation, we submit that the weak economic performance of Hungary is *partly* due to her unfavourable resource endowments.

2.2.2 Inept economic policies do harm

The importance of appropriate fiscal and monetary policies in determining the growth trajectory of a given country has also become commonplace since the 1960s. This understanding has been forcefully supported by the recent worldwide calamities of the post-Lehman period. Partly due to her size and poor resource endowment, Hungary has been traditionally a very open economy. Currently, the combined value of her exports and imports is equal to 140% of annual GDP. In this context, it is important to refer back to those years – already mentioned above – when the Hungarian GDP growth figures were two times higher than in the EU. This is precisely when the country's balance-of-payments displayed a deficit of 7–8% in four consecutive years. Moreover, during the last 10 years, the central government, the local governments, the business sector and even the household sector pursued the same strategy of reaching for low-hanging fruit. Everybody was borrowing and – apart from the central bank – nobody was willing and/or capable to accumulate significant foreign (reserve) assets. As a result, Hungary has the worst position among the EU-27 countries concerning net international positions (Figure 11-3). The country's total net debt was equal to 113% of its annual GDP, a figure

---

[6] This is not a new idea in Sachs' academic oeuvre. See also Gallup and Sachs and Mellinge (1998).

far more worrisome than those of Romania or Poland (64%) or the Czech Republic (49%). Thus, considering the entire 1990–2010 period, the contribution of these regulatory policies was not positive – to say the least.[7]

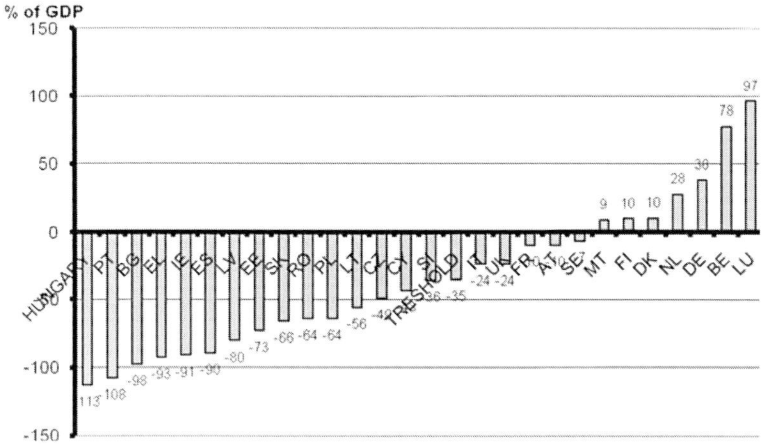

Fig. 11-3 Net international positions of the EU-27 in 2010
Source: European Commission (2012a, 4)

With the benefit of hindsight, we can apprehensively state that in terms of GDP growth the ballooning indebtedness of Hungary brought very disappointing results. As we will discuss, the borrowed money was primarily used to sustain consumption rather than to finance productive capital investments. With this strategy, the country reached a fiscal wall. Neither the markets nor the international financial institutions are likely to be willing to finance additional (net) borrowing. A long and painful period of deleveraging lies in wait for Hungary.

[7] From the recent Hungarian assessments available in English language, see e.g. Antal (2004), Szapáry (2006), Győrffy (2009), Csillag and Mihályi (2006), Török (2010) and EEAG (2012).

2.3 A simple decomposition

Let us start our analysis with a trivial identity:

$$\frac{GDP}{Head} = \frac{GDP}{Total\ population} =$$

$$\frac{GDP}{Workers} \times \frac{Workers}{Population\ in\ working\ age} \times \frac{Population\ in\ working\ age}{Total\ population} \qquad (1)$$

Where

$$\frac{GDP}{Workers} = \text{productivity}$$

$$\frac{Workers}{Population\ in\ working\ age} = \text{employment rate}$$

$$\frac{Population\ in\ working\ age}{Total\ population} = \text{dependency ratio,}$$

and then take the first derivatives of the three components in Equation (1):

$$\Delta\frac{GDP}{Head} = \Delta\frac{GDP}{Total\ population} =$$

$$\Delta\frac{GDP}{Workers} \times \Delta\frac{Workers}{Population\ in\ working\ age} \times \Delta\frac{Population\ in\ working\ age}{Total\ population} \qquad (2)$$

From the evidence presented in the previous sections, we can state without any additional investigation that Hungary suffers from two (not necessarily related) problems expressed in equations (1) and (2) – the low level of economic development and its slow annual increase.

Analysing the three components in reverse, the assessment of the dependency ratio (as defined here for our purposes) is relatively straightforward. In 1980, 10 years before the regime change, the share of the working (15–64) age in the total population was 64.6%. This number rose to 66.2% by 1990 and 68.7% by 2011. This is a change in the right direction; the growth problem of Hungary did not originate from here! During the last 10 to 15 years, participants in Hungarian policy discussions have heavily focused on the *employment rate*, the second component of Equation (1). Even those economists who fundamentally disagree on each and every detail of fiscal and monetary policies tend to accept without further analysis that this is the largest problem in Hungary. Indeed, the EU-wide international comparisons unequivocally show that Hungary "excels" with its lowest figure. According to the Eurostat methodology, the Hungarian rate was 55.4% in 2010, exactly 10 percentage points lower than the EU-15 average (66.4%) and the absolute lowest figure among the EU member states.[8]

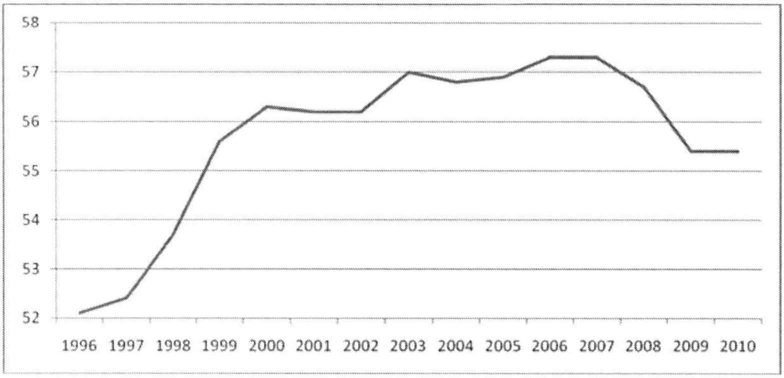

Fig. 11-4 Changes in the Hungarian employment rate, 1996–2010 (In percentage of the 15–64 age group)
Source: Eurostat

However, what matters for the volume of production (GDP) is not the absolute number of workers but the amount of work these people perform in terms of working hours. The employment rate is low in Hungary because part-time employment is unpopular.[9] For those who do work in Hungary, they do so for 1,961 hours a year on average, which is well above the OECD average of 1,749 hours. Perhaps it is surprising that Greece is the only country that has a higher figure. As Figure 11-5 on the next page shows, the Dutch, the Germans and the Norwegians are all below 1,500 hours. If Hungary's GDP is low, the problem must be hidden elsewhere.

[8] Malta used to be ranked lower than Hungary, but lately their figure rose from 55.0% in 2009 to 56.1% in 2010. Among the OECD countries, however, Italy and Turkey have slightly worse numbers than Hungary (OECD 2012, 25).

[9] In 2010, the share of part-time workers was 5.5% in Hungary and 21.4% in the EU-15.

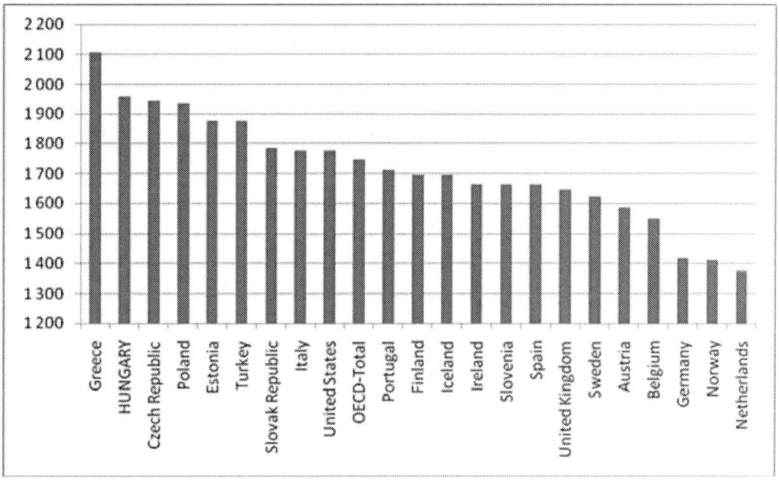

Fig. 11-5 Average annual working time in selected OECD countries, 2010 (Hours per worker)
Source: OECD (2011)

As the numbers in Table 11-1 show, the variation of annual working hours around the calculated base for comparison (Hungary = 100) is in a rather narrow range (87–127%) and the absolute numbers in col. [1] are not correlated with the broadly varying GDP/head figures. Take, for example, Norway, Austria and Poland. The number of working hours per head of the total population is almost exactly the same in the three countries, while the GDP/head figure in Austria is twice as high as in Poland, and the Norwegian figure is three times higher than the Polish one. Thus, we can now safely state as a conclusion that the low level and the weak dynamics of *labour productivity* are responsible for the Hungary's poor overall economic results.

Table 11-1 The relationship between total working time and economic development in 2008–2009

Country	Annual working hours per population		GDP/Head
	Hours	Percentage	1990. international dollars (PPP)
	[1]	[2]	[3]
Czech Republic	946	127	12 868
Portugal	900	121	14 436
Slovakia	837	113	13 033
Romania	832	112	4 895
Norway	816	110	28 500
Austria	816	110	24 131
Poland	816	110	10 160
Greece	811	109	16 362
…	…		
HUNGARY	744	100	9 500
France	707	95	22 223
Belgium	702	94	23 655
Italy	692	93	19 909
Turkey	650	87	8 066

Source: [1] and [2] own calculations from Eurostat (2009), [3] Maddison (2010)
Notes: Annual working hours are calculated in [1] for the entire population, including everyone. Data reflect the amount of work performed in the first quarter of 2009. Thus, the data show the state of the labour market before the international financial crisis. GDP/head data in [3] refer to the year 2008.

3. The problem is labour productivity

3.1 Education is not the answer

Many policy makers and good-willed political commentators honestly believe that more *higher education* is the No. 1 recipe for growth. The opposite is true.

In search for explanations and solutions to combat relative economic backwardness, most observers tend to overlook the positive legacy of socialist central planning. From the vantage point of the present paper, it is important to note that higher education was a top priority of the fallen system. As a result, 20 years after the fall of communism the population of the former socialist countries still has significantly more years of schooling than capitalist countries of similar development levels. Russia is a perfect illustration. According to OECD (2009), 54% of the 25–64 age cohorts in Russia possess a higher education degree, in stark contrast with Japan and the US (40%) or the Swiss (30%). Because socialist planning systems looked at higher education as having merit, it was provided free of charge. From the perspective of Hungary, the comparison with neighbouring Austria is noteworthy. The share of adults with a university degree is about 18% in both countries, while the difference in per capita GDP levels is more than 2:1.

Table 11-2 The number of independent tertiary education institutions, 1970–2008

Year	Number of institutions
1970	74
1980	57
1989	57
1990	77
2000/2001	62
2004/2005	69
2005/2006	71
2007/2008	71
2010/2011	69

Source: Central Statistical Office. Statistical yearbooks, various years

In this regard, the situation has only worsened since 1990. In the 2010/2011 academic year, 1 out of 3 university students was enrolled in some kind of part-time, distance learning program rather than a regular, full-time program. In 1990/1991, this proportion was only 1:4 (Figure 11-6).[10] This tendency has led to a numerical overproduction of university graduates, which is a further fragmentation of the higher educational system and – as Polónyi and Timár (2001) warned long ago – to deteriorating quality throughout the entire network.[11] Anecdotal examples suggest an

[10] It is noteworthy that there are only few degrees that can be earned in full-time university programs only, such as medicine and architecture.

[11] It is more appropriate to state that Hungary, similar to many other former socialist countries, is suffering from a "quasi-development" problem (Jánossy

additional problem: part-time university students are usually not very effective workers because they must divide their attentions and energies between two places – the workplace and the university.

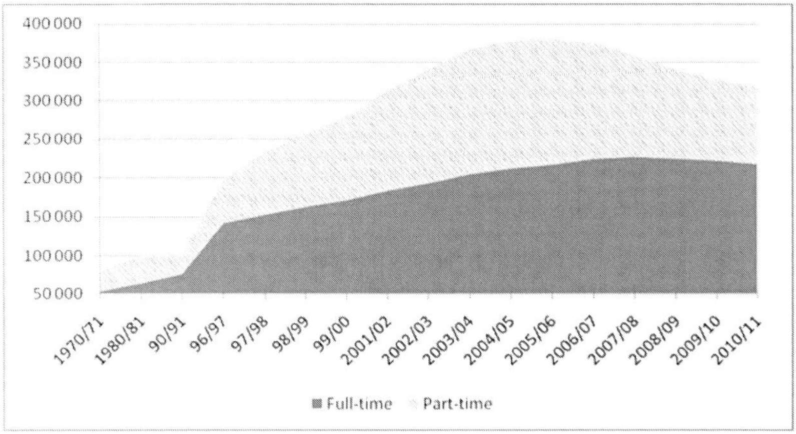

Fig. 11-6 The composition of students in higher education, 1970–2011 (Number of students)
Source: Central Statistical Office. Statistical Yearbook (1991, 254), Fazekas and Kézdi (2011, 203)

Since the regime change, many Hungarian workers possessing only 8 years of schooling are unable to find jobs because the jobs they would traditionally fill are now filled by others possessing a degree from middle-schools (8 + 4 years). On the basis of this finding, many experts are convinced that the government must channel additional resources to expand the network of secondary schools. The argument is that without a good middle-school education the upcoming generation of young people will not meet the diverse skill requirements of the labour market. This paper is not the proper place to go into the details of this debate. However, perhaps it is enough to state that while in Hungary only one-third of this social stratum are employed, in other EU countries, such as Portugal, Greece and Denmark, two-thirds of the workers with 8 years of schooling find a job.

We have a precise and detailed picture regarding the knowledge levels and the competencies of the future generation Hungarian workers, i.e.,

1969). A lot of education has been obtained, but a poor economy has resulted because of the poor quality of teaching.

those who have just completed the 8-year long mandatory *elementary schools*. The results of the 2009 PISA-test Program[12] show that the competencies of average Hungarian 15-year-old students in reading, mathematics and natural sciences are comparable with the OECD country averages. In most comparisons, the Hungarian students are on par with their peers studying in Sweden, Denmark and France. In 2009, the Hungarian students were even ahead of Americans in science and mathematics.

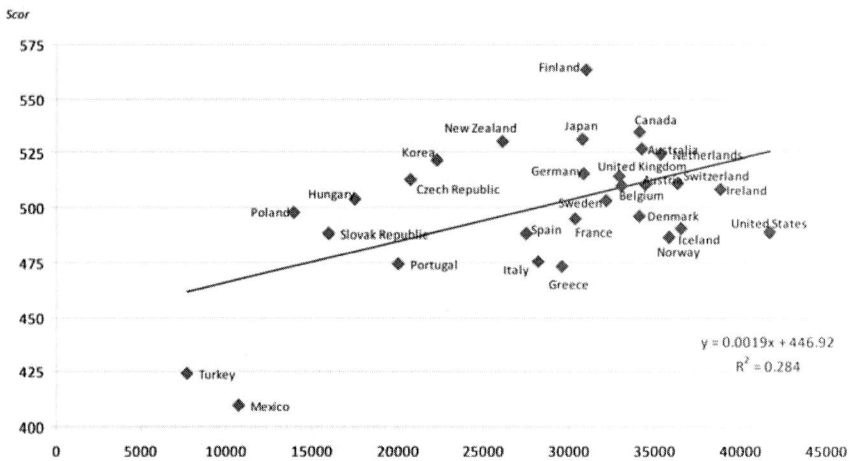

Fig. 11-7 PISA-test results and the OECD countries' economic development levels (Results from science for 15-year-old students in 2006 and per capita GDP levels at purchasing parity rates)
Source: OECD PISA 2006 database, Table F2.12a

As the regression calculation in Figure 11-7 shows, there is a logic according to which some countries are significantly above the regression line (Hungary, Czech Republic and Poland), while others are below it (Italy, Greece and Norway). The former group of countries are all transitional economies with a long tradition of socialist central planning. The second group proves that in striving for economic growth and development, countries with favourable natural endowments can compensate for the lower quality of their labour force.

---

[12] The Program for International Student Assessment (PISA) is a worldwide evaluation in 65 countries of 15-year-old school pupils' scholastic performance, performed first in 2000 and repeated by the organizer (OECD) every three years.

3.2 In- and outward migration – an underutilised potential

In many countries, outward migration is an important source of economic growth. In such cases, the economic rationale is that the migrating labourers can generate more added value in a more advanced economy than at home, and their home country benefits from this higher income through the repatriation of the higher earnings (remittances). It is a well-known example that, at the turn of the 19th and 20th centuries, such migration greatly contributed to the overall development of Hungary. This was also the policy that was successfully applied by Italy during the late 1950s and by Yugoslavia in the 1960s. After joining the EU in 2004, the legal conditions of outward migration have changed favourably, but Hungarians did not move in significant numbers unlike other post-communist countries. In 2009, Romanian and Polish workers sent home €2.9 billion and €2.7 billion, respectively, while in Hungary the net balance of remittances was *minus* €50 million.

Another way of enhancing a country's growth potential is the import of labour. After World War II, Germany, Spain, the UK and Ireland used slightly different policies, but they all benefitted from the use of under-qualified inexpensive workers from Southern Europe. Such a strategy is currently being pursued by Russia and to a smaller extent by the Ukraine, exploiting the labour reservoir of the ex-Soviet republics (Tajikistan, Kyrgyzstan, etc.). The United States is also a net importer, but her strategy is – not fully, but to a large extent – based on brain drain. Highly qualified intellectuals are imported from Europe, the Middle East, China and India.

While some experts have already started to make forecasts about Hungary's future immigration needs,[13] the present situation is unfavourable both in the labour market and social-cultural dimensions. To become an attractive country for immigration, unskilled foreign workers should calculate *net savings* of €500–1,000 per month. However, Hungary's tax and benefit policies (that compress wage distribution) are a major hurdle. Depending on the exchange rate, the average net wage is €460, and the official gross minimal wage is €320. In Hungary today, for a single worker without children earning the average wage, take home pay is only half of what it costs to employ him. From such a low net income, there is no way to save enough to provide for the family back home. Qualified foreign workers, in theory, could aspire to higher amounts of savings, but the barriers of the Hungarian language are almost insurmountable for them. In addition, the Hungarian public is notoriously intolerant vis-à-vis foreigners

[13] Polónyi and Timár (2001) calculated that the Hungarian labour market would need 20,000 immigrants per year for the next 40 years.

and towards ethnically different people in particular. Therefore, it is highly unlikely that any political party would dare to start a political discussion on the benefits of immigration in the near future.

While the politicians' caution and fear from public sentiments are understandable, discarding the possibility of both types of migration (inward and outward) is a luxury that Hungary can hardy allow for itself in the future.

3.3 Our answer: Far too many micro-firms

As previously stated, the main problem in Hungary is the low average level of productivity. The next step is to analyse its variation. There are two dimensions where these variations are obtrusive. First, productivity differs drastically according to the size of firms. Second, but chiefly as a consequence of the first finding, there are huge territorial differences within the country.

3.3.1 The missing increasing returns to scale

During the last 20 years, many studies proved that there were large and growing productivity differences in Hungary between the large firms and small- and medium-sized companies (SMEs). As a static fact, this is not a specific Hungarian puzzle; the same was found in international comparisons (Lewis 2004, McKinsey Global Institute 2010, EC Enterprise and Industry 2010). However, it is important to note that, prior to 1990, large (state-owned) enterprises played a dominant role in the Hungarian economy and the regime change brought a reversal in this regard. Partly, this was unavoidable. Moreover, similar to nearly all industrialised nations, Hungary has also witnessed a shift in labour from the secondary sector, where firms were generally larger, to the tertiary sector (services), where they are smaller.[14]

There are other factors. According to a Hungarian saying, policy makers fell from the other side of the horse, i.e., the country moved from

[14] In Kaldor's time, the share of the secondary sector (manufacturing + construction) was 31% in UK's total employment, but it started to fall rapidly. By 2010, it was somewhere around 15% only. In Hungary, after the rapid restructuring of the entire economy, the contraction of the secondary sector did not start until 2002, and it was very slow even after that. In relative terms within total employment, the share was 29.6% in that year and the 2010 figure was only slightly lower (27.1%). In other words, it still matters what is happening in these two traditional sectors of the Hungarian economy.

one extreme position to the opposite. In 1989, there were approximately 2,500 enterprises with more than 250 employees; the latest figure for 2009 was 870. The number of sole proprietors in 1988 was 300,000; today the number is 1.4 million (2010). In other words, there is a continuing fragmentation of the nation's entrepreneurial capital stock. In 2008, the annual value added of a Hungarian micro-enterprise was HUF 4.5 million per employee, while the same figure was HUF 8.2 million in large firms. The trend is negative. In 1998, the difference was only 150%; it was 182% in 2008 (Pitti 2010a). If we look at the 2009 data of the top 200 non-financial Hungarian firms, the average per capita output in this elite group was HUF 67 million, while the corresponding figure was HUF 21 million, which is a three-fold difference, in the rest of the economy. It is alarming that since 2000 the absolute number of middle-size and large companies has been falling. The same holds for the changes in the structure of employment. This is the opposite of European trends. While elsewhere the process of concentration prevails, in Hungary the fragmentation of resources are to be observed almost everywhere.[15] (The Hungarian categorisation of micro, small, medium-size and large firms is fully in line with the methodology of Eurostat. For detailed comparative data in all four enterprise categories used in the EU, see Appendix).

The size problems also have a very important sectorial dimension. The productivity gap is not so worrisome in *industry* because many firms today are run as subsidiaries of western multinational companies. Foreign-owned manufacturing companies still operate, and anecdotal evidence suggests that the productivity of the Hungarian employees in these subsidiaries is the same or even higher than in countries such as Germany and Austria where the mother companies have their own plants. However, the situation in the *construction industry* is alarming. Currently, there are 100,000 domestic companies operating (at least on paper) within the sector; in 1990, that number was slightly more than 5,000. Among the construction firms today, there are only 250 that are large enough to be qualified as a shareholding company – all of the other enterprises are limited liability companies owned by a single proprietor, a family or a very small number of connected entrepreneurs. The situation is even worse in *agriculture*, where 40% of the country's agricultural land is cultivated by people who call themselves "farmers," although only 3% of them have a specialised degree from a tertiary educational institution. This is a politically vocal

[15] At the very top of the company pyramid – firms with more than 5,000 employees – there is a positive change, but not sufficiently strong. In 2004, the number of such privately owned firms was 11, while 14 such firms were registered in 2009.

and therefore important social group of 5–600,000 agrarians.[16] Because these "farmers" are under-qualified, they continue to produce what they have seen from their fathers – grain. There are approximately 180,000 farmer households currently registered as grain producers. In a country of the size of Hungary, 180 large farms would most likely be too many. Under such conditions, it is fully understandable why the total output of the Hungarian agricultural sector has been in free fall since 1990. In 2010, the level was the same as in the early 1970s, despite gigantic government and EU subsidies. The productivity gap is also substantial in certain parts of the *service sector*, where 63% of the jobs are to be found. In some areas, the multinationals have a strong and exclusive presence (e.g., banking, telecommunication), but in other areas (e.g., catering, retail trade) small Hungarian firms and public institutions dominate the job market. The problem in retail trade or catering is striking for any client with open eyes. In small Hungarian-owned shops and restaurants, one can often see assistants and waiters doing nothing because the premises are simply empty. By contrast, has anyone ever seen a McDonald's or a Tesco hypermarket in which employees were not busy all the time? And these observations are not just anecdotal. According to the Central Statistical Office (KSH 2010), the number of retail trade outlets in 2009 was 2.5 times more than in 1989, while the total turnover at constant prices grew by only 5%! The same source shows the same tendency in catering. In 2009, there were almost twice as many functioning restaurants and cafes than in 1989, although the turnover in terms of volume actually fell by 15%. The same holds for public sector employees, which is very high by international comparison.[17] Two-thirds of these employees are working in very fragmented Hungarian local government institutions (e.g., general administration, education, health).

The issues discussed above also have important territorial (regional) dimensions. Since 1996, the Hungarian Statistical Office has been regularly publishing a GDP/head time series for the country's seven administrative *regions*. Figure 11-8 shows the disparity in these inter-

---

[16] Land ownership is even more fragmented than land cultivation. The number of registered farm land owners is 3.3 mn. According to the 2010 National Farm Survey, 60% of them are subsistence farmers, i.e. they do not even intend to market their own produce. From the total amount of labour used in Hungarian agriculture, only 25% is wage labour, 75% is provided by the land-owner and his family members.

[17] According to the 2008 OECD data, 20% of the Hungarian labour force is in the public sector, surpassed only by France and four Scandinavian countries. OECD (2012, 46).

regional differences. Without going into a detailed demographic analysis, we note that the employment ratios and the dependency ratios do not display large variations among the regions. The variation is caused by the variation in labour productivity.

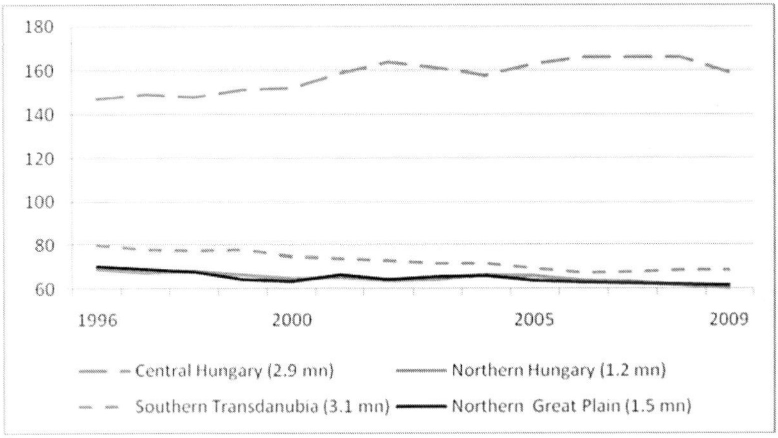

Fig. 11-8 Regional GDP/head differences
Source: Fazekas and Kézdi (2011, 312)
(In percentage. National average = 100)
Note: For the sake of visibility only four of the seven regions are shown. The numbers in brackets show the population size.

The advantage of Central Hungary, which includes the capital city of Budapest, is one of historical heritage. However, ethnically speaking, Hungary is a homogenous country; the differences cannot come from such differences among the seven regions. We strongly believe that the labour productivity gap is caused by the law of increasing returns to scale. Apart from Budapest, there is no other city in Hungary that is large enough to be successful in Europe-wide competition. Almost all big firms are located in Budapest or in Central Hungary. In other towns, everything is too small, narrow and disconnected: the labour market, the local demand, the logistic network, and the spectrum of amusements offered.[18] For a long time, it

[18] The country is too small to make a domestic airline network viable. Only Budapest has an international airport deserving its name. In 1990, the nation's capital had more than 2 million inhabitants; it has only 1.7 million today. The other larger towns have been also shrinking in size. The second and the third largest cities are Debrecen and Szeged with populations of 208,000 and 170,000, respectively. Compared with the US, according to a recent McKinsey (2012) report

was a widely shared opinion that the construction of motorways from Budapest towards the seven most important border-crossing points would equalise the investment climate throughout the country. The motorways are now up and running, but the hopes did not materialise. Most of the time, many new highways are almost empty.

3.3.2 The consequences

The low level and the slow growth of productivity in the SMEs – and in micro-firms in particular – have at least three devastating dynamic corollaries at the macroeconomic level. Each of them is important, but only the third point will be discussed in this paper:

(1) SMEs cannot play a serious role in vocational training;
(2) SMEs cannot be properly taxed; therefore, the authorities have to rely on other taxable sources;
(3) SMEs have weak incentives to invest and to grow.

If production capacities are under-utilised (as in retail trade) and yields are low (as in agriculture), then unit cost – and therefore prices – are bound to be excessive, which then inhibits the growth of demand. If there is no demand, the firm or the farm cannot grow. As Gábor (1994) noticed early on, the Hungarian SMEs have been suffocating in this vertiginous vicious circle for two decades. There are very few successful SMEs capable of growth to reach the size and maturity of a publicly traded firm. Between 2000 and 2009, there were only 22 initial public offerings (IPOs) on the Budapest Stock Exchange, while Prague can take pride in 95 such transactions.

In societal terms, the size distribution of firms has a strong influence on the distribution of the fruits of economic growth. Because SMEs are operating with narrow profit margins, they will not generate sufficient investable funding. This is the explanation for the downward sloping investment curve in Figure 11-9. At this point, we again invoke the concept of circular causation. If the level of investment is low for a prolonged period of time, the capital stock will be outdated and this will negatively impact labour productivity. This relationship holds strictly not only at the firm level but also at the macro level if externalities are taken into account.

---

using data for 2010, 84% of the American GDP was generated in the largest 259 US cities, with a population of 150,000 or more.

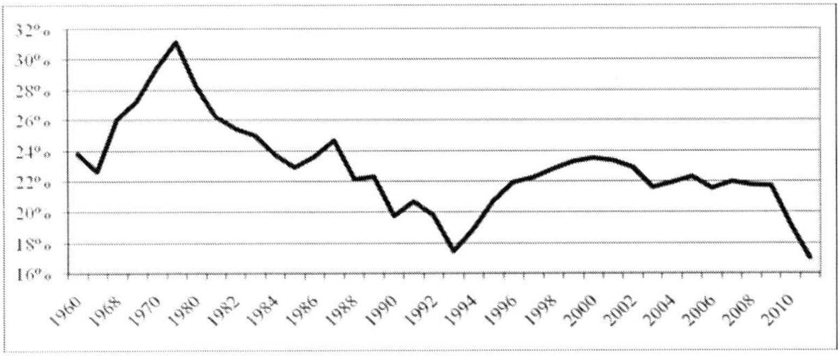

Fig. 11-9 The share of gross accumulation within GDP, 1960–2011
Source: Central Statistical Office

In a European EU-27 comparison, the Hungarian SMEs have the weakest record in innovation. In the latest 2011 edition of the Innovation Union Scoreboard, four statistical measures are used to assess the SME sector's contribution to innovation (Table 11-3). Of these four, Hungary occupies the very last position in two, and its scores and rankings are disappointingly weak in the other two categories as well.[19]

[19] Those who know the Hungarian economy may object to the above presented causation by saying that there are many *large* publicly owned companies and institutions, particularly in such capital intensive industries such as transport, healthcare and education; thus, a lot of investments and R&D must be financed by these public actors. Unfortunately, this objection does not hold. These companies and institutions – precisely because they are publicly owned – have been forced by the government to operate with low profit margins to keep their prices and/or fees low.

Table 11-3 The relative position of Hungarian SMEs as enablers of innovation, around 2010

Share of … (in percentage of the total number of SMEs)	EU-27 average	Best performing country	Hungary's absolute figure and ranking among EU-27
…SME's innovating in-house	30.31	46.03 (Germany)	12.60 (27th)
…innovative SME's collaborating with others	11.16	22.23 (Belgium, Denmark, Estonia and UK)	7.15 (19th)
… SME's introducing product or process innovation	34.18	53.61 (Germany)	16.82 (27th)
…SME's introducing marketing or organisational innovations	39.09	53.02 (Luxembourg)	20.52 (24th)

Source: European Commission (2012b, 62–63) (Annex A)

3.3.3 How did we get here?

If the consequences are so serious, it is imperative to understand how micro-firms became so weighty in the Hungarian economy so soon after the regime change and why they could preserve their positions up to present times. The problem is also known to other countries. As shown in the Appendix, Portugal and Greece also have many small firms, and this finding may explain their anaemic growth and low productivity to a great extent. Furthermore, the Portuguese story is similar to the Hungarian case to the extent that after the fall of the Salazar dictatorship, consecutive governments had pursued a deliberate policy of demonopolisation. However, the similarities most likely end there. It has been shown convincingly by Braguinsky et al. (2011) that in Portugal the survival of inefficient small firms is chiefly explained by the strong protection for regular workers in their labour code and other legislation, which was instituted as a reaction to the anti-democratic constraints of the overthrown dictatorship.

The labour code does cause problems in Hungary too; however, in our view, it is not the main explanation of the distorted company structure. In Greece, rigid product market rules seem to be the culprit. As a recent

McKinsey & Company (2012) report shows, Greek licensing and operating processes are extremely cumbersome. In a direct, regression-based comparison the Hungarian data look better (McKinsey 2012, 20). While these international comparisons are always informative, we must look for explanations elsewhere to understand the Hungarian case. In our view, there are at least four other causational mechanisms that mutually reinforce each other and thus fatally undermine productivity growth at the macro level.

During the first period of the socialist planned economy, the state merged all the previously existing privately owned SMEs into newly created state-owned enterprises. Subsequently, the administrative prices guaranteed that profits were all taxed away from the society and then redistributed as investments for the benefit of state-owned enterprises. Under such circumstances, the service sector shrank, causing a deterioration of the quality of life for consumers. As SMEs disappeared, many consumer goods and services became either inaccessible or accessible in only a few places. As is well known, there were long queues in shops, and diners could not find a free table in restaurants. After 1973, the situation improved somewhat in this regard, particularly in Hungary as compared with other socialist countries. However, only the regime change in 1989 opened the gates in front of the owners of SMEs. The huge pent-up demand quickly created its own supply.[20] The mushrooming SMEs made a significant contribution to consumers' welfare, although this was not – and for methodological reasons could not be – measured as a part of output. This kind of statistical distortion holds even today, when wage or consumption figures from the pre-1990 figures are compared with current data.

After the initial boom, the continued hypertrophy of micro- and small firms was largely due to the new legal environment. As land ownership had been constrained since 1994 and lax tax and credit rules and subsidised investment moneys were continuously pumped into the system, the micro-ventures looked competitive from the consumers' perspective. The explanation is that half to two-thirds of the activities of micro- and small enterprises are in the grey and black economy, and this allows them to offer bargain prices. Hence, the large firms operating in the "white" economy cannot translate their higher productivity levels into lower prices and thus compete with the small firms. In addition, the small firms use fixed capital sparingly, which is logical from their perspective. This is even more logical if the aging of the owners is also taken into account. As

[20] By 1994, the first year when such figures were released in comparable form with later data, the number of registered business units was already above 1.0 million.

tax returns show, the small firms write off more fixed capital than they actually replace. These mechanisms, as already mentioned, do not cause much obstruction in the manufacturing sector, but they are strongly present in agriculture, retail trade, the construction industry and in the areas of health and culture. Because the manufacturing sector is relatively small today (15–17% of GDP), its high and growing productivity cannot sufficiently improve the economy-wide average.

The third reason that explains the survival of so many SMEs is that the customary market-clearing mechanism (the big fish eat the small fish) does not work effectively. Due to the lax accounting rules, the owners of small firms are able to hide their families' personal consumption costs as costs of their enterprises.[21] This is possible because in small firms the bookkeeping and the access to a firm's bank accounts are typically controlled by the owner-manager, which is inconceivable in middle-size firms with more than 50 employees. In this way, the true proceeds of the small firms can be 50 to 100% more than the reported profits. The flip side of this situation is that the more competitive, larger firms cannot buy these smaller firms because the owner of the small firm would like to receive 5–10 times his *true* annual proceeds, while the potential buyer (a larger company) can offer only 5–10 times the *reported* annual profits. Moreover, these widely used cost-hiding practices prevent *horizontal cooperation* among farmers, shopkeepers and even professional service providers, such as physicians, nurses, translators and artists. Because everybody has something to hide from the eyes of the taxman, they are all afraid to show their contracts, invoices and bills to each other. Without openness and transparency in their administration, they cannot fully cooperate with each other in their actual daily work.[22]

Finally, the honest but erroneous conviction of Hungarian policy makers needs to be mentioned in which their continued support of SMEs is necessary to create new jobs. As in many other countries, there is a widespread and repeated claim, both in the business community and in government, that most new jobs are created by small businesses. In static terms, this is true for Hungary as well. However, "young" firms should not be confused with "small" firms. As everyday Hungarian experience suggests – and rigorous econometric investigation for the US proves

[21] A few typical examples: the office is operating in the apartment or the family house of the owner, the family car is legally owned by the firm, the phone costs of the entire family are assumed by the family company, eating-out costs of the family are billed as client-related expenses, etc.

[22] For a general discussion on the importance of cooperation, see also Győrffy (2009) and Szalavetz (2010).

(Haltiwanger et al. 2010) – most new jobs are created by young firms that happened to be small at the beginning and not by those small firms that remained small even 5–10 years after their establishment.

4. Summary and conclusions

This paper argues that Hungary has no other growth reserves than a more efficient allocation of the existing human and capital stock. Overall labour resource utilisation is comparable to our peers because the low participation rates are fully compensated by the higher average hours worked. Inward and outward migrations are promising but untapped channels. As for capital, the country today lacks large enterprises, which can maximise workers' output through economies of scale and scope. Thus, there is a need for ownership concentration of fixed capital and natural resources (e.g., agricultural land and forests). Such a strategy would require a fast consolidation of micro- and small enterprises into transparently functioning middle-size and large firms. Paraphrasing the famous Marxist slogan, the new slogan should be, "*Small entrepreneurs of Hungary, unite!*"

Once this is achieved by means of legal and administrative changes, Hungary will be once again an attractive investment opportunity to foreign investors. If the Hungarian labour force in the service sector, agriculture and elsewhere can generate extra profits for the owners of capital, the necessary financial means will be amply supplied by international capital markets. In practice, this will mean green field investments and privatisation of existing assets as well.

In other words, low productivity in certain – but not in all – parts of the Hungarian economy is the primary structural barrier to overall economic growth. The labour participation issue is merely a symptom and – to a considerable extent – the result of government induced administrative distortions. The country's low employment rate cannot be addressed before a massive productivity and profitability boost. This boost can no longer come from debt- and consumption-driven output growth, but rather from private sector investments in machinery and infrastructure. No doubt, a shift from consumption to investments, from wages to profits is politically difficult. Thus, there is a price to be paid for the acceleration of economic growth, just as there is a price to pay for the failure of catching up with the EU-15. The society has to change its mind-set. The majority of Hungarians today do not understand that production per se, good intentions, and diligence do not represent true values. If they as consumers do not buy something that is being produced (e.g., expensive Hungarian agricultural products) or do not buy tickets to half-empty passenger trains in the countryside or do not enrol into the small countryside universities – then the continuation of such production or service provisions is simply a waste. Eventually, the price we pay is that the country as a whole will remain unable to catch up with our envied neighbours, such as Austria or even Slovakia. Both the public and the political elite of Hungary should understand and accept that there is no societal objective for which it is worth sacrificing the growth of labour productivity. At present, we are very far from this.

References

Antal, L. 2004. *Fenntartható-e a fenntartható növekedés?* [Is sustainable growth really sustainable?] Budapest: Közgazdasági Szemle Alapítvány.

Aumann, B. and Scheufele, R. 2010. „Is East Germany catching up? A time series perspective." *Post-Communist Economies* 22, 2: 177–192.

Braguinsky, S. and Branstetter, L. G. and Regateiro, A. 2011. "The Incredible Shrinking Portuguese Firm." *NBER Working Series*, no. 17265, July.

Csillag, I. and Mihályi, P. 2006. *Double Bond (The 18 Month of Stabilization and Economic Reforms)*. Budapest: Global Knowledge Foundation (in English and Hungarian); reprinted in 2007, as a separate volume in East European Economics under the title *Last Chance* 44, 6: 1–102.

Darvas, Zs. 2011. "Exchange Rate Policy and Economic Growth after the Financial Crisis in Central and Eastern Europe." *Corvinus University Working Paper*, no. 3.

EC Enterprise and Industry. 2010. "SBA Fact Sheets 2009." http://ec.europa.eu/enterprise/policies/sme /facts-figures-analysis/performance-review/index_en.htm#h2-2

EEAG. 2012. *Report of the European Economy – The Hungarian Crisis (2012)*. Munich: CESifo Group, 115–130.

European Commission. 2012a. Alert Mechanism Report. Brussels, 14 February, COM(2012) 68 final.

—. 2012b. "Innovation Union Scoreboard 2011." Brussels: Pro Inno Europe – Innometrics.

Eurostat. 2009. Data in Focus, no. 35. Labour Market Latest Trends 1Q2009.

Fazekas, K. and Kézdi, G., eds. 2011. *Munkaerőpiaci tükör 2011* [Labour Market Survey]. Budapest: MTA Közgazdaságtudományi Intézete – Országos Foglalkoztatási Közalapítvány.

Gábor, R. I. 1994. "Modernity or a new kind of duality? Second thoughts about the second economy." In *Transition to capitalism? The communist legacy in Eastern Europe* edited by Kovács, J. M., 3–20. New Brunswick, New Jersey: Transaction Publishers.

Gallup, J. L. and Sachs, J. D. and Mellinge, A. D. 1998. "Geography and Economic Development." NBER Working Paper, no. 6849, December.

Győrffy, D. 2009. "Structural Change without Trust: Reform Cycles in Hungary and Slovakia", *Acta Oeconomica*, 59, 2: 147–178.

Haltiwanger, J. C. and Jarmin, R. S. and Miranda, J. 2010. „Who Creates Jobs? Small vs. Large vs. Young." NBER Working Papers, no. 16300, August.

Jánossy F. 1969. "Wiedersprüche in der Ungarischen Wirtschaftsstruktur – Wie sind sie enstanden un wie können sie überwunden warden." *Acta Oeconomica* 4, 4: 351–377.

Kaldor, N. 1966. *Causes of the slow rate of economic growth of the United Kingdom: An Inaugural Lecture*. Cambridge: Cambridge University Press.

Kornai, J. 1972. *Rush versus Harmonic Growth*. Amsterdam: North-Holland.

KSH. 2010. *Magyarország 1989–2009* [Hungary 1989–2009]. Budapest: KSH.

Lewis, W. W. 2004. *The Power of Productivity: Wealth, Poverty, and the Threat to Global Stability*. Chicago: University Of Chicago Press.

Maddison, A. 2010. "Historical Statistics of the World Economy: 1–2008 AD." http://www.ggdc.net/maddison/

Mihályi, P. 2011a. "Utolérési kísérletek Magyarországon, 1870–2030" [Catching-up experiments in Hungary, 1870–2030]. Institute of Economics, Hungarian Academy of Sciences, Discussion Papers, MT-DP – 2011/1.

—. 2011b. "Nem a foglalkoztatás szintje a döntő kérdés" [What matters is not the level of employment]. *Munkaügyi Szemle* (short electronic version). www.munkaugyiszemle.hu, 2. June.

—. 2011c. "Nem a foglalkoztatás szintje a döntő kérdés" [What matters is not the level of employment]. *Munkaügyi Szemle* 55, 3: 13–19.

McKinsey Global Institute. 2010. "Growth and competitiveness in the United States: The role of its multinational companies." June.

—. 2012. "Urban America: US cities in the global economy." April.

McKinsey & Company, Athens Office. 2012. "Greece 10 Years Ahead. Defining Greece's new growth model and strategy." March.

OECD. 2011. "Average annual working time Hours per worker. Employment and Labour Markets." http://www.oecd-ilibrary.org /employment/average-annual-working-time-2011_annual-work-table-2 011-1-en

—. 2012. *OECD Economic Surveys – Hungary*. Paris: OECD.

Pitti, Z. 2010a. "A hazai és nemzetközi vállalati szféra a válság előtt és után" [The Hungarian and foreign firms before and after the crisis]. Lecture delivered at an Ecostat conference on January 28.

Polónyi, I. and Timár, J. 2001. *Tudásgyár vagy papírgyár* [Knowledge or paper factory]. Budapest: Új Mandátum.

Szalavetz, A. 2010. "Transformation and Catching-up Issues in Hungary – From a Network Alignments Perspective." *Acta Oeconomica*, 610, 2: 197–216.

Szapáry, Gy. 2006. "Experience with inflation targeting in Hungary", *Public Finance Quarterly* 51, 4: 471–482.

Török, Á. 2010. "Fiscal policy in the service of sustainable growth." *Public Finance Quarterly*, 55, 4: 746–752.

Van Valen, L. 1973. "A New Evolutionary Law." *Evolutionary Theory* 1: 1–30.

Young, A. 1928. "Increasing Returns and Economic Progress", *Economic Journal* 38, September: 527–542.

Appendix

The number of micro, small, medium and large firms in selected EU member countries in 2009 (Per 10.000 of population)

Micro firms
(Employment: 1–9 workers, Annual revenue: > €2 million)

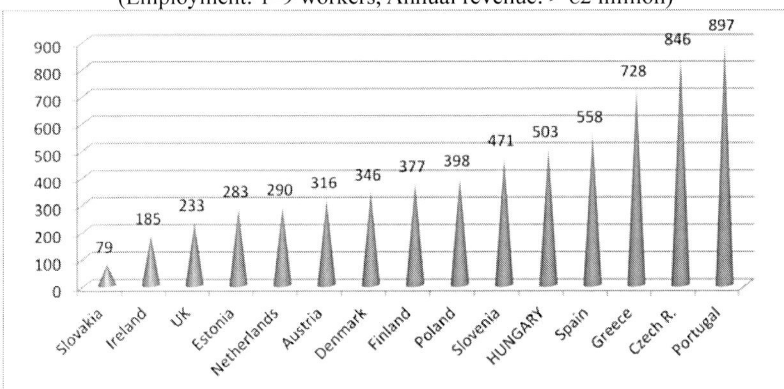

Small firms
(Employment: 10–49 workers, Annual revenue: > €10 million)

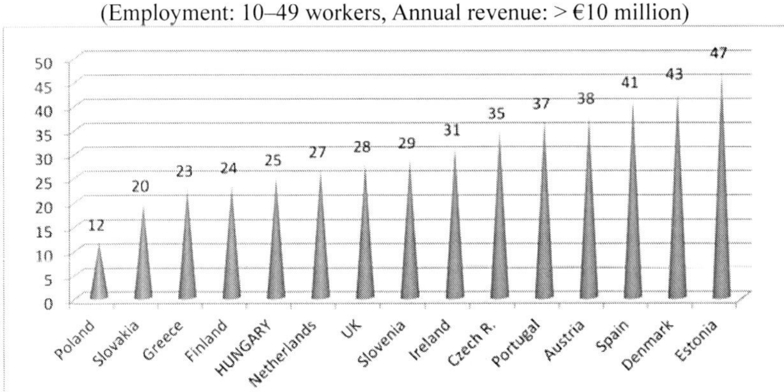

Medium-sized firms
(Employment: 50–249 workers, Annual revenue: > €50 million)

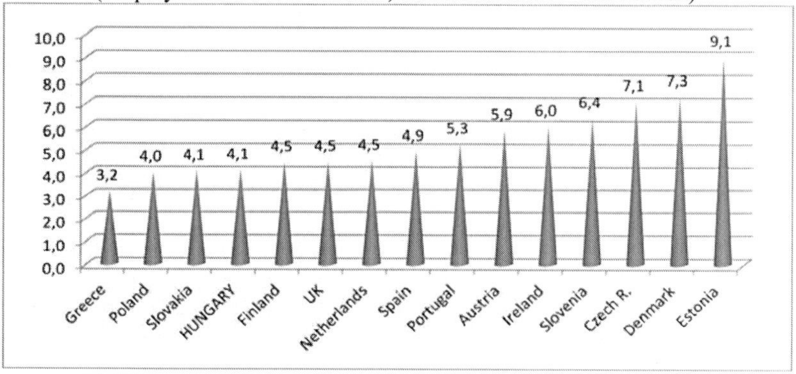

Large firms
(Employment: > 250 workers)

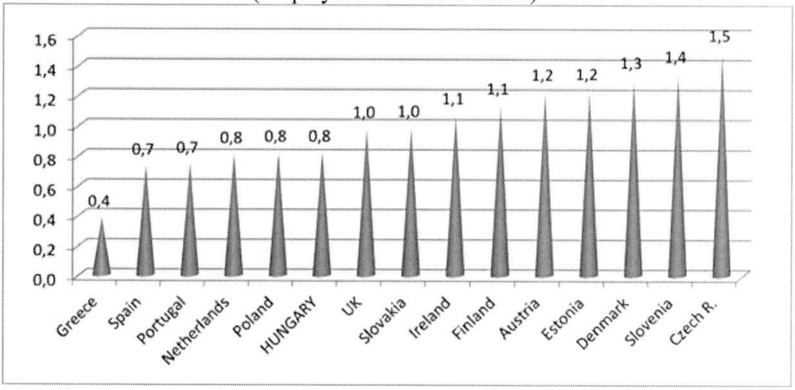

Source: Author's calculation based on EC Enterprise and Industry (2010) Small Business database

CONTRIBUTORS

Gabriele Cipriani is Director of the European Court of Auditors in Luxembourg. He has over 30 years of experience in EU public finances and is the author of several publications and conference papers in this field. After obtaining a PhD in Political Science (University of Bologna, Italy) and a Master's degree in European law (College of Europe – Bruges, Belgium), he joined the European Court of Auditors in 1978 and has been employed there since that time. He is currently the Director of the Court's Chamber responsible for Structural policies, Transport and Energy.

Zsolt Darvas joined the Bruegel Institute (Brussels, Belgium) as a Visiting Fellow in September 2008 and continued his work at Bruegel as a Research Fellow beginning in January 2009. He is also a Research Fellow at the Institute of Economics of the Hungarian Academy of Sciences and Associate Professor at Corvinus University of Budapest (Hungary). He holds a PhD in Economics from Corvinus University of Budapest. He has taught courses in Econometrics there and at other institutions since 1994. His research interests include macroeconomics, international economics, central banking and time series analysis.

Beáta Farkas is an associate professor at the University of Szeged (Hungary). She is the Head of the Institute of Finance and International Economic Relations. After obtaining degrees in Law (University of Szeged) and in Economics (Corvinus University of Economics, Budapest), she joined the University of Szeged and holds a PhD in Economics. She was the founding Dean of the Faculty of Economics and Business Administration. Her current research interest is in the Comparative Economics of European economies.

Gábor Dávid Kiss is an assistant professor at the University of Szeged (Hungary), Faculty of Economics and Business Administration. He holds a PhD in Finance from the University of Szeged. His research interests include international finance, time series analysis, and the economic and monetary union.

Andreász Kosztopulosz is an associate professor at the University of Szeged (Hungary), Faculty of Economics and Business Administration. He holds a PhD in Finance from the University of Szeged. His research interests include both international and corporate finance.

Árpád Kovács is a Professor at the University of Szeged (Hungary), and the President of the National Budgetary Council of Hungary. He is the President of the Editorial Committee of the bilingual Journal of Public Finance and has been the President of the Hungarian Economic Association since 2008. He was the President of the State Audit Office of Hungary between 1998 and 2009 and the President of the International Organization of Supreme Audit Institutions between 2004 and 2007. He obtained his Habilitation in Economics at the Budapest University of Technology and Economics in 2003. His research interests include public finance and fiscal policy.

Miklós Losoncz is Research Professor at the Budapest University of Technology and Economics (Hungary). He habilitated at the Széchenyi István University (Győr, Hungary), where he was Jean Monnet professor between 2009 and 2011. He was awarded the scientific degree of "Doctor of the Hungarian Academy of Sciences" in 2007. His research interests cover European integration in general and the Economic and Monetary Union and the EU's external relations in particular. He conducts research on the sovereign debt crisis and the Hungarian economy and economic policy.

Péter Mihályi is a Professor of Economics, the Head of the Department of Finance at the University of Pannonia (Veszprém, Hungary), a visiting Professor of Economics at the Central European University (Budapest) and an external Research Fellow at the Institute of Economics, Hungarian Academy of Sciences, Budapest. He was an invited lecturer at the European Institute of Public Administration (Maastricht, The Netherlands) between 1985 and 1993 and economic affairs officer at the United Nations Economic Commission for Europe (Geneva, Switzerland) from 1983 to 1993. He participated in the preparation of health care and municipal finance reforms as an Assistant Secretary of State in the Ministry of Finance between 1997 and 1998 and as a Senior Adviser to the Minister of Health in 2008.

Matti Viren is a Professor of Economics and the Head of the Economics Department at the University of Turku (Finland). He is also a consultant at the Bank of Finland. As an analyst he worked for the United Nations Economic Commission for Europe (Geneva, Switzerland) and for the European Free Trade Association. He became a Member of the Finnish Academy of Sciences in 1997. He worked with the Polish Ministry of Finance, Warsaw, as a pre-accession advisor from November 2001 to April 2003. His current research interests include applied macroeconomics, applied monetary economics, fiscal policy and the size of government.

Anna Visvizi is an independent political and economic analyst and an associate professor at DEREE – The American College of Greece, Athens. Prior to joining DEREE, she was a Marie Curie Research Fellow at the University of Ålborg (Denmark) and at the Centre for Globalization and Regionalization (CSGR) at the University of Warwick (United Kingdom). Anna Visvizi holds a PhD in Politics and International Studies (University of Warwick). Currently, the main focus of her research is directed at European economic governance, on the causes and implications of the sovereign debt crisis in Greece and the empirical pattern of the IMF's intervention in Greece.

Masahiko Yoshii has been a Professor at the Graduate School of Economics at Kobe University (Japan) since 2000 and the President of the EU Institute in Japan since April 2011. He is also the editor of the Japanese academic journal: Comparative Economic Studies (Kyoto). He holds a Doctor of Economics degree from Kobe University. His research interest includes Russian and Central and Eastern European Economies, Economic Systems and Comparative Economics.

Fabian Zuleeg is the Chief Economist at the European Policy Centre (EPC, Brussels, Belgium), in charge of the Europe's Political Economy Programme. He holds a PhD in the Political Economy of EU enlargement from Edinburgh University (United Kingdom). He leads the EPC's work in the Economic Policy Forum, working closely with decision makers in European institutions. He is responsible for the EPC's work on the Economic and Monetary Union, the European Single Market (in particular the Digital Single Market), European labour markets, the EU budget and PPPs, health and well-being, and environment and energy issues. His current work focuses on the economic and Euro crises, Europe's economic future and the future sustainability of Europe's economic and social models in light of challenges such as demographics.

Index